For Dummies

COMPUTER BOOK SERIES FROM IDG

Windows® CE 2 For Du

D1539749

Helpful Hints

- You can find hidden menus on your device by holding down the Alt key and tapping a location with the stylus. For example, to access the hidden menu that provides options for organizing the layout of your desktop, hold down the Alt key and tap in the center of the desktop. To quickly empty the Recycle Bin, hold down the Alt key and tap the Recycle Bin icon. On the menu that pops up, tap the Empty Recycle Bin option.

- Press Shift+Caps Shift to turn on the All Caps option, which makes every letter you type appear as an uppercase letter. To turn off the All Caps option, press Shift+Caps Shift again.

- When you change the batteries in your CE device, make sure that you always change the main batteries before changing the backup battery. Never remove both the main and backup batteries at the same time — doing so erases everything on your device.

- To move icons around on your desktop, simply tap the desired icon and drag it across the screen to the desired location.

- To minimize a window on your device, simply tap the button for that window on the taskbar. When you want to open the window again, tap the same button on the taskbar.

- If an OK button appears in the upper-right corner of a window, you need to tap that button to save any changes you make in the window. If you tap the X button to close the window, the changes you make may not be saved.

Keyboard Editing Options

Press These Keys	To Do This
Ctrl+A	Select the entire document
Ctrl+C	Copy a selected block of information from a document
Ctrl+F	Locate information
Ctrl+H	Find and replace specific information
Ctrl+N	Create a new document
Ctrl+O	Open an existing document
Ctrl+P	Print the current page or selected information
Ctrl+S	Save the current document
Ctrl+V	Paste the last information that was copied or cut
Ctrl+W	Close the current document
Ctrl+X	Cut a selected block of information from a document
Ctrl+Z	Undo the last action you performed

Navigating Documents

Press These Keys	To Do This
Alt+up-arrow key	Move up one page in the document
Alt+down-arrow key	Move down one page in the document
Alt+left-arrow key	Move to the left side of a document
Alt+right-arrow key	Move to the right side of a document
Ctrl+Alt+ left-arrow key	Move to the top of a document
Ctrl+Alt+ right-arrow key	Move to the bottom of a document

Copyright © 1997 IDG Books Worldwide, Inc. All rights reserved.

IDG BOOKS WORLDWIDE

Cheat Sheet $2.95 value. Item 0322-7.

For more information about IDG Books, call 1-800-762-2974.

...For Dummies: #1 Computer Book Series for Beginners

Windows® CE 2 For Dummies®

Windows CE Keyboard Shortcuts

Press These Keys	To Do This
Alt+Tab	Display the Task Manager window
Alt+Esc	Switch between open windows
Alt+H	Display a Help window for the current program
Ctrl+Tab	Switch between tabs in dialog boxes
Windows key*	Pop up the Start menu
Windows key+C	Open the Control Panel folder
Windows key+E	Open the main folder on your CE device (the My Handheld PC folder on a hand-held PC)
Windows key+H	Display the Help window for Windows CE
Windows key+I	Open the Stylus Calibration option
Windows key+K	Open the Keyboard Properties option
Windows key+R	Open the Run window

* The Windows key resembles the Windows CE logo. It is usually located between the Ctrl and Alt keys on the keyboard of your CE device.

Frequently Encountered Buttons

Tap on This Button	To Do This
✂	Remove, or *cut,* an item so that you can move it somewhere else by using the Paste command
📋	Copy the selected item so that you can insert a copy somewhere else by using the Paste command
📋	Paste the last thing you cut or copied into the current location of the cursor
✕	Delete the selected item
🔍	Locate the desired item
B	Make the selected text bold
I	Make the selected text italic
U	Underline the selected text
📁	View the contents of the parent folder
📁	Create a new folder

...For Dummies: #1 Computer Book Series for Beginners

 ®

References for the Rest of Us! ®

COMPUTER BOOK SERIES FROM IDG

Are you intimidated and confused by computers? Do you find that traditional manuals are overloaded with technical details you'll never use? Do your friends and family always call you to fix simple problems on their PCs? Then the *...For Dummies*® computer book series from IDG Books Worldwide is for you.

...For Dummies books are written for those frustrated computer users who know they aren't really dumb but find that PC hardware, software, and indeed the unique vocabulary of computing make them feel helpless. *...For Dummies* books use a lighthearted approach, a down-to-earth style, and even cartoons and humorous icons to diffuse computer novices' fears and build their confidence. Lighthearted but not lightweight, these books are a perfect survival guide for anyone forced to use a computer.

> *"I like my copy so much I told friends; now they bought copies."*
>
> **Irene C., Orwell, Ohio**

> *"Quick, concise, nontechnical, and humorous."*
>
> **Jay A., Elburn, Illinois**

> *"Thanks, I needed this book. Now I can sleep at night."*
>
> **Robin F., British Columbia, Canada**

Already, millions of satisfied readers agree. They have made *...For Dummies* books the #1 introductory level computer book series and have written asking for more. So, if you're looking for the most fun and easy way to learn about computers, look to *...For Dummies* books to give you a helping hand.

IDG BOOKS WORLDWIDE ™

5/97

WINDOWS® CE 2 FOR DUMMIES®

by Jinjer L. Simon

IDG
BOOKS
WORLDWIDE

IDG Books Worldwide, Inc.
An International Data Group Company

Foster City, CA ♦ Chicago, IL ♦ Indianapolis, IN ♦ Southlake, TX

Windows® CE 2 For Dummies®

Published by
IDG Books Worldwide, Inc.
An International Data Group Company
919 E. Hillsdale Blvd.
Suite 400
Foster City, CA 94404
www.idgbooks.com (IDG Books Worldwide Web site)
www.dummies.com (Dummies Press Web site)

Copyright © 1997 IDG Books Worldwide, Inc. All rights reserved. No part of this book, including interior design, cover design, and icons, may be reproduced or transmitted in any form, by any means (electronic, photocopying, recording, or otherwise) without the prior written permission of the publisher.

Library of Congress Catalog Card No.: 97-72412

ISBN: 0-7645-0322-7

Printed in the United States of America

10 9 8 7 6 5 4 3 2

1O/TR/QT/ZY/IN

Distributed in the United States by IDG Books Worldwide, Inc.

Distributed by Macmillan Canada for Canada; by Transworld Publishers Limited in the United Kingdom; by IDG Norge Books for Norway; by IDG Sweden Books for Sweden; by Woodslane Pty. Ltd. for Australia; by Woodslane Enterprises Ltd. for New Zealand; by Longman Singapore Publishers Ltd. for Singapore, Malaysia, Thailand, and Indonesia; by Simron Pty. Ltd. for South Africa; by Toppan Company Ltd. for Japan; by Distribuidora Cuspide for Argentina; by Livraria Cultura for Brazil; by Ediciencia S.A. for Ecuador; by Addison-Wesley Publishing Company for Korea; by Ediciones ZETA S.C.R. Ltda. for Peru; by WS Computer Publishing Corporation, Inc., for the Philippines; by Unalis Corporation for Taiwan; by Contemporanea de Ediciones for Venezuela; by Computer Book & Magazine Store for Puerto Rico; by Express Computer Distributors for the Caribbean and West Indies. Authorized Sales Agent: Anthony Rudkin Associates for the Middle East and North Africa.

For general information on IDG Books Worldwide's books in the U.S., please call our Consumer Customer Service department at 800-762-2974. For reseller information, including discounts and premium sales, please call our Reseller Customer Service department at 800-434-3422.

For information on where to purchase IDG Books Worldwide's books outside the U.S., please contact our International Sales department at 650-655-3200 or fax 650-655-3295.

For information on foreign language translations, please contact our Foreign & Subsidiary Rights department at 650-655-3021 or fax 650-655-3281.

For sales inquiries and special prices for bulk quantities, please contact our Sales department at 650-655-3200 or write to the address above.

For information on using IDG Books Worldwide's books in the classroom or for ordering examination copies, please contact our Educational Sales department at 800-434-2086 or fax 817-251-8174.

For press review copies, author interviews, or other publicity information, please contact our Public Relations department at 650-655-3000 or fax 650-655-3299.

For authorization to photocopy items for corporate, personal, or educational use, please contact Copyright Clearance Center, 222 Rosewood Drive, Danvers, MA 01923, or fax 978-750-4470.

LIMIT OF LIABILITY/DISCLAIMER OF WARRANTY: AUTHOR AND PUBLISHER HAVE USED THEIR BEST EFFORTS IN PREPARING THIS BOOK. IDG BOOKS WORLDWIDE, INC., AND AUTHOR MAKE NO REPRESENTATIONS OR WARRANTIES WITH RESPECT TO THE ACCURACY OR COMPLETENESS OF THE CONTENTS OF THIS BOOK AND SPECIFICALLY DISCLAIM ANY IMPLIED WARRANTIES OF MERCHANTABILITY OR FITNESS FOR A PARTICULAR PURPOSE. THERE ARE NO WARRANTIES WHICH EXTEND BEYOND THE DESCRIPTIONS CONTAINED IN THIS PARAGRAPH. NO WARRANTY MAY BE CREATED OR EXTENDED BY SALES REPRESENTATIVES OR WRITTEN SALES MATERIALS. THE ACCURACY AND COMPLETENESS OF THE INFORMATION PROVIDED HEREIN AND THE OPINIONS STATED HEREIN ARE NOT GUARANTEED OR WARRANTED TO PRODUCE ANY PARTICULAR RESULTS, AND THE ADVICE AND STRATEGIES CONTAINED HEREIN MAY NOT BE SUITABLE FOR EVERY INDIVIDUAL. NEITHER IDG BOOKS WORLDWIDE, INC., NOR AUTHOR SHALL BE LIABLE FOR ANY LOSS OF PROFIT OR ANY OTHER COMMERCIAL DAMAGES, INCLUDING BUT NOT LIMITED TO SPECIAL, INCIDENTAL, CONSEQUENTIAL, OR OTHER DAMAGES.

Trademarks: All brand names and product names used in this book are trade names, service marks, trademarks, or registered trademarks of their respective owners. IDG Books Worldwide is not associated with any product or vendor mentioned in this book.

is a trademark under exclusive license to IDG Books Worldwide, Inc., from International Data Group, Inc.

About the Author

Jinjer Simon started her computer career in 1984 when she entered college and took her first computer programming class. Since that time, it seems that very little transpires in her life without somehow being associated with a computer. She rarely ventures far without a computer of some type — which makes her handheld PC such a welcome addition to her life because it gives her the freedom to take a computer everywhere.

In addition to this book, Jinjer is also the author of *Windows CE 2 For Dummies Quick Reference,* published by IDG Books Worldwide, Inc.

Jinjer has worn several hats in the computer industry, ranging from computer programmer to end-user support and documentation development. She currently works as a consultant designing online computer documentation for Microsoft Windows software, writing user manuals, creating software training guides, and developing Internet Web sites.

Jinjer lives in Carrollton, Texas, a suburb of Dallas, with her husband Richard, and their two children, Alex and Ashley. In her spare time, when she is not writing books or playing mom, she enjoys traveling with her family and scuba diving.

ABOUT IDG BOOKS WORLDWIDE

Welcome to the world of IDG Books Worldwide.

IDG Books Worldwide, Inc., is a subsidiary of International Data Group, the world's largest publisher of computer-related information and the leading global provider of information services on information technology. IDG was founded more than 25 years ago and now employs more than 8,500 people worldwide. IDG publishes more than 275 computer publications in over 75 countries (see listing below). More than 60 million people read one or more IDG publications each month.

Launched in 1990, IDG Books Worldwide is today the #1 publisher of best-selling computer books in the United States. We are proud to have received eight awards from the Computer Press Association in recognition of editorial excellence and three from *Computer Currents'* First Annual Readers' Choice Awards. Our best-selling *...For Dummies*® series has more than 30 million copies in print with translations in 30 languages. IDG Books Worldwide, through a joint venture with IDG's Hi-Tech Beijing, became the first U.S. publisher to publish a computer book in the People's Republic of China. In record time, IDG Books Worldwide has become the first choice for millions of readers around the world who want to learn how to better manage their businesses.

Our mission is simple: Every one of our books is designed to bring extra value and skill-building instructions to the reader. Our books are written by experts who understand and care about our readers. The knowledge base of our editorial staff comes from years of experience in publishing, education, and journalism — experience we use to produce books for the '90s. In short, we care about books, so we attract the best people. We devote special attention to details such as audience, interior design, use of icons, and illustrations. And because we use an efficient process of authoring, editing, and desktop publishing our books electronically, we can spend more time ensuring superior content and spend less time on the technicalities of making books.

You can count on our commitment to deliver high-quality books at competitive prices on topics you want to read about. At IDG Books Worldwide, we continue in the IDG tradition of delivering quality for more than 25 years. You'll find no better book on a subject than one from IDG Books Worldwide.

John Kilcullen
CEO
IDG Books Worldwide, Inc.

Steven Berkowitz
President and Publisher
IDG Books Worldwide, Inc.

Eighth Annual Computer Press Awards ≥1992

Ninth Annual Computer Press Awards ≥1993

Tenth Annual Computer Press Awards ≥1994

Eleventh Annual Computer Press Awards ≥1995

IDG Books Worldwide, Inc., is a subsidiary of International Data Group, the world's largest publisher of computer-related information and the leading global provider of information services on information technology. International Data Group publishes over 275 computer publications in over 75 countries. Sixty million people read one or more International Data Group publications each month. International Data Group's publications include: **ARGENTINA:** Buyer's Guide, Computerworld Argentina, PC World Argentina; **AUSTRALIA:** Australian Macworld, Australian PC World, Australian Reseller News, Computerworld, IT Casebook, Network World, Publish, Webmaster; **AUSTRIA:** Computerwelt Osterreich, Networks Austria, PC Tip Austria; **BANGLADESH:** PC World Bangladesh; **BELARUS:** PC World Belarus; **BELGIUM:** Data News; **BRAZIL:** Annuário de Informática, Computerworld, Connections, Macworld, PC Player, PC World, Publish, Reseller News, Supergamepower; **BULGARIA:** Computerworld Bulgaria, Network World Bulgaria, PC & MacWorld Bulgaria; **CANADA:** CIO Canada, Client/Server World, ComputerWorld Canada, InfoWorld Canada, NetworkWorld Canada, WebWorld; **CHILE:** Computerworld Chile, PC World Chile; **COLOMBIA:** Computerworld Colombia, PC World Colombia; **COSTA RICA:** PC World Centro America; **THE CZECH AND SLOVAK REPUBLICS:** Computerworld Czechoslovakia, Macworld Czech Republic, PC World Czechoslovakia; **DENMARK:** Communications World Danmark, Computerworld Danmark, Macworld Danmark, PC World Danmark, Techworld Denmark; **DOMINICAN REPUBLIC:** PC World Republica Dominicana; **ECUADOR:** PC World Ecuador; **EGYPT:** Computerworld Middle East, PC World Middle East; **EL SALVADOR:** PC World Centro America; **FINLAND:** MikroPC, Tietoverkko, Tietoviikko; **FRANCE:** Distributique, Hebdo, Info PC, Le Monde Informatique, Macworld, Reseaux & Telecoms, WebMaster France; **GERMANY:** Computer Partner, Computerwoche, Computerwoche Extra, Computerwoche FOCUS, Global Online, Macwelt, PC Welt; **GREECE:** Amiga Computing, GamePro Greece, Multimedia World; **GUATEMALA:** PC World Centro America; **HONDURAS:** PC World Centro America; **HONG KONG:** Computerworld Hong Kong, PC World Hong Kong, Publish in Asia; **HUNGARY:** ABCD CD-ROM, Computerworld Szamitastechnika, Internetto online Magazine, PC World Hungary, PC-X Magazin Hungary; **ICELAND:** Tolvuheimur PC World Island; **INDIA:** Information Communications World, Information Systems Computerworld, PC World India, Publish in Asia; **INDONESIA:** InfoKomputer PC World, Komputek Computerworld, Publish in Asia; **IRELAND:** ComputerScope, PC Live!; **ISRAEL:** Macworld Israel, People & Computers/Computerworld; **ITALY:** Computerworld Italia, Macworld Italia, Networking Italia, PC World Italia; **JAPAN:** DTP World, Macworld Japan, Nikkei Personal Computing, OS/2 World Japan, SunWorld Japan, Windows NT World, Windows World Japan; **KENYA:** PC World East African; **KOREA:** Hi-Tech Information, Macworld Korea, PC World Korea; **MACEDONIA:** PC World Macedonia; **MALAYSIA:** Computerworld Malaysia, PC World Malaysia, Publish in Asia; **MALTA:** PC World Malta; **MEXICO:** Computerworld Mexico, PC World Mexico; **MYANMAR:** PC World Myanmar; **NETHERLANDS:** Computer! Totaal, LAN Internetworking Magazine, LAN World Buyers Guide, Macworld Netherlands, Net, WebWereld; **NEW ZEALAND:** Absolute Beginners Guide and Plain & Simple Series, Computer Buyer, Computer Industry Directory, Computerworld New Zealand, MTB, Network World, PC World New Zealand; **NICARAGUA:** PC World Centro America; **NORWAY:** Computerworld Norge, CW Rapport, Datamagasinet, Financial Rapport, Kursguide Norge, Macworld Norge, Multimediaworld Norge, PC World Ekspress Norge, PC World Nettverk, PC World Norge, PC World ProduktGuide Norge; **PAKISTAN:** Computerworld Pakistan; **PANAMA:** PC World Panama; **PEOPLE'S REPUBLIC OF CHINA:** China Computer Users, China Computerworld, China InfoWorld, China Telecom World Weekly, Computer & Communication, Electronic Design China, Electronics Today, Electronics Weekly, Game Software, PC World China, Popular Computer Week, Software Weekly, Software World, Telecom World; **PERU:** Computerworld Peru, PC World Profesional Peru, PC World SoHo Peru; **PHILIPPINES:** Click!, Computerworld Philippines, PC World Philippines, Publish in Asia; **POLAND:** Computerworld Poland, Computerworld Special Report Poland, Cyber, Macworld Poland, Networld Poland, PC World Komputer; **PORTUGAL:** Cerebro/PC World, Computerworld/Correio Informático, Dealer World Portugal, Mac*In/PC*In Portugal, Multimedia World; **PUERTO RICO:** PC World Puerto Rico; **ROMANIA:** Computerworld Romania, PC World Romania, Telecom Romania; **RUSSIA:** Computerworld Russia, Mir PK, Publish, Seti; **SINGAPORE:** Computerworld Singapore, PC World Singapore, Publish in Asia; **SLOVENIA:** Monitor; **SOUTH AFRICA:** Computing SA, Network World SA, Software World SA; **SPAIN:** Communicaciones World España, Computerworld España, Dealer World España, Macworld España, PC World España; **SRI LANKA:** Infolink PC World; **SWEDEN:** CAP&Design, Computer Sweden, Corporate Computing Sweden, Internetworld Sweden, it.branschen, Macworld Sweden, MaxiData Sweden, MikroDatorn, Natverk & Kommunikation, PC World Sweden, PCaktiv, Windows World Sweden; **SWITZERLAND:** Computerworld Schweiz, Macworld Schweiz, PCtip; **TAIWAN:** Computerworld Taiwan, Macworld Taiwan, NEW ViSiON/Publish, PC World Taiwan, Windows World Taiwan; **THAILAND:** Publish in Asia, Thai Computerworld; **TURKEY:** Computerworld Turkiye, Macworld Turkiye, Network World Turkiye, PC World Turkiye; **UKRAINE:** Computerworld Kiev, Multimedia World Ukraine, PC World Ukraine; **UNITED KINGDOM:** Acorn User UK, Amiga Action UK, Amiga Computing UK, Apple Talk UK, Computing, Macworld, Parents and Computers UK, PC Advisor, PC Home, PSX Pro, The WEB; **UNITED STATES:** Cable in the Classroom, CIO Magazine, Computerworld, DOS World, Federal Computer Week, GamePro Magazine, InfoWorld, I-Way, Macworld, Network World, PC Games, PC World, Publish, Video Event, THE WEB Magazine, and WebMaster; online webzines: JavaWorld, NetscapeWorld, and SunWorld Online; **URUGUAY:** InfoWorld Uruguay; **VENEZUELA:** Computerworld Venezuela, PC World Venezuela; and **VIETNAM:** PC World Vietnam. 3/24/97

Dedication

This book is dedicated to my husband and best friend, Richard, for all his love and support over the past ten years.

Acknowledgments

I want to thank John Pont for doing such a great job of pulling together everything in this book and keeping the project on track. I also want to acknowledge Felicity O'Meara for the great job she did copyediting the book, and Mary Corder and Suzanne Thomas for their support and guidance during the development of this book.

I want to thank Jill Pisoni for providing me the opportunity to get involved with IDG, and for asking me to write this book.

I want to give a special thanks to James Cummiskey, my technical editor, not only for the hours he spent reviewing the book to make sure that everything was accurate, but also for his willingness to help me figure out how certain things had changed in Windows CE 2.0.

Finally, I want to acknowledge the efforts of all the people at IDG who were involved in making this book a success by doing everything from cover design to page layout and indexing.

Publisher's Acknowledgments

We're proud of this book; please register your comments through our IDG Books Worldwide Online Registration Form located at: http://my2cents.dummies.com.

Some of the people who helped bring this book to market include the following:

Acquisitions, Development, and Editorial

Project Editor: John Pont

Senior Acquisitions Editor: Jill Pisoni

Copy Editor: Felicity O'Meara

Technical Editor: James Cummiskey

Editorial Manager: Mary C. Corder

Special Help

Suzanne Thomas, Associate Editor; Constance Carlisle, Copy Editor; Elizabeth Netedu Kuball, Copy Editor; Stephanie Koutek, Proof Editor

Production

Project Coordinator: E. Shawn Aylsworth

Layout and Graphics: Jonathon Andry, Steve Arany, Lou Boudreau, Linda M. Boyer, J. Tyler Connor, Angela F. Hunckler, Todd Klemme, Brent Savage, Janet Seib, M. Anne Sipahimalani, Michael A. Sullivan

Proofreaders: Vickie Broyles, Christine Berman, Michelle Croninger, Joel K. Draper, Robert Springer, Janet M. Withers

Indexer: Cynthia D. Bertelsen

General and Administrative

IDG Books Worldwide, Inc.: John Kilcullen, CEO; Steven Berkowitz, President and Publisher

IDG Books Technology Publishing: Brenda McLaughlin, Senior Vice President and Group Publisher

Dummies Technology Press and Dummies Editorial: Diane Graves Steele, Vice President and Associate Publisher; Mary Bednarek, Director of Acquisitions and Product Development; Kristin A. Cocks, Editorial Director

Dummies Trade Press: Kathleen A. Welton, Vice President and Publisher; Kevin Thornton, Acquisitions Manager

IDG Books Production for Dummies Press: Beth Jenkins Roberts, Production Director; Cindy L. Phipps, Manager of Project Coordination, Production Proofreading, and Indexing; Kathie S. Schutte, Supervisor of Page Layout; Shelley Lea, Supervisor of Graphics and Design; Debbie J. Gates, Production Systems Specialist; Robert Springer, Supervisor of Proofreading; Debbie Stailey, Special Projects Coordinator; Tony Augsburger, Supervisor of Reprints and Bluelines; Leslie Popplewell, Media Archive Coordinator

Dummies Packaging and Book Design: Patti Crane, Packaging Specialist; Kavish + Kavish, Cover Design

◆

The publisher would like to give special thanks to Patrick J. McGovern, without whom this book would not have been possible.

◆

Contents at a Glance

Cartoons at a Glance

By Rich Tennant

page 53

page 335

page 313

page 215

page 265

page 7

Fax: 978-546-7747 • E-mail: the5wave@tiac.net

Table of Contents

Introduction

· ·

You are about to embark on quite an adventure as you explore one of Microsoft's newest creations, the Windows CE 2 operating system. *Windows CE 2 For Dummies* introduces you to the world of Windows CE in a very friendly manner, providing examples that you can easily relate to your everyday life.

Windows CE was designed to be a user-friendly operating system, not some complicated thing for all the self-proclaimed computer nerds. On that basis, this book illustrates the simplicity of using Windows CE, leaving the technical jargon for those who really thrive on it. Although I do occasionally offer you a few bits of Windows CE trivia, you can simply ignore this information as you use this book.

About This Book

Windows CE 2 For Dummies provides you with an in-depth reference for answering all your questions when working with Windows CE. Don't feel pressured to read this book from cover to cover. You only need to read the information that explains the features you want to understand.

This book's design makes it easy to use. Whenever you come across something in Windows CE that you don't understand, simply flip to the table of contents or the index in this book to locate the topic you want to read about. You can quickly gather the information you need and get back to work in no time.

Conventions Used in This Book

To help you quickly spot the information you need, I use consistent terminology when I refer to actions that you can perform.

If you've used any other Windows operating system, or even a Macintosh, you're probably familiar with the action of *clicking* on an item by using your mouse. Because Windows CE runs on devices that have a touch screen and stylus, you encounter the terms *tap, double-tap,* and *drag-and-drop* in this book. Here's how to tap dance:

  ✔ **Tap.** If instructions tell you to tap an item, you need to take the stylus (the funny little pencil that came with your CE device) and use it to tap the item on the screen.

  ✔ **Double-tap.** When I tell you to double-tap a specific location, you simply take your stylus and tap the item twice in a fairly short amount of time. I also show you how you can customize your CE device's settings based on the speed at which you tap.

  ✔ **Drag-and-drop.** One more new thing you get to try out is how to perform a drag-and-drop operation under Windows CE. It probably makes more sense to call this the tap, drag, and release operation, but to maintain the common computer lingo, I still refer to it as *drag-and-drop* in this book. To do this, touch the desired item with your stylus, drag the stylus across the screen to the new location, and then pick up the stylus to release the item.

Of course, because you read about connecting to your personal computer in some of the chapters in this book, be prepared to click an item with your mouse.

I occasionally instruct you to press certain keys simultaneously on the keyboard — both your CE device and personal computer keyboards. Instead of always saying "simultaneously press both the Alt and R keys on the keyboard," I say something like this:

  Press Alt+R

You also want to make sure that you understand the shorthand I use for telling you to select an option on a menu on your CE device or personal computer. Instead of saying something long like "choose the Copy option on the Edit menu," I tell you to perform the task in the following manner:

  Choose File⇨Open

By using this method to express menu selections, I help you to quickly look at a description and spot the options you need to choose.

The underlined letters in the preceding command are called *hot keys*. As a keyboard alternative to using the stylus, you can quickly activate a menu command or option by pressing Alt and the underlined letter. For example, you can choose the preceding command by pressing Alt+F, O.

What You're Not to Read

As you may have already noticed, this book contains sections labeled with the Technical Stuff icon. Anytime you see this icon, feel free to ignore the information contained in that section. I include this technical information for computer-nerd-wannabes. You don't need to read these sections if you are simply trying to figure out how to perform a specific task.

On the other hand, if you aspire to impress your friends, you can always thumb through the book and read one of the sections with the Technical Stuff icon. You are sure to impress even the nerdiest of computer nerds with this information.

Foolish Assumptions

I foolishly assume that you're reading this book because you either recently purchased or will soon purchase a CE device. I also assume that you are looking for pointers on how to make this CE device become a useful tool and not just another one of those must-have gadgets that you never use.

You are probably someone who is frequently on the go and needs to take important information with you, such as information about appointments, copies of proposals and budgets, and even lists of important contacts.

You may even be looking for a good communication device that enables you to keep up with e-mail messages from the office as well as dive into the vast world of the Internet without hauling around a big computer.

How This Book Is Organized

I divide the information in this book into six parts. Each part contains chapters that relate to the topic of the part. Grouping related information in the book makes for an easy search when you try to locate information about the topic that interests you.

Part I: Windows CE Basics

Before diving into the middle of Windows CE, this part provides some of the basic information about Windows CE, such as how to set up your CE device and how to work with your Windows CE desktop. You also figure out the importance of the taskbar and how to monitor your Recycle Bin.

Part II: What Can I Do with My CE Device?

Now that you've spent all that money on this new little gadget, figure out how to perform various tasks on it, such as maintaining your daily schedule, keeping track of tasks, maintaining a current list of contacts, and even creating different documents. This part covers most of the free programs that come already installed on your CE device.

By exploring the information in this part, you quickly find out how to make your new CE device a useful tool. You won't find it sitting on some shelf collecting dust like other gadgets you may have purchased.

Part III: Interfacing with Your Personal Computer

Do you have Microsoft Word documents that you want to take to a meeting? Or perhaps you want to work on your budget at home. You can connect your CE device to a personal computer to copy files, load new programs onto your CE device, and even back up the information on your CE device.

This part covers the various tasks that you can perform by simply connecting your CE device to a personal computer that runs the Windows CE Services program.

Part IV: Getting Online with Windows CE

Probably one of the most fascinating uses for a CE device is the capability to connect to the Internet from this small device. With the aid of a modem, you can quickly connect to the Internet and send e-mail messages from anywhere as long as you have access to a phone line.

You can also use your CE device to connect to other locations, such as a company server, where you can send and receive e-mail messages.

Part V: Personalizing Your CE Device

Find out how you can quickly personalize your CE device by displaying your personal information when you turn on your device. You can also password-protect your CE device to eliminate the possibility that someone else may gain access to your information.

Part VI: The Part of Tens

Based on the title of this part, it is probably fairly easy to guess that this part has something to do with the number ten. This part provides lists of useful information, such as ten ways to spend money on your Windows CE device and ten common problems you may encounter with Windows CE.

Icons Used in This Book

If you have taken the time to flip through this book, you have probably noticed the little pictures that frequently appear in the margins of the book. You use these little pictures (commonly referred to as *icons*) as guides when you explore the information this book contains. If you have read other ...*For Dummies* books, you are probably already familiar with these icons.

Nerd alert! This icon immediately signals you that the information in the section targets aspiring computer nerds. You can feel free to avoid this information. However, if you are bored and looking for a way to impress your friends, you may want to take a quick peek at the information in this section.

When you're reading a section in the book, make sure you look at the information covered here. You find handy pointers that simplify using Windows CE.

Don't forget about these points when you use Windows CE.

Make sure you carefully follow any information that the Warning icon highlights. By paying close attention to this advice, you can avoid pitfalls that you may encounter when working with Windows CE.

Where to Go from Here

Well, you are ready to start exploring the world of Windows CE. Remember, this book is your reference. Feel free to mark commonly used pages, highlight useful paragraphs, and even make notes in the margins. The more you personalize this book, the more useful it will be.

Remember to use the table of contents and the index when you're looking for information about a specific topic. By using these simple tools, you can quickly locate what you need without spending hours thumbing through the book page by page.

And don't forget about the Cheat Sheet at the beginning of the book. You can remove this card from the book and place it in a location where you can quickly refer to it while working in Windows CE.

Part I
Windows CE
Basics

The 5th Wave
By Rich Tennant

"OH THOSE? THEY'RE THE SEAT-CUSHION-MOUSE. BOUNCE ONCE TO ACCESS A FILE, TWICE TO FILE AWAY — KEEPS THE HANDS FREE AND THE BUTTOCKS FIRM."

In this part . . .

This part explains the basics of Windows CE 2, one of the newest operating systems to hit the market. No matter what your background, you need to understand some of the basic features of Windows CE before you attempt to do much with your CE device.

In this part, you get a tour of the basic features of the CE device, as well as advice regarding what to look for in purchasing one. Most important, you find out all you need to know about working with the Windows CE desktop and navigating the world of Windows CE.

Chapter 1

What Is Windows CE?

*W*indows CE devices have invaded the computing market. You can find them not only in large computer stores, but also in almost any store that sells computers or handheld organizers. One thing these new CE devices have in common is that they all run Windows CE 2.0, a new operating system from Microsoft.

CE devices are meant to be used by the everyday person, such as the real estate agent who needs to keep track of his or her appointments, the salesperson who wants to quickly check e-mail, and even the casual user who would like to play a game of Solitaire while waiting to see the dentist. If these devices create the type of excitement that the developers anticipate, distinguishing the computer nerds from the everyday people will be difficult, because everyone will be carrying one of these little gizmos.

This chapter hopefully eases some of the confusion about this surge of excitement by providing a brief overview of Windows CE and taking a close look at the most popular CE devices, including an explanation of each part on the device. The chapter also walks you through setting up your CE device for the first time.

Understanding Windows CE

Windows CE is essentially a scaled-down version of Microsoft's popular Windows 95 operating system. (An *operating system* is a program that controls all the stuff that occurs on a computer.) Microsoft created Windows CE to provide an operating system that could be used on a hardware system with very modest memory requirements, such as the most widely used type of Windows CE device, the handheld PC.

Handheld PCs (handheld personal computers, often called *handhelds*) are designed to be small enough to carry in your front pocket yet powerful enough to be useful. Wow, these things almost sound like something you've seen in all those space movies, right? I like to describe a handheld PC as a laptop that is about the same size as a checkbook (assuming that your checkbook is roughly the same size as mine). The dimensions of the units are approximately 7 inches long by 3 inches wide and about 1 inch thick (unopened). Of course, when you open the device to use it, it measures about 7 inches square and about $1/2$ inch thick.

Because these CE devices are so small, you can easily carry one with you. Think of all the places you have hauled — or should have hauled — a laptop just to finish a proposal or adjust the budget figures. Now you can carry one of these small CE devices and work on your documents at your leisure.

Each CE device comes with the monitor and keyboard built in. The major downside is that the keyboard on most CE devices is much smaller than a normal keyboard and, therefore, more difficult to use.

All the stuff that occurs from the time you turn on the CE device until you turn it off again is managed and controlled by Windows CE. (Remind you of anyone you know?) In other words, Windows CE keeps track of the location of each program, determines where to store a document, knows which programs you are currently using, and keeps track of the current date and time.

Windows CE provides all the essential elements of Windows 95 and enables you to add only the extra bells and whistles that are relevant to your situation. In fact, Windows CE looks a lot like Windows 95 (see Figure 1-1). A good analogy for comparing the two operating systems would be looking at the menu in a pizza parlor: Windows 95 is a pizza with the works; Windows CE is a cheese pizza.

One frequently mentioned feature of Windows CE is its capability to *interface* with Windows 95 or Windows NT. (That is, you can connect your CE device

Figure 1-1:
Windows
CE looks
a lot like
Windows 95.

to a personal computer running either Windows 95 or Windows NT.) This way, you can take important information from your personal computer and carry it with you on your CE device. For example, you can copy your appointments from your personal computer and place them on your CE device. Then you can carry your schedule home or into a meeting. In fact, you can even take a spreadsheet or a word processing document into a meeting and make changes to it on your CE device as decisions are made.

With Windows CE, you also have the capability of moving information from your CE device onto your personal computer so that you can access the same information under Windows 95 or Windows NT. The chapters in Part III explain how to transfer your data, load new software onto your CE device, synchronize your Calendar and Tasks with your personal computer, and more.

Windows CE devices appear on store shelves next to other well-known handheld devices. To make a CE device easy to spot, the Microsoft Windows CE logo appears on the box, identifying the product as a device that runs Windows CE. The Windows CE logo looks like a small windowpane and is basically the same logo that Microsoft uses for Windows 95; the main difference is that you see "Microsoft Windows CE" under the logo. The logo can also be found on most of the CE devices themselves. Windows CE comes already installed on these devices. Therefore, when you purchase a CE device, you don't have to concern yourself with the hours of frustration caused by installing a new operating system — it has been done for you.

Locating Installed Windows CE Programs

Windows CE comes with several useful programs already installed on your CE device. You soon notice that most of the programs that come with Windows CE resemble the programs that are available on other versions of Windows.

Keep in mind that these are not the only programs you can use with Windows CE. One of the major advantages of owning a handheld PC that runs Windows CE is that the Windows CE operating system makes it much easier to add new software to your CE device than it is with other types of handheld devices.

Table 1-1 lists the programs that you can find already installed on your CE device. Icons for most of these programs are already sitting on the desktop of your CE device. (Don't despair if you can't immediately find the program you want; I discuss each of these programs in detail in the appropriate chapter in this book.)

Table 1-1	Windows CE Programs (The Freebie Stuff)
Program	*Description*
Microsoft Pocket Word	This word processing program very closely resembles the much-acclaimed Microsoft Word. With this program, you can create and review memos, letters, reports, and so on. For more information about Microsoft Pocket Word, see Chapter 6.
Microsoft Pocket Excel	This spreadsheet program is a scaled-down version of Microsoft Excel. You can use this program to create spreadsheets to keep track of expenses, manipulate data, and so on. For more information about Microsoft Pocket Excel, see Chapter 7.
Microsoft Pocket PowerPoint	This scaled-down version of Microsoft PowerPoint enables you to deliver a PowerPoint presentation from your CE device. With some CE devices, this program comes on the Windows CE Services CD; if this is the case for yours, you need to install Pocket PowerPoint if you want to use it. For more information about Microsoft Pocket PowerPoint, see Chapter 8.
Calculator	This little program lets you perform calculations. It keeps track of the last calculation performed on an on-screen paper tape, similar to that of an adding machine. This program very closely resembles the Calculator program in other Windows operating systems.
Tasks	This program resembles an electronic to-do list. It enables you to create entries for and keep track of tasks that you need to perform. For more information on Tasks, see Chapter 4.

Program	Description
Calendar	You can use this program to keep track of appointments and events. You can also view your current tasks from within the Calendar program. For more information about using Calendar, see Chapter 3.
Contacts	You can create an electronic address book of all your important contacts. For more information, see Chapter 5.
World Clock	You can not only keep track of the current time, but also simultaneously track the time in another location. This feature enables you to quickly switch your CE device to the current time as you travel into a different time zone. For more information, see Chapter 19.
Pocket Internet Explorer	This program lets you use your CE device to surf the Internet. For more information, see Chapter 16.
Solitaire	Of course, no Windows operating system would be complete without Solitaire. You will find that the Windows CE version closely resembles other Windows versions of the popular game, shown in Figure 1-2.
Inbox	With the use of a modem, you can use the Inbox program to send and receive e-mail messages from any location. For more information, see Chapter 17.

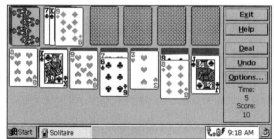

Figure 1-2:
No version
of Windows
would be
complete
without
Solitaire.

Examining a CE Device

Each CE device comes equipped with its own unique set of bells and whistles. These added features, such as modems and extra memory, are designed to influence you to select one CE device over another. Some basic items, however, are common to all CE devices. This section looks at each of these items and describes how each one was designed specifically for use with Windows CE.

The touch screen and stylus

Your CE device comes equipped with a *touch screen,* meaning that to make a selection on your CE device, you simply touch, or *tap,* the option you want to select. Windows CE offers touch-screen capabilities for all programs that run on your CE device.

CE devices come with a stylus to make tapping on-screen items an easy task. The *stylus,* which looks like a little pencil, replaces the mouse used with other Windows operating systems. Anytime you want to make a selection on your device, simply use the stylus to tap the option you want to select.

Depending on the item you are selecting (an icon, button, menu option, and so on), you may need to tap twice on the item, or *double-tap.* For example, you need to double-tap an icon to start the corresponding program. Unfortunately, no exact science exists for determining when to tap or double-tap; the best recommendation is to first tap the item, and if you don't get the results you want, try double-tapping.

With touch-screen capabilities, you can even drag items across the screen. Simply place the stylus on the item you want to select and then *drag* by moving the stylus across the screen to where you want to place the item.

You can tap the screen with anything, including your finger. Keep in mind, though, that fingers do leave fingerprints on the screen, so this method may not be the best one.

The size of most screens is approximately $4^1/_2$ inches by $2^1/_2$ inches (some CE devices have hit the market with larger screens), and most of them have monochrome displays, although some devices have color displays. A *monochrome* display means that everything appears in shades of gray on the screen. So looking at a monochrome monitor is like looking at a black-and-white photo of an item rather than a color photograph.

If you ever lose your stylus, you can purchase a replacement. Be sure to locate a stylus that fits in the stylus storage location on your device. Several styles of styluses are available, most of them much fancier-looking than the one that comes with the CE device. The only problem is that the fancier ones probably will not fit the location where your original stylus was stored — if you purchase one of these, you have to find another place to keep it.

The screen is hard to read

Depending on the lighting conditions, you may find that reading the screen of the CE device is difficult. This problem usually occurs when either the display is too dark or everything displayed on-screen is too light. You can't see the screen because the contrast settings are not appropriate for the current lighting conditions.

Each CE device provides a way to adjust the contrast settings of the screen. This adjustment may be either a dial or a specific key combination on the keyboard. By changing the contrast settings, you can adjust the brightness of the items on-screen. You will probably need to adjust this setting frequently as you move from one location to another, depending on the lighting conditions.

If you have adjusted the contrast and the screen is still blank, your batteries may be dead. Try changing the main batteries, or if you are using a rechargeable battery, recharge it. If you are still unable to see anything on-screen, you may need to press the Reset button. Occasionally, just like a personal computer, the CE device locks up and needs to be reset. If this still does not solve the problem, contact the manufacturer.

The keyboard

Each Windows CE device comes with a fully functional keyboard. Unlike the standard 101-key keyboards that come with most personal computers, the CE device keyboard has approximately 61 keys. The CE device does not have all the weird function keys and the extra set of numbers (affectionately referred to as the numeric keypad) that clutter up standard personal computer keyboards. But you can still find all the other standard keys.

Okay, so you have a standard keyboard, but look at how small those keys are! Obviously, the keyboard has been condensed so that more keys could be placed in a smaller amount of space. So unless you have extremely small fingers, you will probably find typing on the keyboard somewhat cumbersome. Don't despair — as you've heard a thousand times, practice makes perfect. The more you use the keyboard, the more comfortable you will become with it and the faster you'll get. I know that was no help, but what else can I say? You just can't use a small keyboard easily. But look on the bright side: You can use the stylus to accomplish many of the tasks you want to perform on your CE device, although you will find the keyboard valuable whenever you want to create an e-mail message or modify a spreadsheet.

If you are really having a difficult time pressing the keys on the keyboard, try pressing the keys with the back of your stylus. This may become tedious if you have a great deal of text that you need to type, however.

If you are accustomed to using a keyboard with your personal computer, you probably understand the function of most of the keys on your CE device. They all have the same functionality as the keys with the same name on the keyboard for your personal computer. Just in case you want a refresher, Table 1-2 provides a quick overview of the major keys on the keyboard of your CE device.

Table 1-2	When Should I Press That Key?
Key	*Description*
Shift	The Shift key has the same functionality as it does on typewriters. If you hold down this key while you type a letter, you get the uppercase version of the letter. The Shift key is also used to access the characters that sit above the numbers on the top row, as well as other characters that are sitting on keys with two characters.
Caps Shift	Pressing Shift+Caps Shift turns on the All Caps option, so that every letter you type is an uppercase letter. To turn off the All Caps option, press the two keys again. Pressing the Caps Shift key by itself provides exactly the same results as the Shift key.
Tab	The Tab key enables you to jump from one location to another on a screen where you are entering information. For example, if you're typing contact information in the Contacts program, you can use the Tab key to move from the Name field to the Title field. You can also use this key in word processing programs, such as Pocket Word, to indent text a specified amount of space.
	You can press Alt+Tab to pop up the Task Manager window, which lists the programs that are currently running on your CE device. You can use this window to jump quickly to a program in the list or to close a program. This key combination can be especially useful if a program locks up on your CE device. You can simply open the Task Manager window and then tap the End Task button to close the task.
Enter	In a word processor, such as Microsoft Pocket Word, you use the Enter key to move the cursor to the beginning of the next line and create a new paragraph in your document. Remember, if you are typing a paragraph, the word processor will automatically move the text to the next line when you get to the end of the current line. It will also move the cursor to the beginning of the next page when you get to the end of the page. This feature is commonly referred to as *word wrap*. Therefore, you only need to press the Enter key when you want to create a new paragraph.

Key	Description
Alt	The Alt key lets you perform alternative functions with certain keys on the keyboard. On some CE devices, the text on the Alt key is a different color, such as pink. The functions that you can use the Alt key to perform are written in the same color on the corresponding keys. For example, to move the cursor up one page, you hold down the Alt key and press the key with the pink label PgUp. On other CE device keyboards, the Alt key functions are simply listed on the keyboard above the corresponding keys.
	You can also use the Alt key to open the first pop-down menu at the top of a screen. As a Windows standard, this menu option is usually called File. This feature is a useful way to access the menus at the top of the screen, but with the touch-screen capability of your CE device, it's probably something you will rarely use.
Ctrl	You use this key, normally referred to as the Control key, similarly to the way you use the Alt key. For example, in Microsoft Pocket Word, you can press Ctrl+F to pop up the Find window so that you can locate text within your document. With the addition of the touch screen, you will probably rarely use this key.
Esc	This key, normally called the Escape key, is basically what its name implies — a way to cancel an operation in progress.
	You also use this key to accept data or an option on the screen. By pressing the Enter key, you inform Windows CE that you agree with the stuff and want to continue.
Delete/Backspace	When you press the Delete/Backspace key, the character to the left of the cursor is removed from the screen. To remove characters on the other side of the cursor, hold down the Shift key and then press this key.

Turning on your night-light

Most CE devices come with a backlight. A *backlight* illuminates the display so that you can read your CE device in dimly lit conditions. This feature is very useful if you want to use your CE device in places such as in your car, at a restaurant, or even in bed at night. The backlight is quite valuable — look for this feature when you purchase your CE device. If your unit has a backlight, you'll find a switch on the CE device, probably near the display. For the exact location of the button, refer to the manufacturer's documentation.

On most CE devices, the backlight stays on for only a short amount of time. Because the backlight uses extra battery power, it turns off to make sure that you don't accidentally forget and leave it on. If you need to use it for a longer amount of time, simply press the backlight button again. If your CE device is plugged in to an electrical outlet or connected to your personal computer, the backlight may stay on indefinitely.

If you use your backlight a lot, your batteries will run down more quickly, because of the battery power the backlight requires. If you intend to use your CE device for an extended amount of time, try to find a location with an adequate amount of light so that you don't need to use the backlight at all.

On some CE devices, you can modify the amount of time that the backlight stays on. Check the hardware documentation that came with your CE device to see if you have this option.

Battery power — How long does it last?

All CE devices are designed to run on battery power. CE devices usually have two types of battery power: the main batteries and the backup battery.

Most CE devices use standard AA-size batteries as the main batteries; you simply replace them when they are no longer working. Some CE devices provide the option of purchasing a rechargeable battery that is designed to replace the AA-size batteries. Most of them also come with (or provide the capability to add) an AC adapter that you can use to plug the CE device into an outlet, thus conserving battery power and renewing the rechargeable battery if installed.

The backup battery is found in another location on the device. This battery is a longer-lasting one that is used to maintain the computer's memory when the main batteries are run down or removed from the unit. Because this battery is only used when the main batteries are no good, it should last much longer than the main batteries. Some manufacturers speculate that the backup battery has a life of about five years, but this information is all based on your usage of the unit and how quickly you replace the main batteries when they are run down.

When the time comes to replace either the main or backup batteries, make sure that you verify the battery size required by your CE device. Each CE device has its own unique battery requirements. For more information, refer to the hardware documentation that came with your device.

That mysterious Windows key

One of the newest keys to appear on a keyboard is the Windows key. The key is so named because it looks exactly like the logo that Microsoft uses to represent the Windows operating systems. This key was added to several new keyboards when Windows 95 was introduced to the market. Unless you ran out and bought a new keyboard after Windows 95 was released, you may not have seen this key yet.

Many of the new CE devices come equipped with this key. If your CE device has this key, it is probably located on the left side of the Alt key. You can use the Windows key by itself or in conjunction with other keys on the keyboard, as I outline in the following table:

Combination	Description
Windows key	Opens the Start menu.
Windows key+C	Opens the Control Panel, which enables you to change your CE device's settings.
Windows key+E	Opens the My Handheld PC folder on your handheld PC, or the corresponding folder on your CE device. This key combination has the same result as selecting the My Handheld PC icon on the desktop.
Windows key+H	Opens the Windows CE help file.
Windows key+K	Runs the Keyboard Properties program so that you can set or modify specific keyboard settings.
Windows key+I	Runs the Stylus Properties program so that you can recalibrate the way the stylus selects stuff on-screen.
Windows key+R	Displays the Run window, in which you can type the name of a specific program that you want to use. If you don't know the name of the program you want to use, you can tap the Browse button in this window and then search for the program that you want to run.

Replacing the batteries

Never remove both the main batteries and the backup battery from your unit at the same time. Without some type of battery in your unit, you will probably lose all the stuff you have stored on the CE device.

If you determine that both the main and backup batteries need to be replaced at the same time, make sure that you replace the main batteries before you replace the backup battery. You need to ensure that the unit has enough battery power to maintain the storage before replacing the backup battery.

Whenever you replace the main batteries, make sure that you use all new batteries. Do not replace them with a mixture of old and new batteries.

Each CE device has a different battery storage location. To determine the exact location of the batteries on your device, refer to the manufacturer's documentation.

What is my battery status?

To ensure that you don't run out of batteries during an important meeting or during a game of Solitaire on a flight to New York, you should periodically check the battery status for your unit. To do so, you use the Windows CE program called Power Properties.

To start the Power Properties program, you double-tap its icon in the Control Panel folder. To open the Control Panel folder, choose the Settings option from the Start menu. In the Control Panel folder, tap the Power icon. The icon looks like a battery with a power plug sitting next to it.

You can also display the Power Properties program by double-tapping the battery icon in the status section of the taskbar.

The Power Properties program provides two tab options. The first tab option, Battery, indicates the status of the main and backup batteries (see Figure 1-3). This tab also tells you when the main batteries were last replaced and the amount of time that your CE device has been turned on since the batteries were last replaced. If the status of both types of batteries is Good, you don't need to worry too much. If either battery type has a status of Very Low, you should change that battery immediately.

Figure 1-3:
The Power
Properties
program
indicates
the power
status for
the main
and backup
batteries.

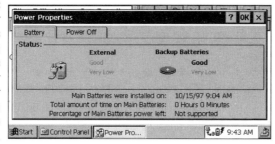

Windows CE is designed to help you conserve the life of your batteries. Windows CE automatically turns off when a predetermined amount of time elapses without the CE device's being used. The options in the Power Off tab allow you to specify the amount of time that your CE device should remain on without activity, as shown in Figure 1-4. The default time is 3 minutes. To change this time frame, tap the down-arrow button and then highlight the amount of time you want. You can also change the amount of time by typing the numeric value on the keyboard; however, keep in mind that the maximum value you can select or type for this field is 5 minutes.

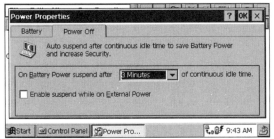

Figure 1-4: Specify the amount of time the CE device should remain idle.

Most people don't care if the CE device turns off when it's plugged into an AC outlet. If you still want your device to turn off in the amount of time specified on the Power Off tab option, tap the box next to the Enable suspend while on External Power field. A check mark in the box indicates that you want the device to turn off within the specified amount of time, even if the device is plugged in.

What is this cable for?

When you unpacked your CE device, you probably noticed that at least one cable had been placed in your box. Three types of cables may be in the box with your device. With some CE devices, you may find all three, but most of the units come with only one standard cable. The other cables are available as accessories.

So what is each cable and how do you use it? Unfortunately, manufacturers seem to assume that you can read their minds and determine which cable is used where, so they rarely label the cables. Table 1-3 describes each of the three types of cables that come with most CE devices and tells you how to determine which cable is which.

Table 1-3	Figuring Out CE Device Cables
Cable	*Description*
Data interface	This cable, which should come with each device, plugs into a 9-pin serial port on the back of your personal computer and then into the data port on your CE device. Without this cable, you cannot interface with a personal computer.
Power	If this cable didn't come with your CE device, you should be able to purchase it as an accessory, either from the manufacturer or at the store where you bought your CE device. This cable lets you plug your CE device into an AC outlet — a good investment if you use your device in one location for an extended amount of time.
	This cable should have the standard two prongs, like anything you plug into the wall, at one end; the other end plugs into the external power port on your device.
Battery charger	You probably have this cable only if you also purchased a rechargeable battery for your CE device. This cable enables you to charge the rechargeable battery while the battery is still in the CE device. With many CE devices, the same cable is used for both connecting to an AC outlet and recharging the rechargeable battery.

Understanding storage capabilities

One issue that will probably haunt you is determining whether your CE device has enough memory. Although all CE devices come with Windows CE already installed, Windows CE is installed in *ROM* (read-only memory), meaning that it does not take up any of the space you use for storing data files and additional programs. Most CE devices have approximately 4MB of ROM. (The size of this memory is not really that important, however, because you cannot add any programs or files to it.)

The area where you store all your extra stuff is commonly referred to as *RAM* (random access memory). This memory is what you need to compare when looking for a CE device. All CE devices come with at least 2MB of RAM, but several of them come with more than 2MB.

If you plan to load several extra programs, think about buying a CE device with a larger amount of RAM. If your device comes with a PC Card slot, you can also consider purchasing a storage card to plug into your CE device and add additional memory. The PC Card slot is available on most CE devices. It provides a location where you can add new options to your CE device, such as a modem or extra storage. So in reality, the options are limitless when it comes to storage capabilities on a CE device.

Another thing to keep in mind when you look at storage for CE devices is that Windows CE uses a compression method for storing all files. Windows CE is able to shrink the size of everything it saves on your CE device. Therefore, a file that takes 2MB to store on your personal computer will be considerably smaller on your CE device.

Before you load new items onto your device, you should know how much memory you have available. You can use the System Properties program to determine the amount of available memory on your device. This program is available on the Control Panel.

Storage memory versus disk memory

If you have stumbled across the System Properties program and looked at the Memory tab option, you've probably noticed that it talks about the storage memory and the program memory. Just when you had the RAM and ROM memory types under control, Windows CE throws in two new types.

Actually, the difference between the two types is fairly simple. Both are part of the RAM in your CE device. Basically, a certain amount of RAM is used to run programs — this is the *program memory*. The other portion of memory, *storage memory,* is where programs and data files are stored.

Here's where confusion sets in: Windows CE already has its own memory location, and now it needs to use some of your storage, too. The reason is that the RAM where the Windows CE operating system is stored does not allow anything to be written in it. When Windows CE

runs, it is just like other operating systems and requires memory space where it can keep track of all the programs you are currently running. Because this information must be written into memory, Windows CE must use some program memory (which can be written to).

Most CE devices come with the RAM divided between the program memory and the storage memory. The more storage memory you allocate, the more programs and documents you can actually place on your CE device. On the other hand, the more program memory you allocate, the more programs you can run simultaneously.

If at all possible, leave this screen set to the default settings. If you find that you don't have the amount of memory you need, try adding a PC Card for additional storage.

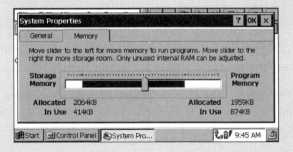

What goes in that slot?

So you found the perfect CE device, or at least you thought you did, but now you discover that it doesn't have enough memory or that you really need a modem, too. Well, don't despair, you can add those features to your CE device.

Most CE devices come with a *PC Card slot,* usually located on the side of the device. This slot enables you to add optional features to your CE device, including memory cards, modems, and serial ports. This slot is the standard size for normal PCMCIA cards, commonly referred to as PC Cards. PCMCIA (which stands for Personal Computer Memory Card Interface Adapter) cards are about the size of a credit card. They are used to add options to a CE device or personal computer, such as a modem, extra storage, or even an extra serial port.

On some CE devices, the slot comes with a plastic card inserted in it. This card helps keep the CE device clean when you don't have a PC Card inserted in the slot.

Placing a PC Card in this slot does have one drawback: It generally causes the CE device to use more battery power. Also, some modem cards require too much memory to work properly on these devices. Your best bet is to find a card that the manufacturer states has a low power consumption. This rating is typically indicated on the box when you buy the modem card. You can even look for a card that the manufacturer states is supported by Windows CE.

Infrared port

On the side of your CE device (or on the back of some devices), you should find a little black shiny window, commonly referred to as the *infrared port.* An infrared port lets you send data to another CE device, computer, or printer that has an infrared port. For example, you can send a document to another CE device, or you can play a game with another CE device. For more information on sending files using the infrared port, refer to Chapter 9.

When you transfer data between two CE devices, the infrared ports on the two devices need to be lined up so they can see each other, and nothing should be blocking either port. To ensure that the files transfer properly, the infrared ports need to be within about three feet of each other.

Because the infrared ports use a light beam to send information back and forth, some types of fluorescent lights may interfere with the data transfer. If you find that you are having problems interacting with the other CE device, try moving to another location.

Besides transferring files between CE devices, another popular use of the infrared port is to play games with users of other CE devices. If you decide to play a game with another person who owns a CE device, the game you select must be designed to work with the infrared port. For more information, refer to the documentation that came with the software game.

With some CE devices, you can send a document to print by using the infrared port. To find out if you have one of these devices, check the hardware documentation that came with your CE device. Even if your CE device has the capability of printing documents, however, you need to locate a printer that has an infrared port to receive the document. If you have both a CE device that can print and a printer that can receive, you're in great shape — you have eliminated the need to transfer the document to your personal computer before printing it.

What is that flashing light?

If you have added any appointments to your Calendar program in Windows CE, you may have noticed a little light flashing on the top of your CE device while it was turned off. If the light is flashing, the device is trying to remind you of something. You may have an appointment at the dentist's office, or it may be time to start cleaning the garage.

You can specify when you want a reminder based on your selection in either the Calendar program or the Tasks program. When you select a reminder, you can also indicate whether you want a flashing light, a beep, or both. You specify this information in the Notification Options dialog box, shown in Figure 1-5.

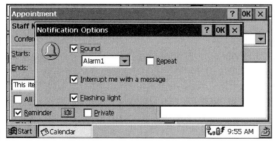

Figure 1-5:
The
Notification
Options
dialog box.

When you turn on your CE device, the flashing light turns off and you get a reminder message of the appointment or task, as shown in Figure 1-6. For more information about setting reminders, see Chapters 3 and 4.

Figure 1-6:
A friendly
reminder
of an
appointment
that is
currently
scheduled.

Most CE devices also have a button you can press to turn off the flashing light without first turning on the unit. This feature is useful because turning your CE device on and looking at the scheduled event may not always be convenient. For more information, refer to the hardware documentation that came with your CE device.

Should I press the Reset button?

Just like a personal computer, each CE device has a Reset button. This button is not intended to be used on a regular basis, but some situations require you to use it. For example, some software demands that the CE device be restarted in order to install the information the program needs to run. The button is recessed and requires extra effort to push, reducing the chance of someone's accidentally pressing it.

When you press the Reset button, the CE device totally shuts down so that when you turn it back on you are essentially rebooting it. (*Rebooting* is a term commonly used when talking about personal computers; it refers to the process of totally restarting a machine.) If a program instructs you to press the Reset button, go ahead and do so, but first make sure that all other programs are closed.

Occasionally, for one reason or another, your CE device may not turn on when you press the On button. Should this problem occur, try pressing the Reset button and then pressing the On button again.

Selecting a CE Device

Buying a CE device can be almost as confusing as determining which personal computer you should purchase. You need to look at these devices for only a few minutes to see that each one is different and comes with its own unique features.

You can find CE devices with built-in modems, extra memory, different processors, and so on. I cannot — actually, I will not — try to guess which CE device is best for you, but Table 1-4 explains these added features and indicates why you may want them.

Table 1-4	Added Features on CE Devices
Feature	*Description*
RAM	The more memory that your device comes with, the more programs and data you can store without adding some type of external card. Obviously, the more memory, the more desirable the CE device. Keep in mind, though, that the more memory you want, the more money you're going to pay for the CE device.
	Remember, a CE device is capable of storing only a few different programs in 2MB of RAM. Another thing to keep in mind is the fact that the RAM on most of the CE devices can be upgraded; you should check to see if this option exists before buying the CE device.
	Be aware of the fact that RAM upgrades are normally installed in the same location where you need to place the upgrade for the Windows CE operating system. The RAM upgrade may have to be removed if you ever want to upgrade your operating system to a new version.
Modem	Some CE devices offer a built-in modem. This feature is definitely worth consideration if you intend to use your CE device to send and receive a great deal of e-mail or connect to the Internet. A built-in modem frees up the PC Card port for other types of PC Cards that can be added to your CE device, such as extra storage.
Rechargeable batteries	You can go through a bunch of batteries by using the CE device on a regular basis. One nice feature to consider is rechargeable batteries. Most CE devices do give you the option of purchasing rechargeable batteries as an added accessory.

Let me ease some fears here by pointing out that all CE devices have been designed specifically to run Windows CE; therefore, you cannot make a wrong decision, as long as you buy a box with the Windows CE logo on it. If all this mention of added-feature stuff causes frustration, forget about it and just buy the one you think looks the nicest. After all, they all run Windows CE.

Turning On Your CE Device for the First Time

Like most new computers, your CE device presents you with some strange screens the first time you turn it on. These screens help you set up your device so that you can use it properly. After you set up the CE device, you won't see most of these screens again.

When you turn on your CE device for the first time, assuming that it has never been turned on before, the Setup wizard appears, as shown in Figure 1-7.

Figure 1-7:
The Setup
Wizard
helps you
set up your
CE device.

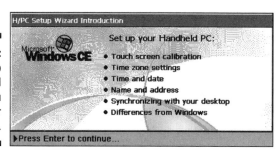

Setting up your CE device

The Setup wizard provides a brief introduction to Windows CE by explaining the touch-screen capabilities, helping you set up your time zone information, letting you set up personal information, and explaining some differences between Windows CE and other versions of Windows. When you start the Setup wizard, the first screen that appears provides an overview of the setup process.

The sooner you set up your CE device, the sooner you can get on to more exciting things, like setting up your calendar. So grab your CE device and follow these steps:

1. **When you see the Setup Wizard Introduction screen, press the Enter key to start the setup process.**

   This screen is the first one displayed when you run the Setup wizard (see Figure 1-7).

2. **Review the information about the stylus on the next screen and press Enter to continue.**

3. On the Calibration screen, shown in Figure 1-8, tap the large + (plus sign) in the middle of the screen.

After you tap, the + will move to another location on the screen. Continue chasing the + around the screen by tapping with the stylus.

Figure 1-8:
To calibrate
your touch
screen, use
the stylus to
touch the +
in the
center of
the screen.

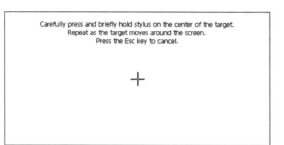

Carefully press and briefly hold stylus on the center of the target.
Repeat as the target moves around the screen.
Press the Esc key to cancel.

You may feel like you're playing cat and mouse, but actually, your CE device is adjusting itself to ensure that your taps are recognized. This process of setting the tapping action is referred to as *calibrating the touch screen.*

4. After you calibrate the screen, press the Enter key to display the World Clock dialog box.

You use the World Clock dialog box to specify a bunch of different information. The Setup wizard is not going to have you specify all the information available on this screen right now; you can return to this dialog box at any time after you run the Setup wizard to add more information. To find out more about the World Clock dialog box, refer to Chapter 19.

5. On the Date & Time tab, select the city where you spend most of your time (Windows CE calls this your home city). To select a city, tap the down-arrow button next to the City field and tap the name of the city closest to where you spend most of your time.

When you select the home city, as shown in Figure 1-9, Windows CE sets up information like the area code you use and time zone information to be used by different programs on your CE device.

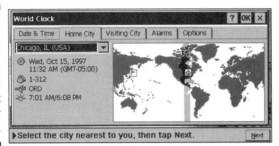

Figure 1-9:
You need to specify the location where you spend most of your time.

6. **After specifying the home city information, tap the Next button at the bottom of the screen to display the Date & Time tab.**

   Here is where you make sure that the date and time settings are correct for your location.

7. **To select a date on the calendar, tap the arrows at the top of the calendar to move from one month to the next. When you locate the correct month, tap the day you want to select.**

8. **To adjust the time, either tap the hand on the clock and drag it to the location you want to select or type the time in the field beneath the clock.**

   Figure 1-10 shows the date and time settings for someone who lives in Dallas, Texas.

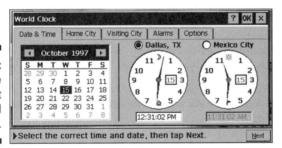

Figure 1-10:
Setting the current date and time.

9. **After you specify the time and date information, tap the Next button at the bottom of the screen to display the Owner Properties screen.**

   This screen enables you to enter your personal information on the CE device. Much like a name tag, this information lets someone figure out who the CE device belongs to if you misplace it.

10. **Type your information in each of the fields on this screen.**

    Make sure that you at least enter a name and phone number so that someone can contact you. You never know when you may accidentally misplace your unit.

11. **If you would like to display your owner information each time the device is turned on, tap the box next to the** Display Owner Identification **field (see Figure 1-11).**

A check mark in the box indicates that the option is selected. With this option selected, when someone turns on your CE device, he or she will immediately see who the owner is. This is particularly important if your CE device is password-protected; if you don't select this option, someone who found your CE device couldn't see your ID information because he or she wouldn't know the password.

Figure 1-11:
The Display
Owner
Identification
field.

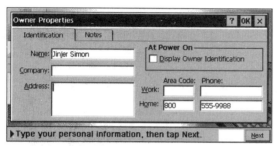

12. **Tap the Notes tab to add any additional personal information that you want displayed when the device is turned on.**

Again, make sure that you tap the box next to the Display Owner Notes at Power on field if you want the information to display when the unit is turned on.

13. **When you finish setting up your personal information, tap the** Next **button to complete the setup program.**

The Setup wizard provides three more screens that provide additional pointers about Windows CE.

14. **When you get to the last screen, tap the** Done **button to close the Setup wizard and save the settings.**

Congratulations! You have successfully set up Windows CE. You are now ready to start exploring your device.

After you use your CE device for a while, you may find that it does not seem to respond to your taps as well as it did when you first set it up. Do not despair; all you have to do is to recalibrate the touch screen. To load the Calibration screen, simply hold down Alt+Ctrl+= (equal sign) on the keyboard.

Rerunning the Setup wizard

You can rerun the Setup wizard at any time. Although you will rarely come across an occasion when you want to do so, the option is available. The only time I would run the Setup wizard again is if I knew I wanted to modify most of the setup information at once; otherwise, all this information can be modified in the Control Panel folder by selecting each individual icon.

 To run the Setup wizard, you need to select the Welcome icon. This icon resembles a light bulb and is located in the Windows folder, which you can access by choosing Programs⇨Windows Explorer from the Start menu and then opening the Windows folder. When you double-tap the Welcome icon, the Setup wizard appears, as discussed in the preceding section.

Upgrading to Windows CE 2.0

If you own a CE device with an earlier version of Windows CE, you probably want to consider upgrading it to Windows CE 2.0. Most existing CE devices can be upgraded. To upgrade a device, you normally have to place a new ROM chip in your device.

To find out the exact details about upgrading your specific CE device, you need to contact your hardware vendor. Many of them will send you the upgrade with instructions on how to do it yourself, although some may require that the upgrade be done in one of their service centers.

Chapter 2

Working with Your Windows CE Desktop

*B*efore you embark on an exciting new adventure, you need to organize your equipment. You need to make sure that you have a map, for example, so that you don't set off in the wrong direction. Similarly, before you use your CE device, you need to organize the items on your Windows CE desktop so that you can easily locate them when you need them.

In this chapter, you explore some of the basic elements of Windows CE and discover the roles these items play in the use of Windows CE. You find out all about the Windows CE desktop and the items that are placed on the desktop when you first set up your CE device. This chapter also covers other extremely useful items that you encounter on your desktop, such as the Recycle Bin, the taskbar, and the Start menu. Finally, this chapter familiarizes you with the elements of a window.

What Are All Those Pictures on the Desktop?

When you run Windows CE, the first thing you see is a screen covered with a bunch of little pictures, as shown in Figure 2-1. If you have used Windows 95, this arrangement probably looks familiar to you. This initial screen is commonly referred to as the *desktop,* and the little pictures are called *icons*. These little icons represent programs that are stored on your CE device. Whenever you want to run the program that is associated with an icon, all you have to do is double-tap the icon with the stylus.

Figure 2-1:
The desktop
displays the
items that
you use
most often.

As shown in Figure 2-1, Windows CE comes with many unique icons. Table 2-1 outlines the icons that are installed on your desktop when you first run Windows CE. These icons are not the only ones that you can place on your desktop; just as with your desk at home or at work, you have the freedom to reorganize the items on your desktop to suit your needs (as I discuss in the next section of this chapter).

Table 2-1	Deciphering the Icons
Icon	*Purpose*
	If you tap this icon, you see everything that exists on your CE device. Tapping this icon is equivalent to choosing Start⇨ Programs⇨Windows Explorer.
	If you tap this icon, you see the contents of the My Documents folder. You normally store your personal files in this folder.
	The Recycle Bin stores all your deleted files until you empty it. **Note:** The fastest way to empty the Recycle Bin is to hold down the Alt key while you tap the Recycle Bin. When the pop-up menu appears, tap the Empty Recycle Bin command.
	This icon is your ticket to the Internet. Tapping this icon opens up the Internet browser that you use to explore the wonders of the Internet.
	This icon represents the Inbox. If you use your CE device to send and receive e-mail messages, you will become very familiar with this icon.
	This icon starts the Calendar program. You can keep track of where you need to be and when you need to be there simply by using this program.

Icon	Purpose
	Tapping this little card file icon opens the Contacts program, which you use to keep track of your personal contacts.
	Use this icon to list tasks you need to complete, such as cleaning the garage or checking out the . . .*For Dummies* home page on the Internet. After you list the tasks, you can also view them by using the Calendar program.
	Tapping this icon displays Microsoft Pocket Word, which enables you to create a new word processing document.
	Tap here to create spreadsheets (called *workbooks* in Windows CE lingo) by using Microsoft Pocket Excel.
	Tap this icon to view a presentation that you created using Microsoft PowerPoint on your personal computer. You can display your presentation on a color screen if you have a VGA adapter card in the PC Card slot on your CE device.

Don't bother memorizing the icon for every program. Each icon is labeled with the name of the program or file to which it corresponds.

Organizing Your Desktop

The Windows CE desktop is kind of like the top of your desk at work or home. Normally, people try to keep the items they use most often on top of their desks — a phone, a stapler, a card file, a calendar, and so on. You use the Windows CE desktop the same way: You set up your desktop so that you can easily access the items you use most often when you use your CE device. For example, you may choose to keep your word processor, the Calendar program, your contact list, and the Recycle Bin within easy reach.

If you think of your Windows CE desktop as the place where you want to keep only the things you use most, it shouldn't become too cluttered. If your desktop does become messy, however, you can always use your handy Recycle Bin to do some spring cleaning.

Arranging your icons

You can arrange the icons on your desktop in many ways. The easiest way is to place the stylus on the icon you want to move and then drag the icon across the screen, just like picking up the phone and putting it on the other side of your desk. Of course, moving items around one by one can become a little tedious. Have you ever wanted to wiggle your nose and have everything in your house move to an appropriate location? With Windows CE, you have almost the next best thing. The desktop menu provides several options for automatically organizing your desktop.

The desktop menu, shown in Figure 2-2, appears when you hold down the Alt key and tap anywhere on the desktop other than where an icon sits. The menu options enable you to have Windows CE arrange and sort your icons in several ways:

✔ If you want to make sure that your icons are always in neat little rows and columns on the desktop, be sure to choose the Arrange Icons⇨ Auto Arrange option. If you choose this option, no matter what you add to your desktop, the icon is placed in the next row or column on the screen. To cancel the automatic arrangement of icons, you need to choose this option again. When the Auto Arrange option is selected, a check mark appears next to it in the menu; when you cancel it, the check mark is removed.

✔ When you move icons around on the screen, you can select the Line Up Icons option to ensure that the icons look uniform in the new layout.

✔ If you have different types of icons on your desktop, such as Pocket Word files, programs, and even worksheets, you may want to sort them so that icons of the same type are placed together. This grouping is often referred to as sorting items based upon their type. To do this, tap the Arrange Icons⇨By Type option on the desktop menu.

✔ You can arrange all the icons on the desktop in alphabetical order, as shown in Figure 2-3. This way, as long as you know your alphabet, you can quickly locate the icon for a program. To arrange the icons alphabetically, tap Arrange Icons⇨By Name on the desktop menu.

Figure 2-2:
To display the desktop menu, hold down the Alt key and tap the desktop.

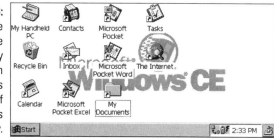

Figure 2-3:
The
Arrange
Icons⇨By
Name option
arranges
most of
the icons
alphabetically.

Note: When Windows CE sorts the icons, it places the My Handheld PC icon and the Recycle Bin icon in the same locations, on the left side of the screen. For some unknown reason — well, the reason is unknown to most of us — these two stubborn icons have decided that they are not going to budge from those locations.

You can create a new folder and place it on the desktop by selecting the New Folder option on the desktop menu. I find this feature useful for keeping track of documents that I use most often.

Adding a new program to the desktop

You can add any new program to your Windows CE desktop. When you add items to the desktop, you are really adding a *shortcut* to the desktop. A shortcut is a link to the actual program or file. The really cool thing about shortcuts is that you can remove the shortcut from your desktop without removing the program from your CE device.

What about the right mouse button?

If you have ever used Windows 95 or Windows NT 4.0, you are probably used to pressing the right mouse button, or *right-click-ing,* when you want to display additional menu options for any option on the screen. Unfortunately, Windows CE does not come with a mouse, so you can't use the right mouse button commands — right?

Wrong. You can access the menus that you get from right-clicking by simply holding down the Alt key while tapping an item with the stylus.

If you are looking for an option but can't find it on the menus that are currently displayed, try holding down the Alt key and tapping. In many places within Windows CE, you can find new menus using this technique.

You can add a shortcut to the desktop in many ways. The easiest method is to use the Desktop as Shortcut option on the Windows CE program's toolbar menu:

1. **Open the Windows CE Explorer program and locate the icon for the program that you want to add to your desktop.**

   The easiest way to open the Windows CE Explorer program is to double-tap the My Handheld PC icon (or the corresponding icon on your CE device) on your desktop.

2. **Tap the program that you want to place on the desktop to select it.**

   The selected program icon appears highlighted on the screen to indicate that you have it selected.

3. **Choose File⇨Send To⇨Desktop as Shortcut.**

   The next time you view the desktop, the new shortcut for the selected icon appears, as shown in Figure 2-4. The little arrow in the lower-left corner of the icon indicates that the icon represents a shortcut to the program.

Figure 2-4:
A small arrow in the lower-left corner identifies the icon as a shortcut.

Use caution when you delete icons within Windows CE. If you remove an icon that does not have a little arrow in the lower-left corner, you remove the actual program.

Recycling Unwanted Items

Everyone has been taught, some better than others, to use a recycle bin when throwing things away. So you may be shocked to find the Recycle Bin icon sitting in the upper-left corner of your screen.

The Recycle Bin is a folder on your system that contains all the items that you have deleted, as shown in Figure 2-5. It works in the same fashion as a real recycle bin. When you delete a file or a program, Windows CE places the specified item in the Recycle Bin. Deleted items remain in the Recycle Bin until you empty the bin or retrieve the item. By using the Recycle Bin, you can recover deleted files as easily as you might salvage the sports section from the household newspaper recycle bin.

Figure 2-5:
Double-tap
the Recycle
Bin to see
the items
you have
deleted.

You can drag items from your desktop into the Recycle Bin by tapping the item you want to delete and dragging it onto the Recycle Bin icon. Anything that you drag onto the Recycle Bin icon is removed from its location on the desktop.

As soon as you add an item to the Recycle Bin, the Recycle Bin icon changes from an empty bin to one that is full of papers. This change is a notification to you that you have trash to empty. The quick and easy way to empty the Recycle Bin is to hold down the Alt key and tap the Recycle Bin icon, and then tap the Empty Recycle Bin option. However, you may want to check the Recycle Bin before emptying it. You never know what you may have hiding in there. Follow these steps:

1. **Open the Recycle Bin by double-tapping its icon.**

2. **To get rid of everything in the Recycle Bin, choose Edit⇨Empty Recycle Bin.**

   If you want to remove a single item from the bin, tap the item in the list and then choose Edit⇨Delete.

You can return items in the Recycle Bin to their original location. Open the Recycle Bin, highlight the item you want to retrieve, and choose Edit⇨Restore. The item is returned to its original location.

Keeping tabs on the Recycle Bin

By default, Windows CE allocates 10 percent of its total storage memory to the Recycle Bin for storing deleted files. You can adjust the amount of storage space that Windows CE has available for deleted files by using the Recycle Bin Properties dialog box. This dialog box appears when you choose File⇨Properties from the Recycle Bin's toolbar menu.

The dialog box indicates the maximum amount of memory available for deleted files. To adjust the percentage of memory that should be used for deleted files, place the stylus on the slider and drag it to the appropriate amount.

If the total size of the items in the Recycle Bin exceeds the allotted amount of storage, a message appears, indicating that you need to remove some of the files from the Recycle Bin before you can add more.

Unless you have a specific reason for changing the size of the Recycle Bin, such as a sudden urge to do some extensive spring cleaning, I suggest leaving the memory setting at the default setting of 10 percent.

In this dialog box, you can also specify that no files are ever placed in the Recycle Bin. If you select this option, you will not be able to recover an item after you delete it. I do not recommend selecting this option.

Recycle Bin Properties	OK	×

Internal

Total storage memory: 576KB
Maximum recycle bin size: 57.5KB

☐ Do not move files to the Recycle Bin, remove immediately on delete.

10%
Maximum size of Recycle Bin (Percent of storage)

Start   Recycle Bin   3:06 PM

Giving the Taskbar Something to Do

If you have played around with Windows CE at all, you have probably noticed the horizontal bar across the bottom of the screen. This bar, shown in Figure 2-6, is commonly referred to as the *taskbar*. The taskbar creates a button for each window that you have open. The button that appears to be pressed down is the window that is currently displayed on-screen. In Figure 2-6, for example, the Calendar program is displayed. To switch to another open program window, tap the window's button on the taskbar.

To minimize an open window, tap the window's button on the taskbar. You can reopen the window by tapping the button a second time. When you *minimize* a window, you are making it invisible so that you can see your desktop; the window remains that way until you tap its button again. Boy, don't you wish you could make things invisible on your real desktop?

Figure 2-6:
The taskbar
monitors
your activity
within
Windows CE.

Taskbar

The right side of the taskbar is the *status area.* You find the clock in this
area. Depending on your settings, you may also find other icons, including
an icon that indicates the current battery status and one that shows
whether the CE device is connected to a personal computer.

 Also located in the right corner of the taskbar is a button that will definitely
come in handy. When you tap the Desktop button, your Windows CE desktop magically appears. Any programs that you have open are minimized,
with buttons for each of them on the taskbar.

Closing programs that won't respond

Sooner or later, a program on your CE device
will stop working, and no matter what button
you tap, it won't do a thing. This experience
can be rather frustrating, but luckily, Windows
CE provides an option for solving this dilemma.

You can force the program to close by using
the Task Manager window. To display this window, press Alt+Tab.

You can highlight a specific program by tapping it and then select the End Task option to
close the selected program.

Keep in mind that if your CE device does not
seem to respond when you press Alt+Tab, you

may need to reset it. Check the hardware
documentation that came with your device for
information about resetting it.

The left corner of the taskbar is where the Start button resides. When you tap this button, a menu of seven options appears. These options help you find different information contained on your CE device. I discuss the Start menu in the section "Unveiling the Start Menu," later in this chapter.

Doing Windows

Each time you run a program, it opens on-screen in a *window*. A window is a box on the screen where each program runs. Actually, I think it looks more like a new page, but I guess it would have sounded kind of strange to name an operating system *Pages*.

All windows have a standard look and feel. This design provides consistency between programs. In other words, a standard blueprint, created by some nerdy computer programmer, is used to design all the windows that appear in Windows CE. After you understand how to locate information on the blueprint, you can quickly familiarize yourself with a new program. Figure 2-7 shows the parts of a typical Windows CE window.

Toolbar

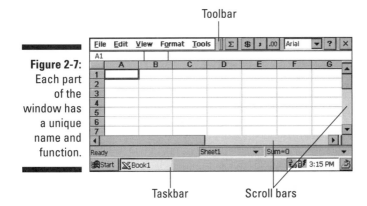

Figure 2-7: Each part of the window has a unique name and function.

Taskbar   Scroll bars

When you open a new window, any other windows that are currently open stay open. You can figure out which windows are open by looking at the buttons on the taskbar. The button that appears to be pressed down is the window that is currently displayed. To switch to another window, tap its button. Or you can switch between windows by pressing Alt+Esc. Windows CE scrolls through the windows that you have open in the order that they are listed on the taskbar.

The toolbar

The toolbar provides the commands you use to do most of the stuff in Windows CE. Notice that the toolbar contains several words, such as *File* and *Edit.* When you tap one of these words, a menu containing a series of options appears. For example, you can tap the word *Edit* to open the Edit menu, and then tap the command you want to use. The toolbar also usually contains several buttons. You tap a button to choose its corresponding command. The exact menu options and buttons displayed on the toolbar vary depending on the program you're running. Figure 2-8 shows the window for Pocket Excel with the Edit menu selected.

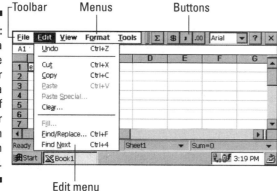

Figure 2-8:
Tapping a word on the toolbar displays a menu of options for the program running in the window.

Toolbar   Menus   Buttons

Edit menu

Sometimes, options appear on a menu in a light gray color. A *grayed-out* option cannot currently be used. If you are using Pocket Word, for example, the Paste option on the Edit menu remains grayed out until you have cut or copied some text.

To close a menu without choosing an option, tap the stylus anywhere else on the screen.

If you misplace your stylus, you can use the keyboard to access the menus on the toolbar. Press the Alt key to open the first menu on the menu bar, which is usually the File menu. After you open the menu, you can use the arrow keys to scroll up and down and from one menu to the others. After you decide which option you want, press the Enter key to choose the highlighted option.

The right side of the toolbar normally contains buttons. Each of these buttons performs a different task. Two standard buttons appear in the right corner of most windows, as discussed in Table 2-2.

Table 2-2	Those Little Buttons
Tap This Button	*To Do This*
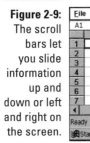 ✕	Close the window. If the OK button is also displayed in the left-hand corner, the window is closed without saving the changes you have made.
?	Display the online help file for the program that is running in the window.

The toolbar may contain other buttons between the menu options and the two buttons outlined in Table 2-2. These buttons are specific to the program you are running. For example, Pocket Excel has a button (which looks like a pair of scissors) that you can use to cut text. If you are not sure what other buttons do on the toolbar, refer to the chapter in this book that provides information about the specific program you are running.

The scroll bars

If the stuff that you are trying to view on your CE device does not all fit on-screen, Windows CE provides a funny-looking bar on the right side of the screen, as shown in Figure 2-9. If the information is too wide to display on-screen, Windows CE places a similar bar at the bottom of the window. These bars are affectionately known as *scroll bars*. If you tap the vertical scroll bar's up-arrow button, the screen moves up one line at a time each time you tap. Tapping the down-arrow button moves the screen down one line at a time. The overall effect is that of rolling through the document.

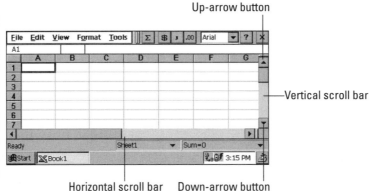

Figure 2-9:
The scroll bars let you slide information up and down or left and right on the screen.

Up-arrow button

Vertical scroll bar

Horizontal scroll bar   Down-arrow button

Scroll bars do not always behave the way you want them to. Depending on where you tap the scroll bar, either the screen scrolls up or down a line at a time, or all the text on the screen may change. Table 2-3 attempts to ease the confusion by explaining the results when you tap various parts of the scroll bar.

Table 2-3	Taming the Scroll Bar
Tap This Part	*To Do This*
Above the box	Display a screenful of information prior to the first line currently displayed on the screen.
Below the box	Display the next screenful of information below the last line displayed on the screen.
Down-arrow button	Scroll the display down one line. When you tap this button, the line that is currently at the top of the screen is no longer visible.
Up-arrow button	Scroll the display up one line. When you tap this button, the last line on the screen is no longer visible.

You can place the stylus on the box in the scroll bar and drag the box up and down to view the information you want.

Doing Dialog Boxes

When you use Windows CE, you frequently encounter windows that appear after you choose an option in a program. You use these windows, commonly referred to as *dialog boxes,* to communicate with Windows CE. Dialog boxes come in all shapes and sizes, and the type of information that they contain varies. They may simply request that you type a numeric value in one field, or you may need to specify values for several different fields. For example, you use the dialog box shown in Figure 2-10 to indicate the height you want a row to appear in a worksheet in Pocket Excel.

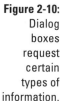

Figure 2-10:
Dialog
boxes
request
certain
types of
information.

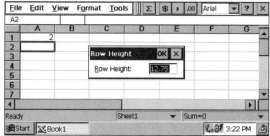

Windows CE also uses dialog boxes to inform you of something, such as the fact that it cannot locate the program you requested or that your batteries are running low. Dialog boxes used for this purpose are called *alert boxes*.

A couple of things are standard on all dialog boxes in Windows CE, however:

- ✔ You always find the name of the dialog box in the upper-left corner of the window.
- ✔ Windows CE always provides a way for you to close the dialog box. Each dialog box has at least two buttons in its upper-right corner. Table 2-4 describes these buttons.

Table 2-4	Buttons for Closing Dialog Boxes
Tap This Button	*If You Want To*
OK	Close the window and save all the changes you have made.
✕	Close the dialog box without saving the changes you have made.

Unveiling the Start Menu

When you tap the Start button, located at the lower-left corner of your screen (on the taskbar), you unveil the Start menu. This menu contains seven options, as shown in Figure 2-11. Each option in the Start menu takes you to a different type of information contained on your CE device, as outlined in Table 2-5.

Figure 2-11:
The Start menu provides tools for searching out different types of information.

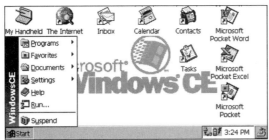

Table 2-5	The Start Menu
Tap This Option	*To Do This*
Programs	View another menu containing the programs that you can select on your CE device.
Favorites	See a list of your favorite Internet locations. You can tap a location to select it.
Documents	See the most recent documents that you created and quickly open a document by tapping the associated icon.
Settings	Adjust system settings for your CE device, such as changing the wallpaper on your desktop or setting a password for your CE device.
Help	Access the Windows CE online help system, where you can find some quick pointers on using Windows CE. Find more information about Windows CE online help later in this chapter.
Run	Quickly run a program, as long as you know the name of the program.
Suspend	Safely shut down your CE device. For details, check out the "Shutting down for the day" section, later in this chapter.

Unlike Windows 95 and Windows NT, Windows CE does not allow you to add items to the Start menu. You can only add items to the menus that appear when you select the Programs, Favorites, or Documents options.

Searching for programs to run

Windows CE keeps track of the different programs that you install on your device — well, most of them — and places them in a menu that displays when you tap the Programs option on the Start menu. I say "most of them" because only the programs that are added using an install program are normally placed on this menu.

To view many of the program files on your CE device, choose the Programs option on the Start menu. Tapping this menu option displays another menu of programs and menus, as shown in Figure 2-12. When you find the desired program, simply tap it to open it. To view the contents of the other menus, tap them and they open.

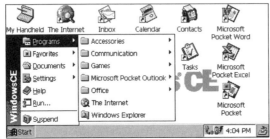

Figure 2-12:
The
Programs
option
displays a
menu of
folders and
programs.

If you do not find the program listed in the Programs menu, it probably was not set up to display on the menu when it was added to your device. You can use the Windows Explorer program, listed on the Programs menu, to find the program that you are looking for.

Selecting a favorite location

Windows CE keeps track of all your favorite Internet sites . . . well, at least the ones you indicate are your favorites. You can select a favorite site either from the Pocket Internet Explorer program or from the Windows CE Explorer program.

After you create a list of favorite sites, you can select a site from the list by simply selecting the Favorites option on the Start menu and then tapping the name of the site you want to visit.

Of course, you need to make sure your modem is set up to connect to your Internet Service Provider so that you can see the site you selected. For more information about connecting to the Internet, refer to Chapter 16.

Customizing the program list

If you have added any programs to your CE device, you may have figured out that some of those programs are not listed on the menu that appears when you choose Start⇨Programs. There is a very good explanation for this, and believe it or not, there is also a way for you to change the Programs menu.

Windows CE displays menu options for only the programs and folders in the Windows/ Programs folder on your device. If you want your program to be added to this group, simply place it in this folder. To do so, either copy or move the program from the current location into this folder. You can find out more about copying files in Chapter 9.

Finding the most recent documents

Have you ever sat down at your computer to work on a proposal you started the previous day but then couldn't remember what you named the proposal when you saved it? Windows CE can tell you the name of the most recent documents that you created, regardless of the program you used to create the documents.

To see the most recent documents that you worked with on your CE device, choose the Documents option from the Start menu. The Documents option opens a menu containing a list of the documents you last worked on, as shown in Figure 2-13.

Figure 2-13: The Documents menu lists the files that you worked on most recently.

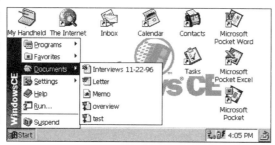

To open a document from the list, simply tap it. The file opens up in the program where you last worked on it. For example, a Pocket Word file opens up in Pocket Word.

If you get tired of seeing all those files listed on the Documents menu, you can quickly clear the menu by choosing Settings⇨Taskbar on the Start menu to display the Taskbar Properties dialog box. In this dialog box, tap the Start Menu tab and then tap the Clear button.

Finding some extra help

You may find yourself in a situation where you need help with your CE device and this book is not sitting by your side. Of course, I can't imagine ever going anywhere without *Windows CE 2 For Dummies,* but the day may come when that is the case.

Fortunately, Windows CE does provide some limited pointers in a help file installed on your CE device. This help file, shown in Figure 2-14, appears when you select the Help option from the Start menu.

Figure 2-14:
The
Windows
CE Help
window
provides
tips for
using the
programs
on your CE
device.

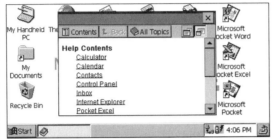

When you first open the help file, you see a list of underlined options. Each underlined option is called a *link*. If you tap an underlined option, the help file jumps to the specified location and the corresponding information appears.

The help file contains five buttons, as described in Table 2-6.

Table 2-6	Help File Buttons
Tap This Button	**To Do This**
▤ Contents	Return to the main screen. You can use this button to return home if you get lost in the help file.
↰ Back	Display the help screen you viewed prior to the current one. Tapping this button is like turning to the previous page in a book.
◈ All Topics	Display a list of all help topics that are available within Windows CE.
▯	View the help file on the full screen. This button provides a better view of the information.
▱	View the help file in a window.

Most Windows CE programs also come with their own unique help file. To open the help file for a program that you're currently running, tap the question mark button in the upper-right corner of the screen.

Running a program

The easiest way to run a program on your CE device is to locate the icon that represents the program. However, if you don't want to search for the icon, you can quickly run a program as long as you know its name.

To run a program, choose the Run option from the Start menu. The Run dialog box appears, as shown in Figure 2-15. Type the program name in the Open text box and tap the OK button. The program runs when you tap the OK button, as long as Windows CE can locate a program with the name you typed.

Figure 2-15:
The Start
menu offers
an option
for running
a program.

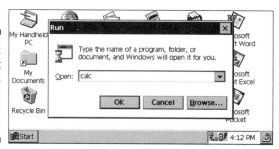

If you don't remember the exact name of the program, you can tap the Browse button and search for the program on your CE device. But if you don't know the program's name, I suggest just using the Programs option on the Start menu to locate the program.

When you open the Run dialog box, the Open text box contains the name of the last program that you ran using the Run option. You can tap the down-arrow button to display a list of programs that you have run in the past by using the Run option. To run one of the programs in the list, tap the name of the program and then tap the OK button.

Shutting down for the day

Probably one of the more confusing issues with any type of computer is figuring out the best way to shut it off. All CE devices come with an Off button on the keyboard, so of course, your first instinct is to press the Off button when you are ready to shut down. Unfortunately, pressing the Off button is not necessarily the best shutdown option for some CE devices. If you have not saved the information in your open files, you could lose this information.

The best way to turn off your CE device is to choose the Suspend option from the Start menu. When you choose this option, Windows CE makes sure that all open files have been saved properly and then turns off the device.

When you use the Suspend option, Windows CE basically goes to sleep, remembering everything you were working on. The next time you turn on your CE device, Windows CE makes sure that all those programs and documents are still open and ready for you to work on them again. If you have any unsaved documents, Windows CE saves the documents and opens them the next time you use your device. Windows CE does not prompt you for a filename before shutting off your CE device, however. After you save the file, Windows CE gets rid of the unnamed version that it saved when you suspended your CE device.

The only way to totally reboot your CE device is to press the Reset button. This action is rarely necessary, but you may have a program that instructs you to press this button to reboot your CE device.

Part II
What Can I Do with My CE Device?

The 5th Wave   By Rich Tennant

"IT'S A SOFTWARE PROGRAM THAT MORE FULLY RE-FLECTS AN ACTUAL OFFICE ENVIRONMENT. IT MULTI-TASKS WITH OTHER USERS, INTEGRATES SHARED DATA, AND THEN USES THAT INFORMATION TO NETWORK VICIOUS RUMORS THROUGH AN INTER-OFFICE LINK-UP."

In this part . . .

*N*ow that you've spent all that money for that new fancy gadget that runs Windows CE, probably the last thing you intend to do is to have it sit on some shelf and collect dust. To help you put your new tool to good use, this part shows you how to use many of the free programs that you have received with Windows CE. In this part, you find answers to the following questions:

✔ How do I remember all my appointments before I get a phone call telling me that I am late?

✔ How do I make sure that I never forget Mom's phone number?

✔ How do I make sure that I remember our anniversary?

✔ How do I work on that proposal without hauling home a big laptop?

✔ How do I adjust the budget figures while dining with a customer?

Chapter 3
Organizing Your Time

· ·

· ·

*W*indows CE comes with a full-blown calendar program, called Calendar, that you can use to schedule all the important stuff in your life. After you set up an appointment, your CE device reminds you when it is time for the appointment with a friendly beep, a flashing light, or both. (When you create the appointment, you decide how you want to be reminded.) Of course, that may ruin some of those good excuses we all have for missing a meeting or a dentist appointment. But at least you can be reminded of the appointment and then decide whether you want to remember it. After all, no one else has to know that you have such a powerful device at your disposal.

This chapter leads you through the process of creating appointments and events for all the important — and not-so-important — things you have to get done.

Locating Your Calendar

 The Calendar program is usually fairly easy to locate. Because Calendar is such an important program, most CE devices are set up by the manufacturer so that the icon is sitting on your Windows CE desktop. The icon resembles a basic wall calendar. To start Calendar, you simply use the stylus to double-tap the Calendar icon.

If you cannot find the Calendar icon on your desktop, don't despair; you can locate it by following these simple steps:

1. **Use the stylus to tap the Start button (located in the lower-left corner of the screen).**

    A pop-up menu containing various selections appears.

2. **Tap the Programs option.**

    Another menu opens containing a list of the programs and other menus on your CE device.

3. **Tap the Microsoft Pocket Outlook option.**

    You see a third menu containing more programs, as illustrated in Figure 3-1.

Figure 3-1:
Tap the
Start button
and find the
Calendar in
the pop-up
menus.

4. **Tap the Calendar option on the menu to display the Calendar program, shown in Figure 3-2.**

    You use this view of the Calendar program to set up all the important stuff you have to do, such as appointments and special events.

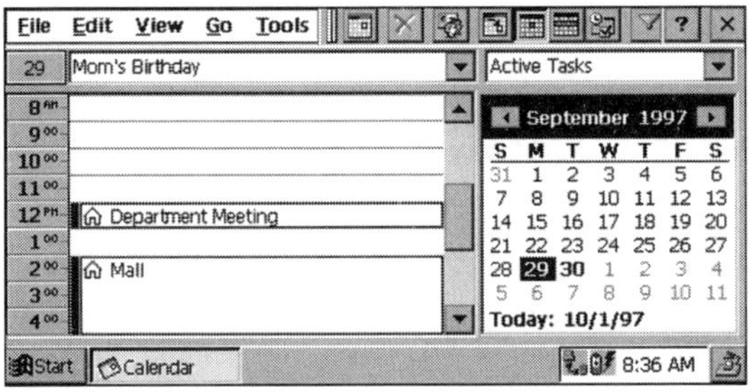

Figure 3-2:
The
Calendar
program
displays the
appointments
you have
scheduled.

If you have been using Microsoft Outlook or Schedule+ 7.0 on your personal computer to keep track of your appointments, you can transfer those appointments to your CE device. I discuss this topic in more detail in the section "Synchronizing Your Calendar with Microsoft Schedule+ 7.0 or Outlook," later in this chapter. For more detailed information about synchronizing with your personal computer, refer to Chapter 12.

Changing Your Frame of View

All right, I realize that I probably can't change your opinion about life on Mars, but at least I can show you how to look at your calendar information in a different way. Windows CE provides several ways to look at the information in the Calendar program; you can look at the calendar for the day, check your agenda, or you can view a week's worth of information on-screen, as shown in Figure 3-3.

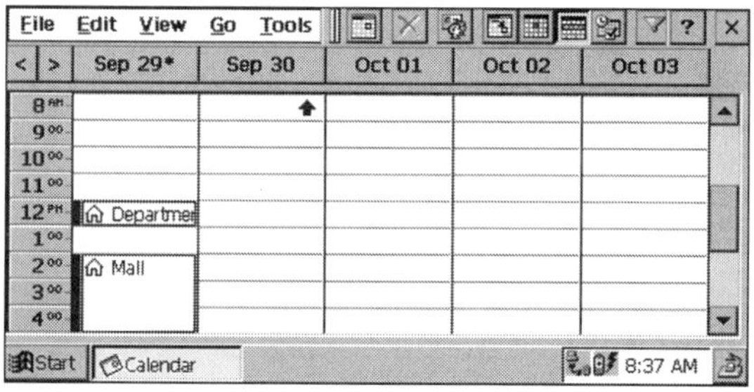

Figure 3-3:
Week view
displays a
five-day
week as a
default.

To view the calendar for a specific day, simply tap the desired date in the calendar on the right side of the screen and then tap the Day button on the toolbar. This view shows you a list of times with any scheduled appointments on the left side of the screen, and a small calendar with the selected day highlighted on the right side of the screen.

To view the agenda for any date, simply tap the desired date in the calendar and then tap the Agenda button on the toolbar. This view shows you the appointments, all-day events, and tasks that are scheduled for the selected date.

To view the week's appointments, you simply tap the Week button on the toolbar at the top of the screen. When you view Calendar in Week view, only the usual five working days (Monday through Friday) are displayed. To see the entire seven-day week, choose View⇨Number of Days⇨7.

You can view any number of days (between 1 and 7) in Week view. To change the number of days you want displayed, simply choose View⇨ Number of Days and then select the number of days you want to see from the menu.

Each appointment appears on the calendar at the specified time. If you look closely, you may see one or more symbols next to each appointment. Each of these little pictures serves a purpose. Table 3-1 describes the six symbols that may be displayed next to an appointment in either Day or Week mode.

Table 3-1	Deciphering the Symbols of an Appointment
Symbol	**Description**
🔔	You set a reminder for the appointment.
📅	You set up a meeting and sent out requests for people to attend.
📝	You have entered additional information about the appointment in the Notes section of the Appointment card.
🔑	You indicated that the appointment is private by selecting the Private check box on the Appointment card. If you connect to a network and others see your appointment, they will not know what you have scheduled, just that you are busy.
🔄	The appointment is a *recurring appointment,* meaning that it occurs on a regular basis.
🏠	You set a location for the appointment.

Creating an Appointment

An *appointment* is something that is scheduled to occur within a specific time frame on a specific date. For example, you may use an appointment to represent the time when you need to be at Mom's house for Sunday dinner.

Before Windows CE can keep track of your appointments, you need to enter them into the Calendar program. Now, if you want to conveniently forget to attend something without feeling guilty about it, you probably don't want to add that appointment to Calendar. Or if you do, make sure that your CE device doesn't remind you of the appointment, and as long as you remember to forget to check your CE device at that time, you will still forget the appointment.

That said, suppose you need to create a dental appointment for Monday, October 6, at 9:00 a.m. You decide to create this appointment in Day view, because using this view is the easiest way to view the stuff happening on a specific day. To create the appointment, simply follow these steps:

1. **On the small calendar in the bottom-right corner of the screen, tap the date of the appointment. For example, locate October 6 for the dental appointment, as shown in Figure 3-4.**

   When you tap a date, a black square appears around it, indicating that the date is selected. An open square box indicates the current date.

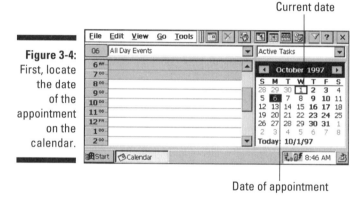

Figure 3-4:
First, locate the date of the appointment on the calendar.

2. **In the time section on the left side of the screen, use the scroll bars to locate the time of the appointment.**

   For the dental appointment example, the time is 9:00 a.m.

3. **Tap the time of your appointment (for example, 9:00 AM) and drag the stylus down the screen to the time when the appointment should be over (for example, 12:00 PM).**

   If you draw a line from one time to another, that time frame appears highlighted on-screen, as shown in Figure 3-5.

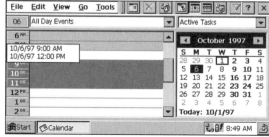

Figure 3-5:
Highlight the time frame of the new appointment.

4. Tap the New Appointment button on the toolbar at the top of the screen.

The New Appointment button is the leftmost button on the toolbar. It looks like a small calendar with a specific date selected. You can also display the Appointment card by choosing File⇨New Appointment.

After you choose the New Appointment button or command, an Appointment card appears, as shown in Figure 3-6.

Figure 3-6:
You create
a new
appointment
on a blank
Appointment
card.

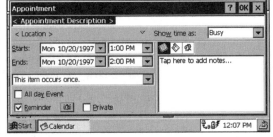

In Day view, you can highlight a time on the calendar for a new appointment and start typing. Windows CE recognizes the fact that you want to create a new appointment and opens a new Appointment card. Whatever you type appears in the field that contains the text <Appointment Description> on the Appointment card.

5. In the field that contains the text <Appointment Description>, **type a description for your appointment.**

If you are adding a dental appointment, for example, type something as simple as **Dentist**.

6. In the field that contains the text <Location>, **enter the location of the appointment.**

If you have had an appointment at this location previously, you can tap the down-arrow button next to the field and then tap the location in the drop-down list that appears; otherwise, type the desired location in the field.

Windows CE has designed the Appointment card so that you do not have to type values for both the description and the location of the appointment. For example, if you plan to be at the mall shopping from 2:00 p.m. to 5:00 p.m., you can simply type **mall** for the location and not type anything for the description. Windows CE just displays your location on the calendar without a description.

7. **In the drop-down list box labeled Sho̲w time as, select the value that identifies how you want this appointment to appear on your calendar to others.**

   This field is important only if you are synchronizing your calendar with a personal computer that is connected to a network. If you set this value, people can look at your calendar and determine whether you are available at a specific time. You can specify that the time is displayed as Free, Tentative, Busy, or Out of Office.

8. **Make sure that the S̲tarts fields contain the correct date (for example, Mon 10/6/97) and the correct time (for example, 9:00 AM).**

   If you need to change the date, tap the down-arrow button next to each field to display the Calendar window, as shown in Figure 3-7. Tap the date you want to add to the Appointment card. To correct the time, tap the down-arrow button and then tap the correct time.

9. **Make sure that the E̲nds fields contain the correct date (for example, Mon 10/6/97) and the correct time (for example, 12:00 PM).**

   When you select a date in the Starts field, Windows CE places the same date in the Ends field. By the same token, if you set the date in the Ends field without setting the date in the Starts field, Windows CE places the same date in the Starts field. Windows CE assumes that you intend to start and complete the appointment on the same date.

10. **Make sure the R̲eminder field contains a check mark so Windows CE will remind you when it is time for your appointment.**

    Windows CE reminds you of the appointment based on the default reminder settings. You can find more information about customizing your reminders in the following section of this chapter.

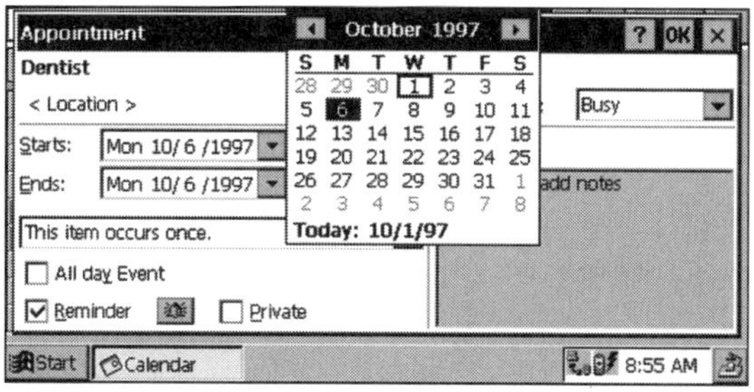

Figure 3-7:
To adjust
the date in
the Starts
or Ends
fields,
use the
Calendar
window.

11. **Tap the OK button in the top-right corner of the screen to save the appointment.**

You can select the Private check box if you have created an appointment that you don't want to let other people see. This setting is necessary only if you are connecting to a network or synchronizing to a personal computer that is connected to a network where people can check your schedule. If you have selected the Private check box, when others look at your schedule, they just see that you are not available at that time.

Setting a reminder for your appointment

You don't do yourself any good if you set up an appointment and then forget to show up for it. This is where Windows CE really shines. Windows CE can remind you of an appointment, even when your CE device is turned off. How your CE device reminds you depends on the settings you specify. For example, if you specify that the light on your CE device should flash and the device should beep 15 minutes prior to an appointment, your CE device beeps to get your attention, and the light flashes until you turn on your CE device and view the Calendar Reminder message. Figure 3-8 shows a sample Calendar Reminder message.

Figure 3-8: A message appears on-screen to remind you of a scheduled appointment.

You set the reminder information by tapping the Reminder Defaults button on the Appointment card. You can set the reminder information when you create the new appointment or after the appointment has been created. Simply follow these steps:

1. **Double-tap the appointment to display its Appointment card.**

2. **Make sure that a check mark appears in the <u>R</u>eminder check box.**

   Windows CE reminds you of an appointment only if you have selected the Reminder check box.

 3. **Tap the Reminder Defaults button to display the Reminder Defaults dialog box, shown in Figure 3-9.**

Figure 3-9:
Use the
Reminder
Defaults
dialog box
to indicate
when you
want to be
reminded.

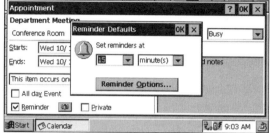

4. **In the first drop-down list box, tap the down-arrow button and tap the amount of time you want.**

   You can select a value of 1, 5, 10, 15, 30, or 45 in this field. If you want to set a reminder for an hour prior to the appointment, for example, tap 1.

   If you want your reminder to be at a time interval that is not available in the list, such as 20 minutes before the meeting, type a value in this field by highlighting the value that is currently in the field and typing a new value.

5. **In the next drop-down list box, tap the down-arrow button and then tap the option you want to select: minutes, hours, days, or weeks.**

6. **Tap the Reminder Options button to set the type of reminder you want for this appointment in the Notification Options window.**

   When you tap the Reminder Options button, the Notification Options dialog box appears (see Figure 3-10).

7. **Tap the reminders you want.**

   When you select a reminder, a check mark appears in the box next to the option.

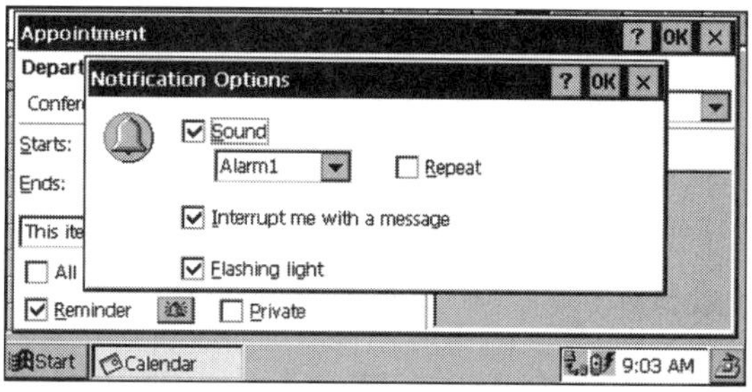

Figure 3-10:
Use the
Notifications
Options
dialog box
to specify
which
reminders
you want.

If you select the Sound option or the Flashing Light option, your CE device reminds you of the appointment even when you've turned off the device.

Windows CE comes with sounds you can select for the Sound option in the Notification Options dialog box. The easiest way to determine which sound you want is to test each one until you find one that you like. To test a sound, simply select the sound in the drop-down list box. To have the sound repeated five times in succession, make sure you select the Repeat check box.

8. **Tap the OK button to save your selections in the Notifications Options dialog box.**

9. **Tap the OK button to save your selections in the Reminder Defaults dialog box.**

10. **Tap the OK button to save your reminder selections on the Appointment card.**

Making an appointment recurring

Most people have appointments they need to attend on a regular basis, such as weekly staff meetings or workouts at the gym. These types of appointments are called *recurring appointments*. With Windows CE, if you set up an appointment as a recurring appointment, it continues to appear on your calendar. You don't need to add a new appointment each time. You can set the information for an appointment when you create the appointment or sometime after you create the appointment. To set up a recurring appointment, simply follow these steps:

1. **Double-tap the selected appointment on the calendar to display its Appointment card.**

2. **Tap the down-arrow button next to the Recurrence field to display a list of different recurrence options, as shown in Figure 3-11.**

Figure 3-11:
Use the
Recurrence
drop-down
list box to
set up a
recurring
appointment.

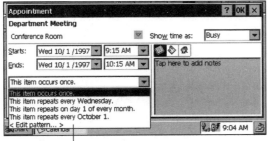

Reccurence drop-down list box

3. **Tap the appropriate option in the Recurrence drop-down list.**

   The recurrence information is placed in the same location where the Starts and Ends fields were originally located on your Appointment card.

4. **Tap the OK button to save the recurring appointment in your calendar.**

If the Recurrence list box doesn't contain the recurrence option you want, you can customize the way the appointment recurs. To customize the way an appointment recurs, simply follow these steps:

1. **Locate the appointment you want to set as recurring and double-tap it to display the Appointment card.**

2. **Tap the down-arrow button next to the Recurrence field and tap the <Edit Pattern> option.**

   When you tap the <Edit Pattern> option, the Edit Pattern wizard appears, as shown in Figure 3-12. If you don't want to create a custom pattern, you can use one of the patterns in the drop-down list box.

Figure 3-12:
Use the Edit
Pattern
wizard to
create a
custom
pattern
for how
often the
appointment
should
recur.

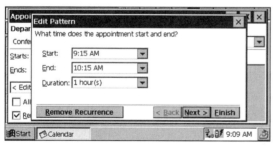

A *wizard* is just a fancy term that some computer nerd came up with to refer to a window that takes you through a series of questions to gather information. You normally tap buttons, such as the Next and Back buttons, to move through the different questions.

3. **On the Edit Pattern wizard, make sure the appropriate times are specified in the Start and End fields.**

   If you need to change the time in either field, simply tap the down-arrow button and select the correct time. The value in the Duration field automatically adjusts itself to reflect the times you select, but you can set that field, too.

4. **Tap the <u>N</u>ext button to display the next question for the wizard, shown in Figure 3-13.**

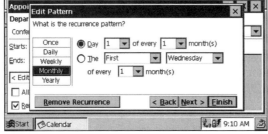

Figure 3-13: The second screen is where you actually select the recurrence pattern.

5. **Tap the button that indicates the frequency with which you want the appointment to occur.**

   If you want to create a task that occurs every month, for example, select the Monthly button. The options that appear differ depending on the button you select.

6. **Use the other fields in this window to define the recurrence pattern.**

   For example, you may want to specify that a monthly appointment should occur on a specific day of the week — say, the second Tuesday of every month. In that case, tap the second radio button, the one next to the word *The*. Next, tap the down-arrow button and highlight the word Second in the drop-down list, tap the down-arrow button next to the second field, and highlight the word *Tuesday* in the drop-down list. Finally, type **1** in the last field.

7. **After selecting the recurrence pattern, tap the <u>N</u>ext button so you can indicate when the appointment starts and ends, as shown in Figure 3-14.**

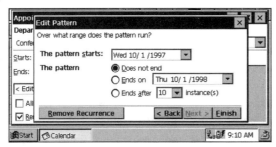

Figure 3-14: Indicate the actual time frame over which the appointments should continue to occur.

8. **In the field labeled The pattern starts, indicate when you want the first appointment to be placed on your calendar.**

   The date in this field comes from the original date you specified for the appointment on the Appointment card. If you want to change this date, simply tap the down-arrow button to display the Calendar window and select the appropriate date.

9. **Select the appropriate radio button to indicate when you want to end the appointments.**

   You can come back and modify these settings at any time. If you want the appointments to continue indefinitely, tap the Does not end radio button.

10. **Tap the Finish button to put the recurrence information on the Appointment card.**

    The recurrence information is placed in the same location where the Starts and Ends fields were originally located on your Appointment card.

11. **Tap the OK button to save the recurring appointments in your calendar.**

If you ever want to get rid of your recurring appointments, display the Edit Pattern wizard and tap the Remove Recurrence button. This button saves you the hassle of deleting any remaining appointments on your calendar.

Entering additional information about an appointment

Have you ever showed up at an appointment and forgotten to bring along some information that you needed, or perhaps remembered that you had an appointment but misplaced the directions to get there? Well, Windows CE provides a solution to these dilemmas. The Calendar program provides a section on each Appointment card where you can include additional information about an appointment. In fact, if you make an appointment to go grocery shopping, you can type your entire grocery list here.

So where is this place? To view it, simply display an Appointment card (either a new or existing card) and then tap the Notes button. This displays the Notes section on the Appointment card, as shown in Figure 3-15.

Perform these simple steps to enter additional information about an appointment you have set up:

Figure 3-15:
Type any
additional
information,
such as the
address
for the
appointment,
in the Notes
section.

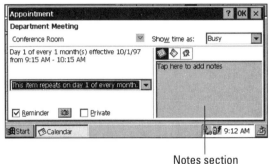

Notes section

1. **Double-tap an appointment to display its Appointment card.**

2. **Tap the Notes button to display the Notes section of the Appointment card.**

   You find the Notes button, along with two other buttons, on the right side of the screen under the Show time as field. The Notes button resembles a miniature notepad.

3. **Tap the highlighted Notes section to display a dialog box in which you can type your notes that relate to the selected appointment, as shown in Figure 3-16.**

   On this screen, you can type text or draw images with your stylus. You can use several formatting options when adding stuff to your notes, as outlined in Table 3-2.

4. **After you finish making your notes, simply tap the OK button and the stuff displays in the Notes section for the appointment.**

Figure 3-16:
You can
design the
notes
for the
appointment
in this
dialog box.

Table 3-2	Useful Notes Buttons
Tap This Button	*If You Want To*
✐	Draw something, such as a map, with your stylus.
Ⓘ	Select text you've entered, or an object you've drawn, so you can format it.
⟻	Insert vertical or horizontal spacing between stuff in your notes. Simply tap the button and then drag to insert the space. As you drag the cursor across the screen, it changes to an arrow indicating the amount of space that will be inserted when you lift up the stylus.
B	Bold the selected text or the text you are going to type.
I	Put the selected text or the text you are going to type in italics.
U̲	Underline the selected text or the text you are going to type.
↰	Undo the last thing you did. You can undo as many as five things you've done.
↱	Undo the last undo you performed.
100% ▼	Select the zoom size for displaying the notes. To change the zoom size, tap the down-arrow button and select a new size.

Assigning a category to your appointment

If you tend to have a lot of different types of appointments, you may want to consider categorizing them. After you categorize your appointments, you can use the Filter option to view only the appointments that relate to a specific category. This option can be extremely useful when you're looking for a specific appointment on your calendar.

 You can specify a category for any appointment by simply tapping the Category button on the Appointment card. When you do this, you get a list of categories that you can assign to your specific appointment, as shown in Figure 3-17. To select a category, simply tap the check box next to the desired category. (You can assign multiple categories to the same appointment, if desired.)

Category list

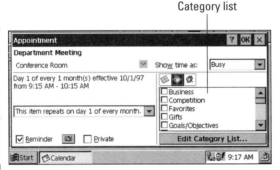

Figure 3-17:
Categories
can be
useful for
keeping
track of
related
appointments.

You can customize the category list by tapping the Edit Category List button. This button displays the Categories dialog box, shown in Figure 3-18, where you can add and delete categories from the list. This dialog box enables you to get rid of all those categories that you don't need and thus create a more meaningful list.

Any changes you make to the category list are reflected on the category lists for the Inbox, Contacts, and Tasks programs.

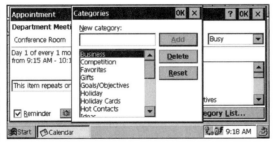

Figure 3-18:
Customize
the
category
list in the
Categories
dialog box.

 After you assign categories to your appointments, you can view appointments within specific categories by tapping the Filter drop-down list on the toolbar and selecting the categories that you want to see. When you tap the Filter drop-down list, you see only the categories that have been associated with appointments on your calendar. When you select a category, only the appointments that meet that category will display on your calendar.

Creating an All-Day Event

An *event* is something that takes place on a specific date but lasts for an indefinite amount of time. If you are like me, you have several events, such as birthdays and vacations, that you need to add to your calendar so that you don't forget them. You add these types of events to the Calendar program in basically the same fashion that you create an appointment.

When you add an all-day event to your calendar, the event appears above the list of appointments (in Day view), as shown in Figure 3-19. If you have multiple all-day events scheduled for that day, simply tap the down-arrow button to view a list of the events.

Figure 3-19:
All-day events are listed at the top of the calendar in Day view.

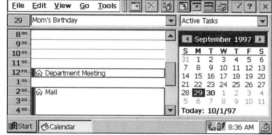

To add an all-day event in Day view, simply follow these steps:

1. Tap the down-arrow button next to the All Day Events field and then tap the New All Day Event option.

As shown in Figure 3-20, a new Appointment card appears with the All Day Event check box selected. Because the All Day Event box is checked, the Starts and Ends fields do not contain time fields.

If you are creating an all-day event that will occur every year on this date, such as a birthday, or an anniversary, you can select the <New Annual All Day Event> option. This option creates a recurring all-day event.

Figure 3-20:
You add an all-day event by selecting the All Day Event check box.

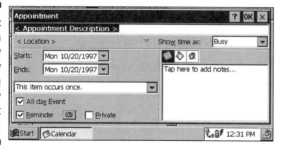

2. **In the field that contains the text** `<Appointment Description>`, **type a description for the event. If you are scheduling a family vacation, for example, you may type** Family Vacation.

Be sure to use a description that lets you easily recognize the event you have scheduled.

3. **In the field that contains the text** `<Location>`, **type a location for the event** — Cancun, Mexico, **for example.**

If you previously had another event or appointment at a location, you can tap the down-arrow button and select the location from the list of other locations.

4. **Make sure that the** <u>S</u>**tarts field contains the date the event starts — for example,** 11/23/1997.

If the date is not correct, tap the down-arrow button to display the Calendar window — shown in Figure 3-21 — and then tap the correct date. If you need to move to the previous or next month on the calendar, tap the month name to display a list of different months and then select the appropriate month from the list, as shown in Figure 3-22. To change the year, tap the year, and use the up and down arrow buttons to select the appropriate year.

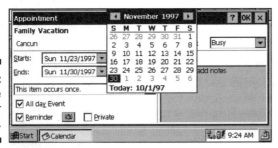

Figure 3-21:
The
Calendar
window.

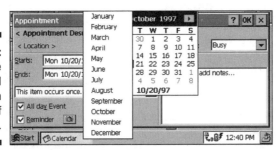

Figure 3-22:
Select the
desired
month from
the list of
months.

5. **Make sure that the Ends field contains the date the event ends — for example,** 11/30/1997.

   If the date is not correct, tap the down-arrow button and then tap the correct date on the Calendar window.

6. **If you want your CE device to remind you prior to the event, tap the Reminder check box so that a check mark appears in the box.**

   As with appointments, you are adding events so that you will remember them. Unless you check your calendar on a regular basis, I recommend always having a reminder for an event. The reminder occurs based on your default reminder settings. For more information about customizing the reminder, refer to the section "Setting a reminder for your appointment," earlier in this chapter.

7. **Tap the OK button to save the new event to your calendar.**

Here are a few points to keep in mind when dealing with all-day events on the calendar:

✔ The days of your scheduled event appear bold on the calendar, just as with an appointment.

✔ All-day events do not appear on the calendar when you view it in Week view. An asterisk appears next to the date if you have scheduled an event for the specified date, however.

✔ If you view the calendar in Agenda view, Calendar lists the all-day events at the top of the summary list of appointments and events.

Setting Up a Meeting

You can use the Calendar program to set up meetings with other people in your Contact list whose e-mail addresses you have. Simply create the meeting within the Calendar program and specify the people you want to invite to the meeting. After you create the meeting and select the people you want to attend, the meeting requests are placed in your Outbox in the Inbox program, waiting for you to connect to your e-mail account and send the messages.

Only the contacts that have e-mail addresses can be invited to your meeting. If they do not have e-mail addresses, they will not appear on the list.

Make sure you connect to your e-mail account after creating a meeting so the meeting requests can be sent out to the appropriate people. After all, if they don't know they are invited, they probably won't show up.

Creating a meeting request is actually just like creating an appointment, with a couple of different steps:

1. **On the calendar, select the date and time when you want to hold the meeting.**

2. **Tap the Make Meeting button on the toolbar.**

   The Appointment card opens up with the names of your contacts with e-mail accounts listed on the right side of the screen, as shown in Figure 3-23. The Make Meeting button is the one that has silhouetted heads on it.

Figure 3-23:
With a meeting request, all the e-mail addresses in your Contact list are displayed.

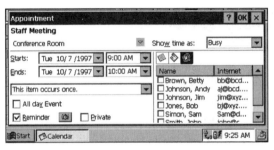

3. **Create your meeting following the same steps you normally use to create an appointment.**

   If you need more information about creating an appointment, refer to the section "Creating an Appointment" earlier in this chapter.

4. **In the e-mail address section, tap the check box next to each person you want to invite to the meeting.**

   The addresses and names in this list are the people you have added to your contact list using the Contacts program. You cannot type any e-mail addresses on this screen — if the people you want to invite are not listed, you need to run the Contacts program and add them to your list of contacts.

5. **When you are finished, tap the OK button to add the meeting to your calendar and place the meeting requests in your Outbox to be sent out.**

If you decide to change the time or date of the meeting, new messages will be sent out indicating an updated meeting request.

Removing Unwanted Appointments and Events

The time will come when you want to remove an appointment or an event from your calendar. Of course, life would be too simple if you were able to use the same steps to delete both appointments and all-day events, so you must remember different steps for each process.

Keep in mind that Windows CE does not remove appointments from your calendar. This way, you can review the previous months and determine what you were doing on a specific date. The drawback is that each appointment and all-day event that is stored uses some of your CE device's storage memory. If you are running low on memory, you may want to consider removing some of the old appointments.

Deleting an appointment

To delete an appointment, all you need to do is follow these simple steps:

1. **Open either Day or Week view, and locate the appointment you want to delete.**

   Make sure that you tap the appointment so that it is highlighted on-screen.

   To use Day or Week view, you must tap one of those buttons in the toolbar. If you are in Agenda view, you cannot delete appointments.

2. **Tap the delete button at the top of the screen in the toolbar.**

   The Delete button resembles a giant X. When you tap it, a message box appears to verify your selection (see Figure 3-24).

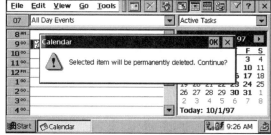

Figure 3-24: To delete the selected appointment, tap the OK button; otherwise, tap the X button.

Deleting an all-day event

Windows CE does not provide a simple way to delete an all-day event from your calendar. If you want to get rid of an all-day event, take the following steps:

1. **Select the date of the all-day event that you want to delete.**

2. **Tap the Agenda button to view the agenda for that date.**

3. **Select the all-day event that you want to delete on the agenda.**

4. **Choose Edit⇨Delete.**

   You see the same message window that displays anytime you delete an appointment (refer to Figure 3-24).

5. **Tap the OK button and the all-day event is removed.**

Viewing Today's Agenda

 You can view all the appointments, events, and tasks you have scheduled for the day by using Agenda view, shown in Figure 3-25. By viewing the agenda, you are able to see a list of all the stuff you have scheduled for the selected day. To open Agenda view, tap the Agenda button in the toolbar.

 You can add or modify appointments or events while viewing the agenda by simply double-tapping the selected event or appointment.

All-day events appear at the top of the appointments list. The list provides only the start time for each appointment.

The Active Tasks section contains the tasks that were either scheduled to be started today or have not yet been completed. **Remember:** You create the tasks by using the Tasks program, which I discuss in Chapter 4.

Figure 3-25:
Agenda
view
summarizes
everything
you have
scheduled
for the
selected
day.

To view the agenda for a different date, you can either tap the down-arrow button next to the current date to display the Calendar window, tap the >> button to display the next date after the current one, or tap the << button to display the previous date.

Finding That Lost Appointment on Your Calendar

 Have you ever set up an appointment and then forgotten when it was scheduled for? The Find button on the toolbar enables you to search for your appointment. When you tap the Find button, the Find dialog box appears, as shown in Figure 3-26.

Figure 3-26:
Use the
Find dialog
box to
search
for an
appointment.

The following steps show you how quickly you can locate an appointment:

1. Make sure the <u>T</u>ype field contains the value Appoint.

Appoint actually stands for appointment, but those programmers at Microsoft did not make the field large enough to display the entire word.

To change the value of the field, simply tap the down-arrow button and highlight the correct value. This little search utility actually looks for something in the Calendar, Inbox, Contacts, and Tasks programs without running those programs.

2. Type the information you want to find in the <u>F</u>ind field.

Make sure you type text that would be found on the appointment you are looking for. For example, if you are looking for your dentist appointment, type **Dentist**.

If you only type a portion of the word, such as **Den**, you see all appointments that contain a word with the characters *den*.

The Find options do not search through any notes that may be attached to an appointment. Therefore, if the text you are searching for is only in the notes, that appointment will not be found.

3. **Make sure the Start and End fields specify an appropriate date range.**

The dates you specify in these fields indicate the range that Windows CE uses to find your appointment. If the appointment is before or after the specified dates, Windows CE will not locate the appointment.

If you want to search through all appointments, simply remove the check marks next to the Start and End fields.

4. **Tap the OK button to perform the search.**

Windows CE looks for all the appointments that contain the text you specified. Any appointments containing that text are listed in the section at the bottom of the Find dialog box, as shown in Figure 3-27.

Figure 3-27:
When you
see the
results of
the find, tap
the desired
appointment
to display its
Appointment
card.

5. **Tap the desired appointment in the list.**

Windows CE displays the corresponding Appointment card for the selected appointment.

Printing Your Calendar

Sooner or later you may want to print out a copy of your calendar. Luckily, Windows CE provides capabilities for printing directly from your CE device if you have the printer connected to the serial port on your CE device (the port you use to connect to your personal computer) or you are able to send stuff to your printer using the infrared port.

Follow these steps to print your calendar information:

1. **Choose File⇨Print Options to display the Print Options dialog box, shown in Figure 3-28.**

   This dialog box is where you select the information that you want displayed on the printout of your calendar. For example, you need to indicate the date range you want to print, whether you want appointments and events or just one of them, and finally what information should print for each appointment or event.

Figure 3-28:
You can specify exactly what you want to print.

2. **Make sure the Start date and End date fields specify an appropriate date range.**

   The dates you specify in these fields indicate the range that Windows CE uses to print the calendar information. Any appointments or events prior to or after the specified dates will not be printed.

3. **In the Fields section, select the fields you want printed for each appointment or event.**

   You probably want to make sure you print the description, so you know what the appointment or event is.

4. **In the Selection section, indicate whether you want to print only events, only appointments, or both appointments and events.**

5. **Tap the OK button to save your print options.**

6. **Choose File⇨Print to display the Print dialog box, illustrated in Figure 3-29.**

Figure 3-29:
You can print out your list of tasks using the Print option.

7. **Make the appropriate selections on the Print dialog box and tap the OK button to send the calendar information to the printer.**

For a complete description of all the information you can specify in each field on the Print dialog box, see Table 6-8 in Chapter 6.

Synchronizing Your Calendar with Microsoft Schedule+ 7.0 or Outlook

If you use your personal computer to maintain your personal calendar, you probably don't want to retype everything onto your new CE device. If you use Microsoft Schedule+ 7.0 or Microsoft Outlook under Windows 95 or Windows NT 4.0 on your personal computer, you are in luck.

Windows CE lets you copy all the calendar information from Schedule+ or Outlook onto your CE device. By the same token, you can copy the calendar information from your CE device back into Schedule+ or Outlook. This process of making sure that both your CE device and your personal computer contain the same personal calendar information is called *synchronizing*.

To synchronize your CE device with your personal computer, a few things are required:

✔ A data cable connected between your CE device and your personal computer

✔ Windows CE Services running on your personal computer

✔ Microsoft Schedule+ 7.0 or Microsoft Outlook on your personal computer

For more detailed information about synchronizing your CE device and your personal computer, see Chapter 12.

Chapter 4

Keeping Track of Everyday Tasks

- -

In This Chapter

▶ Figuring out when to create a task

▶ Locating the Tasks program

▶ Creating a new task

▶ Creating recurring tasks

▶ Adding notes to a task

▶ Downloading tasks from your personal computer

▶ Sorting your tasks

▶ Indicating that a task is completed

▶ Modifying tasks

▶ Checking today's tasks in the Calendar program

- -

*W*ith the Tasks program, you can quickly create your own personal to-do lists. After you add tasks to your CE device, you can view the current tasks on your personal calendar, and your CE device reminds you to either start or complete a task.

This chapter shows you how to set up all your tasks by using the Tasks program that comes with Windows CE. You also see how to use the Calendar program to view all the tasks that you need to work on for a particular day. Most important, you see how to set your CE device to remind you to perform a task.

Is It Really a Task?

The difference between a task and an appointment (or a recurring appointment or an all-day event) can be confusing until you get the hang of thinking in Windows CE-speak. You create a *task* for something that you need to accomplish but not necessarily at a specific time; you create an *appointment*

for an event that occurs at a set time. If you have a doctor's appointment tomorrow at 2:00 p.m., for example, you should create an appointment. If you intend to clean the garage sometime this weekend, you should create a task — perhaps called Clean the garage — and assign a time frame of Friday through Sunday.

You create tasks by using the Tasks program, which I discuss in this chapter. You create appointments, recurring appointments, and all-day events by using the Calendar program, which I discuss in Chapter 3.

Locating the Tasks Program

Before you can create a task, you need to locate the Tasks program on your CE device. The Tasks program provides a central location where you can keep track of all your individual tasks. This program is fairly easy to find.

 The Tasks program is probably sitting on the desktop of your CE device. The icon for the Tasks program looks like a clipboard with a big check mark on it. When you locate the icon, double-tap it to open the Tasks program.

If you cannot find the Tasks program icon on your desktop, you should be able to locate it by following these simple steps:

1. **Use the stylus to tap the Start button (located in the lower-left corner of the screen).**

   A pop-up menu containing various selections appears.

2. **Tap the <u>P</u>rograms option.**

   You see another menu containing a list of the programs and other menus on your CE device.

3. **Tap the Microsoft Pocket Outlook option.**

   You see a third menu containing more programs, as illustrated in Figure 4-1.

4. **Tap the Tasks option on the menu to display the Tasks program, shown in Figure 4-2.**

   You use this program to create, modify, and view your list of tasks.

Figure 4-1:
You can
find the
Tasks
program on
the pop-up
menus
available
when you
tap the
Start
button.

Figure 4-2:
The Tasks
program
displays a
list of the
existing
tasks on
your CE
device.

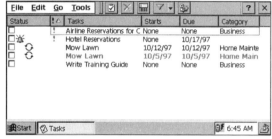

If you use Schedule+ 7.0 or Outlook on your personal computer to keep track of your tasks, you can transfer those tasks to your CE device. You can even transfer tasks from your CE device to your personal computer. I discuss these topics in more detail later in this chapter.

A check mark in the box in the Status column indicates that you have completed the corresponding task. You can add and remove check marks by simply tapping the box.

Creating a New Task

You can use the Tasks program to create your own electronic to-do lists. You do not need to be concerned about the order in which you add your tasks to the Tasks program. After you add tasks to your CE device, you can sort them any way you want. Simply follow these steps to enter a new task:

1. **Open a new Task card, shown in Figure 4-3, by tapping the New Task button, located on the toolbar at the top of the screen.**

The New Task button is the leftmost button on the toolbar. It looks like a clipboard with a check mark on it.

You can also open a new Task card by choosing File⇨New Task.

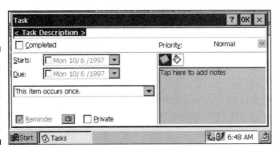

Figure 4-3: Use the Task card to create a new task.

2. **Type the description for your new task in the field that contains the text** `<Task Description>`.

Although Windows CE lets you type a fairly lengthy description in this field, you are going to have a difficult time reading it without manually scrolling the line by moving the cursor. The best recommendation for this field is to type a description that fits within the field without the text scrolling. If you want to say more about this task, try adding that information to the Notes section. (See the section "Adding notes to a task," later in this chapter.)

3. **Tap the down-arrow button in the Priority field and assign a priority to this task.**

If you do not select the priority value, Windows CE assigns a priority of Normal to the task. You can use the Priority field to sort out the most important tasks. For example, if you assign a priority value of High to the most important tasks, all the high-priority tasks appear first on the Tasks screen.

 Technically, you don't have to prioritize your tasks. If you don't want to prioritize the tasks, simply maintain a consistent value in the Priority field for all tasks that you create. You can just leave the default value of Normal in the field.

4. **Tap the check box next to both the Starts and Due fields if you want to indicate the date when the task should begin, be completed, or both.**

If you don't have a start or due date, the task just sits on your calendar until you mark it as completed. If you specify a date, the task does not appear on your calendar until the specified date.

5. **To select a date, tap the down-arrow button next to either the Starts field or the Due field to open the Calendar window, as shown in Figure 4-4, and then tap the date you want to add to the Task card.**

The down-arrow button is located on the right side of each date field. When the Calendar window first appears, it contains either today's date or the last date selected on the current Task card. You can scroll to a different month by tapping the left and right arrows that appear next to the name of the month.

You can manually type the date in both the Starts and Due fields, although this is probably not the best way to enter the dates. You cannot just type 2/14/97. If you type the **2**, the program automatically fills in the rest of the date, based on today's date. (For example, if today is December 18, 1996, and you typed **12**, the date would be 12/18/1996.) To change the day, you need to either tap that portion with the stylus and then type over it or use the arrow keys on the keyboard to move to that portion of the date.

When you select a date in the Starts field, the same date automatically appears in the Due field. If you want the task to be completed by a different date, you need to select a date for the Due field.

If you set the date in the Due field without setting the date in the Starts field, Windows CE does not change the date in the Starts field.

Figure 4-4:
The
Calendar
window
enables you
to easily
select the
date.

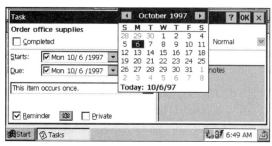

6. **Select the Reminder check box to make sure that Windows CE reminds you on the date when you should either start or complete the task.**

When you actually get reminded depends on whether you specify a start or due date.

You can find more information about customizing your reminders for each task in the following section of this chapter.

7. **Tap the OK button to save the new task.**

Select the Completed check box only if you have finished the task. When you select this box, a check mark appears in that box and one also appears next to the task in the Tasks window.

You can select the Private check box if you have created a task that you don't want to let other people see. This is only necessary if you are connecting to a network or synchronizing to a personal computer that is connected to a network where people can check your schedule. If you select the Private check box, other people look at your schedule and just see that you are not available at that time.

Setting task reminders

How many times have you made a list of things you need to do and then forgotten to look at your list? If you use the Tasks program to create your list, your CE device can remind you when you need to complete a task. How your CE device reminds you depends on the settings you specify. If you set your CE device to flash its light and beep 0 days prior to the start date for the task, on the start date for the task, your CE device beeps to get your attention and then flashes its light until you turn on the device and see the reminder message, shown in Figure 4-5.

Figure 4-5:
A friendly
reminder to
complete
a task.

You set the reminder information on the Task card by tapping the Reminder Defaults button. You can set the reminder information either when you create the new task or after you create the task by double-tapping the selected task. You can modify this information anytime after you create the task. Here's how you set a reminder for a task:

1. Open the Task card for a task in your list.

To open the Task card, locate the task you want to open and double-tap it with the stylus.

2. Make sure that a check mark appears in the <u>R</u>eminder check box.

Windows CE reminds you of a task only if you select the Reminder check box. Also keep in mind that you are only reminded of the task if you have selected a date in the Starts or Due fields and the associated check boxes are checked.

 3. Tap the Reminder Defaults button to display the Reminder Defaults dialog box, illustrated in Figure 4-6.

Figure 4-6: Indicate when you want to be reminded of the task that you need to complete.

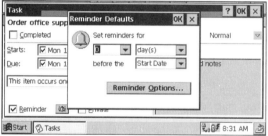
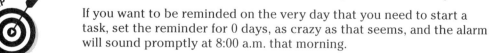

4. In the first drop-down list box, tap the down-arrow button and tap the amount of time you want.

You can select a value of 1, 5, 10, 15, 30, or 45 in this field, or you can manually type a value in this field by highlighting the value that is currently in the field and typing a new value (between 0 and 99).

If you want to be reminded on the very day that you need to start a task, set the reminder for 0 days, as crazy as that seems, and the alarm will sound promptly at 8:00 a.m. that morning.

5. In the next field, tap the down-arrow button and select the day(s) option.

Again, you can select any of the values available in this field. But with a task, you probably want to get a nice reminder on either the day it is due or the day that you should start working on it; so the day(s) option is probably the one you want to use.

6. In the final field, tap the down-arrow button and select either the Start Date or Due Date option.

7. **Tap the Reminder Options button to set the type of reminder you want for this appointment on the Notification Options window.**

   When you tap the Reminder Options button, the Notification Options dialog box appears (see Figure 4-7).

Figure 4-7:
Use the
Notifications
Options
dialog box
to specify
the
reminders
you want
for the
Task.

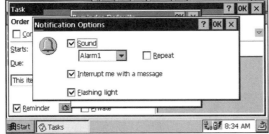

8. **Tap the reminders you want.**

   When you select a reminder, a check mark appears in the box next to the option.

   If you select the Sound option or the Flashing Light option, your CE device reminds you of the task even when you've turned off your device.

   Windows CE comes with sounds you can select for the Sound option in the Notification Options dialog box. The easiest way to determine the sound you want is to test each one until you find one that you like. To test a sound, select the sound in the drop-down list box. To have the sound repeated five times in succession, make sure that you select the Repeat check box.

9. **Tap the OK button to save your selections in the Notifications Options dialog box.**

10. **Tap the OK button to save your selections in the Reminder Defaults dialog box.**

11. **Tap the OK button to save your reminder selections on the Task card.**

Creating recurring tasks

We all have different tasks — such as washing the car, mowing the lawn, or even taking a bath — that need to be done on a regular basis. Instead of creating a new task each time you need to get the oil changed in the car, you can create one task that reminds you to do it every three months.

To set up the information about the recurring task, you use the Recurrence drop-down list box on the Task card, as shown in Figure 4-8. You can set this information when you create the task or after you create the task. To set the time frame for a recurring task, simply tap the down-arrow button to display the list of options and then tap the option you want.

Figure 4-8:
Use the
Recurrence
drop-down
list box to
set the time
frame for a
recurring
task.

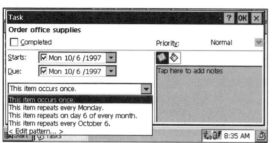

If this list box does not contain the recurrence option you want, you can even customize the way the task recurs. To customize the way a task recurs, follow these steps:

1. **Locate the task you want to set as recurring and double-tap it to display the Task card.**

2. **Tap the down-arrow button next to the Recurrence field and tap the <Edit Pattern> option.**

    When you tap the <Edit Pattern> option, the Edit Pattern wizard appears, as shown in Figure 4-9. If you don't want to create a custom pattern, you can use one of the patterns in the drop-down list box.

    A *wizard* is just a fancy term that some computer nerd came up with to refer to a window that takes you through a series of different questions to gather information. You normally tap buttons, such as the Next and Back buttons, to move through the different questions.

3. **On the Edit Pattern wizard, make sure that the appropriate times are specified in the Start and Due fields.**

    If you need to change the time in either field, simply tap the down-arrow button and select the correct time. Depending on the times you select, the value in the Duration field automatically adjusts itself, although you can set that field, too.

Figure 4-9:
Use the Edit
Pattern
wizard to
create a
custom
pattern for
how often
the task
should
recur on
your
calendar.

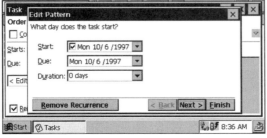

4. **Tap the Next button to display the next question for the wizard.**

5. **Tap the button that indicates the frequency with which you want the task to occur.**

   If you want to create a task that occurs every month, for example, select the Monthly button. The options that appear differ depending on the button you select.

6. **Use the other fields in this window to define the recurrence pattern.**

   For example, you may want to specify that a monthly task should occur on a specific day of the week — say, the second Tuesday of every month. In that case, tap the second radio button, next to the word The. Next, tap the down-arrow button and highlight the word Second in the drop-down list, tap the down-arrow button next to the second field, and highlight the word Tuesday in the drop-down list. Finally, type **1** in the last field.

7. **After selecting the recurrence pattern, tap the Next button so that you can indicate when the task starts and ends.**

8. **In the field labeled** The pattern starts, **indicate when you want the first task to be placed on your calendar.**

   The date in this field comes from the original date you specified for the task on the Task card. If you want to change this date, simply tap the down-arrow button to display the Calendar window and select the appropriate date.

9. **Select the appropriate radio button to indicate when you want to end the tasks.**

You can come back and modify these settings at any time. If you want the tasks to continue indefinitely, simply tap the Does not end radio button.

10. **Tap the Finish button to put the recurrence information on the Task card, as shown in Figure 4-10.**

Figure 4-10:
When you
set a
pattern for
the task to
recur, the
pattern
displays in
place of the
Starts and
Due fields.

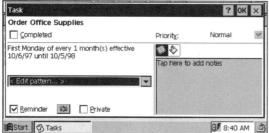

The recurrence information is placed in the same location where the Starts and Due fields were originally located on your appointment card.

11. **Tap the OK button to save the recurring tasks in your calendar.**

If you ever want to get rid of your recurring tasks, simply display the Edit Pattern wizard and tap the Remove Recurrence button. This saves you the hassle of deleting any remaining appointments on your calendar.

Adding notes to a task

If you are like me, most of your tasks probably need more information than you can enter in the <Task Description> field. One of my most frequent tasks is grocery shopping, and it doesn't do any good to go shopping without a list, does it? Well, those wise little computer programmers thought of that when they designed the Tasks program. You can enter all the information that you want about each task in the Notes section. It is available when you view the Tasks card, shown in Figure 4-11.

You can enter an unlimited amount of information in the Notes section. You can format the information any way you want; you can even draw pictures, but you can't use different fonts.

Notes section

Figure 4-11:
Use the
Notes
section for
additional
information,
such as
your
grocery list.

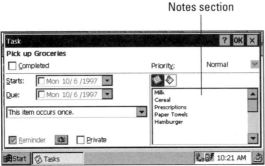

Perform these simple steps to enter additional information about a task you
have set up:

1. **Double-tap a task to display its Task card.**

2. **Tap the Notes button to display the Notes section of the Task card.**

   You find the Notes button, along with the Category button, on the right
   side of the screen under the Priority field. The Notes button resembles
   a miniature note pad.

3. **Tap the highlighted Notes section to display a dialog box in which
   you can type your notes that relate to the selected task, as shown in
   Figure 4-12.**

   On this screen you can type text or draw images with your stylus. You
   can use several formatting options when adding stuff to your notes, as I
   outline in Table 4-1.

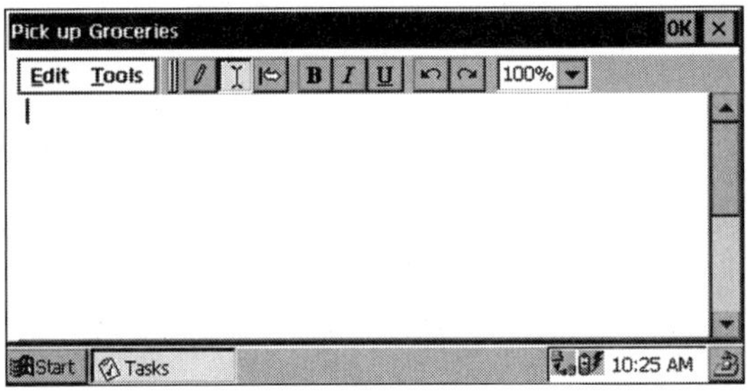

Figure 4-12:
Using the
Notes
dialog box,
you can
create
custom
notes for
each of
your tasks.

Table 4-1	Useful Notes Buttons
Tap This Button	**If You Want To**
✎	Draw something, such as a map, with your stylus.
I	Select the text you've entered or an object you've drawn so that you can format it.
↤	Insert vertical or horizontal spacing between stuff in your notes. Simply tap the button and then drag to insert the space. As you drag the cursor across the screen, it changes to an arrow indicating the amount of space that will be inserted when you lift the stylus.
B	Bold the selected text or the text you are going to type.
I	Italicize the selected text or the text you are going to type.
U	Underline the selected text or the text you are going to type.
↰	Undo the last thing you did. You can undo the last five things you have done.
↱	Undo the last undo you performed.
100% ▼	Select the zoom size for displaying the notes. To change the zoom size, tap the down-arrow button and select a new size.

4. **When you finish making your notes, simply tap the OK button and the stuff displays in the Notes section for the task.**

   If the notes are too large for the section, you can use the scroll bars to view the information.

Categorizing your tasks

To keep track of different types of tasks, you can assign a category to each task. For example, you may put tasks that deal with upkeep of your house into the Home Maintenance category. By assigning a category to the tasks, you can use the Filter option to see a list of all the tasks that deal with a specific category. This capability comes in handy when your task list gets long.

You can specify a category for any task by simply tapping the Category button on the Task card. (You can find it next to the Notes button.) When you do this, you get a list of categories that you can assign to your specific task, as shown in Figure 4-13. To select a category, tap the check box next to the desired category.

Category list

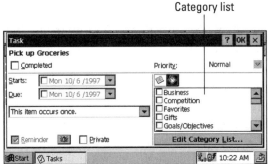

Figure 4-13: Categories can be useful for keeping track of related tasks.

If you look at the list of available categories, you will probably find that it contains several that you never use and that others you want are not even on the list. You can customize the category list by tapping the Edit Category List button. This displays the Categories dialog box, shown in Figure 4-14, where you can add and delete categories to and from the list. This dialog box allows you to get rid of all those categories that don't mean anything to you and create a more meaningful list.

Figure 4-14: Customize the category list in the Categories dialog box.

To add a new category, type the category name in the New category field and tap the Add button. The new category will be available on the list for any new tasks that you create.

To remove a category, locate the desired category in the list and tap the Delete button.

If you tap the Reset button, you get the original list of categories that were available when you first set up Windows CE 2.0. Any additional categories that you have created are removed.

Keep in mind that Windows CE uses this same category list for all the Outlook programs (Inbox, Contacts, Tasks, and Calendar). Consequently, any changes you make to the category list within the Tasks program are reflected on the category list for the Inbox, Contacts, and Calendar programs.

Removing Tasks

The time will come when you want to remove a task from the list. No matter what your reasoning, deleting a task is rather easy.

Keep in mind that Windows CE does not remove tasks that have been completed so that you can look back and see when you finished a particular task. You may want to remove old tasks, however, because each task hogs some of your CE device's memory. You also may want to delete some old tasks because the more tasks you have in your list, the more difficult it is to see which tasks you have yet to complete.

To delete a task, follow these simple steps:

1. In the task list, locate the task you want to delete.

Make sure that you tap the task so that it is highlighted on-screen.

 2. Tap the Delete button at the top of the screen in the toolbar.

The Delete button resembles a giant X. When you tap the Delete button, a message box appears to verify your selection, as shown in Figure 4-15.

3. Tap the OK button to delete the task.

Figure 4-15:
To delete the selected task, tap the OK button; otherwise, tap the X button.

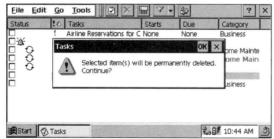

In case you are really in a spring-cleaning mood, you can quickly remove all the tasks that you have completed by choosing Edit➪Delete Completed Tasks.

Examining Your List of Tasks

As you add more and more tasks to the task list, the list becomes increasingly difficult to read. Fortunately, you can change the way the list appears so that it is easier to read. You can sort the list by any of the columns of information, or you can even indicate that you want to see only the tasks related to a specific project.

Customizing the columns

When you look at the display of your tasks, notice that several different columns of information are listed. You may find that you want to add or remove columns from the display or at least change the order in which the columns display. You can accomplish all this by using the Customize Columns dialog box, shown in Figure 4-16. This dialog box displays when you choose Tools➪Customize Columns.

Figure 4-16:
Indicate which columns you want to see when you look at the list of tasks.

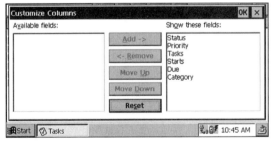

If you have not modified the columns before, you will probably find that all the options are listed in the Show these fields column. You can remove columns from the list by highlighting the desired column name and tapping the Remove button; this moves the column to the Available fields list, and it no longer appears with the list of tasks. Table 4-2 gives you an overview of the results you get when you select each button in the Customize Columns dialog box.

Table 4-2	Buttons for Customizing Columns
Tap This Button	*If You Want To*
Add	Take a column listed in the Available fields list and add it to the Show these fields list so that it displays on your list of tasks.
Remove	Take a column listed in the Show these fields list and place it in the Available fields list. This column will not display when you view your list of tasks.
Move Up	Move a column so that it displays before the column listed above it.
Move Down	Move a column so that it displays after the column listed below it.
Reset	Reset the columns to the original Windows CE default settings.

Sorting the tasks

On your mark, get set, alphabetize your list of tasks. Okay, I'm just joking — Windows CE can alphabetize the list of tasks probably before you can figure out what comes after A.

You can sort the list of tasks based on any of the columns of information that appear in the Tasks program. Simply tap the column's name, and Windows CE sorts the tasks by the information in that column. For example, simply tap the word *Tasks* at the top of the column to sort the list of tasks based on the task names. Windows CE sorts the tasks alphabetically based on their names (see Figure 4-17).

Figure 4-17:
To sort the
list of tasks
based on
the value in
a column,
simply tap
the column
name.

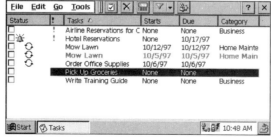

The first time you tap a column, the list is sorted in ascending order (A to Z) based on the values in that column. If you tap a second time, the list is sorted in descending order (Z to A), based on the values in the column.

Viewing only specific tasks

You can view only the tasks that meet specific criteria. For example, you can view only the tasks that have been completed, the tasks that need to be completed, or the tasks for a specific project.

You can view only tasks within specific categories by tapping the Filter drop-down list on the toolbar and selecting the categories you want to see, as shown in Figure 4-18. When you select a category, only the tasks that meet that category appear. You can either select a category or view only active or completed tasks.

Figure 4-18: Use the Filter drop-down list to indicate which tasks you want to view.

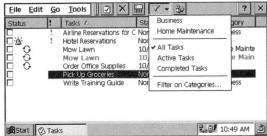

If you want to filter more than one category, select the Filter on Categories option. This displays the Filter dialog box, illustrated in Figure 4-19, in which you can select each of the categories of tasks that you want to see. Keep in mind that only the categories for which you have created tasks will display in this list.

Figure 4-19: Select the check box next to the categories you want to see.

Indicating That a Task Is Completed

The most exciting part of having a list of things to do is crossing items off the list as you finish them. Windows CE makes it quite simple to indicate that you have completed a task.

You use the Status column in the Tasks program to indicate whether you have completed a task (see Figure 4-20). If the check box in the Status column is empty, you still need to complete the task. If the check box contains a check mark, Windows CE knows that you have completed the task. To place a check mark in the check box, simply tap the box next to the task.

Figure 4-20:
The Status
column
indicates
exactly
which tasks
you have
completed.

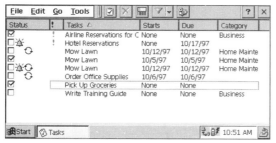

When you mark a task as completed, Windows CE removes the task from the Active Tasks field on your calendar.

I'm sure that you would be disappointed if I didn't tell you that Windows CE provides another way to indicate that the task is completed. If you select the Task card for the task, you can tap the check box next to the Completed field. This method is useful when you want to view the Task card before you mark it as complete.

Modifying Tasks

 For some reason, few of us can create tasks without having to modify them. Of course, you can always double-tap the task in the list and make modifications to the Task card. In my opinion, this is the easiest way to modify a task because you can edit everything about the task in one location. But if you do that all the time, you never get to use the other button on the toolbar, the Edit Panel button.

In Edit Panel view, you can change the task name, priority, category, and start and end dates of the highlighted task (see Figure 4-21). You must change any other information about a task on its Task card.

Figure 4-21:
Tap the Edit Panel button to quickly view basic information about each task.

This view is useful if you want to change something, such as the Priority, in several tasks. You can simply scroll down the list to display one task after another in the Edit Panel.

You can create a new task in the Edit Panel mode by tapping the New Task button and then entering the information identifying the task. If you create a task in this mode, you can only specify information for the fields that are displayed. If you want to add information that is not available in this mode, you need to open the Task card for the task.

Checking Today's Tasks in the Calendar Program

One cool thing about Windows CE is how programs seem to all work together. If you create tasks by using the Tasks program, for example, you can view the tasks that you need to do on a particular day by tapping the down-arrow button above the calendar in the Calendar program (see Figure 4-22). You can also view your daily tasks by tapping the Agenda button (see Figure 4-23).

The scheduled task continues to show up in Calendar for each day, until you indicate that the task has been completed.

From the Calendar program, you can view the details of a task by double-tapping the task name in the list. When you double-tap the task, the Task card for the selected task appears.

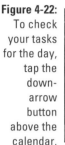

Figure 4-22:
To check
your tasks
for the day,
tap the
down-
arrow
button
above the
calendar.

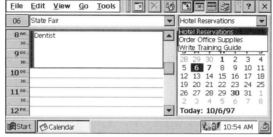

Figure 4-23:
In Agenda
view,
scheduled
tasks
appear on
the right
side of the
screen.

Printing Your Tasks

You may want to print out your tasks from time to time. This is possible if
you either have the printer connected to the serial port on your CE device
(the port you use to connect to you personal computer) or you are able to
send stuff to your printer using the infrared port.

To print out your tasks, choose File⇨Print to display the Print dialog box,
illustrated in Figure 4-24. For a complete description of all the information
you can specify on the Print dialog box, see Table 6-8 in Chapter 6.

Figure 4-24:
You can
print out
your list of
tasks using
the Print
option.

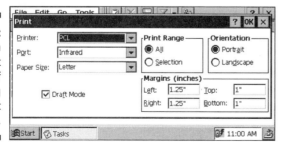

Synchronizing Tasks with Your Personal Computer

If you use your personal computer to maintain your tasks, you probably do not want to reenter everything onto your CE device. If you use Microsoft Schedule+ 7.0 or Microsoft Outlook under either Windows 95 or Windows NT 4.0, you don't have to.

With Windows CE, you can copy all the to-do information from your personal computer onto your CE device. You also can turn around and copy the task information on your CE device back to your personal computer. This process of making sure that the CE device and the personal computer contain the same task information is called *synchronizing*.

To synchronize your CE device with your personal computer, you need a few things:

- ✔ A data cable connected between your CE device and your personal computer
- ✔ Windows CE Services running on your personal computer
- ✔ Microsoft Schedule+ 7.0 or Microsoft Outlook on your personal computer

For more-detailed information about synchronizing your CE device and your personal computer, see Chapter 12.

You should create and modify recurring tasks on your CE device — not your personal computer. Recurring tasks marked as completed in Schedule+ on your personal computer will not show as completed on your CE device. Recurring tasks marked as completed on your CE device, however, will show up as completed in Schedule+ on your personal computer.

Chapter 5

Maintaining an Electronic Address Book

- -

In This Chapter

▶ Locating the Contacts program

▶ Creating a new contact

▶ Locating a contact in the list

▶ Sharing contact lists with other CE devices

▶ Adjusting the display options for the contact list

▶ Backing up and restoring a contact list

- -

*U*nless you are a hermit, you probably have a list of people with whom you correspond on a regular basis. To help you keep track of these people, Windows CE provides a program called Contacts that resembles an electronic address book. You can store all kinds of information about the people and businesses that you contact regularly, and you can find the person you are looking for without manually flipping through an actual address book or card file.

This chapter discusses the various ways you can use the Contacts program to create, view, and modify your contacts' information. It also discusses how you can even obtain contact information from other sources, such as your personal computer or another CE device.

Finding the Contacts Program

Before you can keep track of information about different people and companies, you must decide where you want to store this information. If you write it down in an address book, you'll probably have to get out the correction fluid to correct an entry when someone moves. If you store the information on your CE device, however, you can simply retype the new information in the appropriate location.

Usually, the Contacts program is fairly easy to locate. Even though the program is called Contacts, not Address Book, its icon resembles a desktop address organizer. The icon should be sitting on the right side of your desktop (unless you have reorganized your desktop). After you locate the icon, double-tap it to display the Contacts program.

If you can't find the Contacts program icon sitting on your desktop, don't despair. You should be able to locate it by following these steps:

1. **Use your stylus to tap the Start button (in the lower-left corner of the screen) to open the Start menu.**

   A pop-up menu containing various selections appears.

2. **Tap the Programs option.**

   This opens another menu containing a list of the programs and other menus on your CE device.

3. **Tap the Microsoft Pocket Outlook option.**

   You see a third menu containing more programs, as shown in Figure 5-1.

Figure 5-1:
Locate the
Contacts
program in
the pop-up
menus
available
when you
tap the
Start
button.

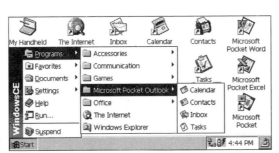

4. **Tap the Contacts option on the menu to display the Contacts program, shown in Figure 5-2.**

   You use this program to create, modify, and view your list of contacts. You can even share contacts with other CE devices using the infrared port.

If you use Microsoft Schedule+ 7.0 or Microsoft Outlook on your personal computer to keep track of your contacts, you can transfer those contacts to your CE device. I discuss this topic in more detail later in this chapter, in the section "Transferring Information Between Your CE Device and a Personal Computer." See the section "Sharing Contacts with Other CE Devices," later in this chapter to find out how to share contacts with other Windows CE users.

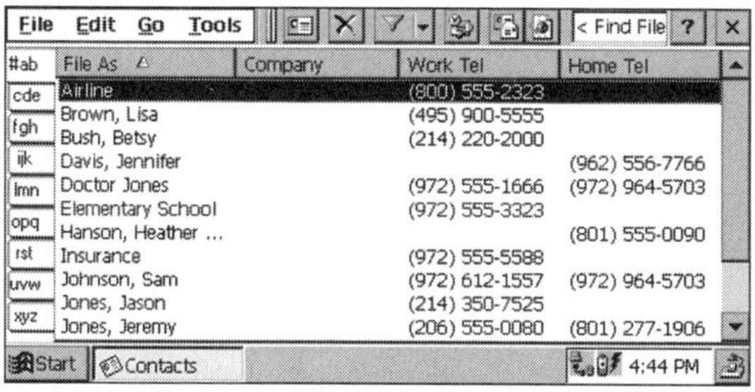

Figure 5-2:
The Contacts program displays an alphabetical list of all your contacts.

Creating a New Contact

You can add any type of contact to your contact list. You may want to add the phone number of your favorite pizza delivery place, keep track of extensions for your coworkers, or maintain a Christmas card list. The contact list can store anything and everything you want to know about each person. If you can't find an appropriate field in which to add the information you want, you can put the extra information in the Notes section of the contact card.

To create a new contact, follow these steps:

1. **Tap the New Contact icon on the toolbar at the top of the screen.**

   The icon resembles an address card. You can also add a new contact by choosing File⇨New.

   The contact card that appears provides options for entering business information, home (or personal) information, and notes about the specific contact. The sections that follow describe in detail how to add each type of information.

2. **Enter information about the new contact and then tap the OK button to save the card.**

   To save a contact card, type either a name or a company name for the contact. If you try to save the card without filling in one of these fields, you receive an error message.

Free-form information?

Each contact card has an open block of space in which you can enter the contact's name and address. Windows CE automatically separates the name into first, middle, and last name segments. It also separates the address into components by street address, city, state, zip code, and country.

If you want to ensure that you enter names and addresses in the correct format, you can open the Confirm screen (see the following figure) and specify each individual piece of the address or name. To display the Confirm screen, tap either the Name or Address field

to highlight it and then tap the Confirm button (see the following figure) that appears next to the field. This button resembles one large field being divided into smaller fields.

When you tap the Confirm button, either the Confirm Address screen or the Confirm Name screen appears so that you can enter the appropriate information. Type the appropriate information in each field and then tap the OK button.

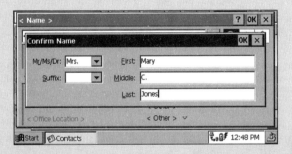

 If you are fortunate enough to have already set up all this information in Schedule+ 7.0 or Outlook on your personal computer, you can copy the information to your CE device. For more information, refer to the section "Transferring Information Between Your CE Device and a Personal Computer," later in this chapter.

Entering business information

 By tapping the contact card's Business Information button on the right side of the screen, you can add business information about a contact, as shown in Figure 5-3. For example, you can enter your favorite computer salesperson or movie theater or information about your coworkers, such as their phone extensions.

Type the information you want in each field. To move the cursor between fields, you can either tap in the field or press the Tab key.

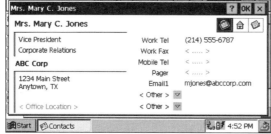

Figure 5-3:
Use the
business
fields
for the
pertinent
business
information
about a
contact.

Two fields are labeled <Other>. In these fields, you can enter some kinds of information — such as the name of the person's assistant or the assistant's phone number — that don't belong in any of the other fields. To add information to an <Other> field, tap either the field name or the down-arrow button next to the field to display a list of the kind of information that you can enter (see Figure 5-4). Highlight the kind of information that you want to enter and then enter the information in the field next to the name.

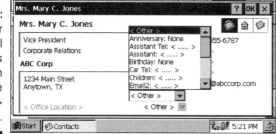

Figure 5-4:
Enter
additional
business
information
in the
<Other>
fields.

Windows CE remembers the values that you enter in each option of the <Other> list. Therefore, you can store a value for each option, even though you can display only one option at a time in each of the <Other> fields.

Entering personal information

 If you want to enter personal information about a contact, as shown in Figure 5-5, tap the Personal Information button and type the information in each field. To move the cursor between fields, you can either tap in the field or press the Tab key.

Figure 5-5:
Tap the
Personal
Information
button for a
contact's
personal
information.

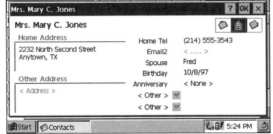

As with business information, the personal information section also has two fields labeled <Other>. You can use these fields to enter personal information about the contact — such as the person's car telephone number or children's names — that does not belong in another field. To add information in one of the <Other> fields, tap either the field name or the down-arrow button next to the field to display a list of the kinds of information that you can add (see Figure 5-6). Tap the kind of information you want to enter and then enter the information in the field next to the name.

Figure 5-6:
Enter
additional
personal
information
in the
<Other>
fields.

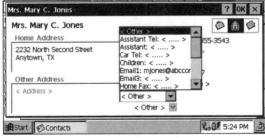

Windows CE remembers what you enter for each option in the <Other> list. Therefore, you can store a value for each option, even though you can see only one option at a time in each of the <Other> fields.

Adding extra information

 If you cannot find a field for some of your information, tap the Notes button and then add any extra information about your contact. When you tap this button, you get a screen containing a notes section and a categories section, as shown in Figure 5-7. You cannot only add custom notes about your contact here but also categorize your contacts so that you can later use the Filter option to view all related contacts.

Notes section   Category section

Figure 5-7:
Type any
additional
information
and assign
a category
to your
contact.

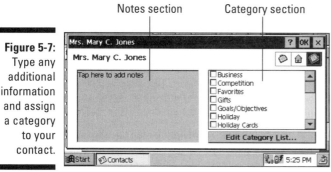

Adding notes

You can create an unlimited amount of notes about your contact. You can format the information in various ways (you can even draw pictures), but you can't use different fonts. Perform these simple steps to enter additional information about your contact on the Notes screen:

1. **Tap the highlighted Notes section to display a dialog box in which you can type your notes that relate to the selected contact, as shown in Figure 5-8.**

   On this screen, you can type text, or draw images with your stylus. You can use several formatting options when adding stuff to your notes, as I outline in Table 5-1.

2. **When you finish making your notes, simply tap the OK button and the stuff displays in the Notes section for the contact.**

   If the notes are too large for the section, you can use the scroll bars to view the information.

Figure 5-8:
Using the
Notes
dialog box,
you can
create
custom
notes for
the contact.

Table 5-1	Useful Notes Buttons
Tap This Button	*If You Want To*
✐	Draw something, such as a map, with your stylus.
I	Select text you've entered or an object you've drawn so you can format it.
|↔	Insert vertical or horizontal spacing between stuff in your notes. Simply tap the button and then drag to insert the space. As you drag the cursor across the screen, it changes to an arrow indicating the amount of space that will be inserted when you lift the stylus.
B	Bold the selected text or the text you are going to type.
I	Italicize the selected text or the text you are going to type.
U	Underline the selected text or the text you are going to type.
↰	Undo the last thing you did. You can undo up to the last five things you have done.
↱	Undo the last undo you performed.
100% ▼	Select the zoom size for displaying the notes. To change the zoom size, tap the down-arrow button and select a new size.

Categorizing the contact

You may want to assign a category — or multiple categories — to each contact. For example, all your work contacts could have a category of business, and your relatives could be assigned a category of family. By assigning a category to the contact, you can use the Filter option to see a list of all the contacts that deal with a specific category — which is useful when your contact list gets fairly long.

You can specify a category on the right side of the Notes screen. To select a category, simply tap the check box next to the desired category.

If you look at the list of available categories, you may find that it contains several that you never use and that others you want aren't even on the list. You can customize the category list by tapping the Edit Category List button. This displays the Categories dialog box, shown in Figure 5-9, where you can add new categories and delete categories from the list. This dialog box lets you get rid of all those categories that don't mean anything to you and thus create a more meaningful list.

Figure 5-9:
Customize
the
category
list on the
Categories
dialog box.

To add a new category, type the category name in the New Category field and then tap the Add button. The new category will be available on the list for any new contacts that you create.

To remove a category, select the desired category in the list and then tap the Delete button.

If you tap the Reset button, you get the original list of categories that were available when you first set up Windows CE 2.0. Any additional categories that you have created are removed.

Keep in mind that Windows CE uses this same category list for most of the Outlook programs (Contacts, Tasks, and Calendar). In other words, any changes you make to the category list within the Contacts program are reflected on the category lists for the Tasks and Calendar programs.

Locating Contacts

As you add more and more names to the contact list, the list gets longer and more difficult to read. Fortunately, you can view the information in several ways. You can sort the list by any of the columns of information, jump to the contacts that begin with a specific letter of the alphabet (if you know what you are searching for), or use the Find command to locate a contact.

Looking at the list alphabetically

You may have noticed the various tabs along the left side of the contact list that have the letters of the alphabet on them. You can use these tabs to jump to the contacts that start with specific letters of the alphabet. If you want to view the contacts that start with the letter T, for example, tap the tab labeled rst. Windows CE highlights the first contact that begins with either the letters *R, S,* or *T* (see Figure 5-10).

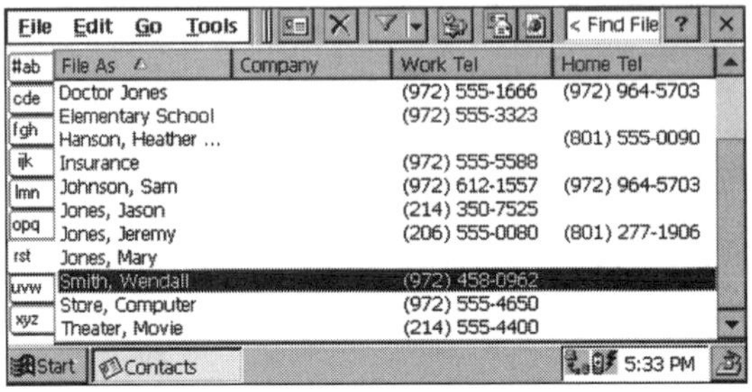

Figure 5-10:
Tap the
tabs on the
left side of
the screen
to jump
alphabetically
through
the list.

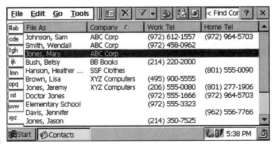

If you tap a tab that doesn't have any matches, Windows CE highlights the
next closest match. For example, if you tap cde and no contact starts with *C*,
D, or *E*, Windows CE jumps to the next name after the letter *E*.

Sorting the contacts

Windows CE automatically sorts the list of contacts alphabetically based on
the values in the first column, which is normally the File As column. (The
File As column contains the name of the contact.) You can, however, sort the
list by another column, such as the Company column, if you want.

To sort the list of contacts by another column, tap the column name. When
you tap a column, a triangle marker moves into the title of the column to
indicate which column you are using to sort the list of names, as shown in
Figure 5-11. The first time you tap a column, the contact list is sorted in
ascending order (from A to Z) based on the values in that column. When you
tap the column a second time, the list is sorted in descending order and the
triangle pointer changes to show the sort order.

Figure 5-11:
To sort the
list based
on the value
in a column,
tap the
column
name.

You can resize the columns so that more information appears on-screen. Simply tap the bar between the column names and drag it left or right.

Quickly locating information in the list

You can use the Quick Find field to find a specific word or name in the sorted column. The Quick Find field is located on the right side of the toolbar at the top of the screen.

To locate a contact, type the name or word you are looking for in the Quick Find field, as shown in Figure 5-12. As you type each character, Windows CE scrolls down the list to find the closest match.

Figure 5-12:
As you enter a value in the Quick Find field, Windows CE finds the closest match.

You can use the Quick Find field only to search the column that is currently being used as the sort column. If you are sorting the list by the File As column, for example, you can use Quick Find to find a specific name.

Finding information on a contact card

You can locate a contact card by using the Find button. The Find button is located on the toolbar at the top of the screen.

When you tap the Find button, the Find window appears (see Figure 5-13). In the Find window, type the text you are looking for in the Find field and then tap the OK button. Windows CE searches all the contact cards until it locates the text you specified. You get a list of the contacts that contain the text you are searching for; to view one, simply tap the desired contact in the list.

Figure 5-13:
The Find
window
shows a list
of the
contacts
that match
the value
you typed in
the Find
field.

You can also open the Find window by choosing Tools⇨Find. And if you have previously searched for a word, you can tap the down-arrow button next to the Find field and select the word rather than enter it again.

To make finding a contact card easier, search for text that is specific to the contact card you are looking for.

Viewing only specific contacts

You can view only the contacts that are part of a specific category. For example, you can view all your personal contacts or even look at your list of hot contacts.

To view only contacts within specific categories, tap the Filter drop-down list on the toolbar and select the categories you want to see, as shown in Figure 5-14. When you select a category, only the contacts in that category are displayed.

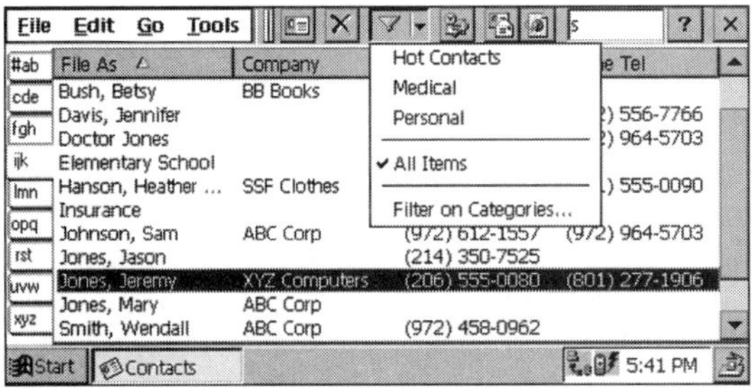

Figure 5-14:
Use the
Filter drop-
down list
to indicate
which
contacts
you want
to view.

If you want to filter more than one category, select the Filter on Categories option. This option displays the Filter dialog box, illustrated in Figure 5-15, where you can select each of the categories for which you want to see contacts. Keep in mind that only the categories for which you have created contacts display in this list.

 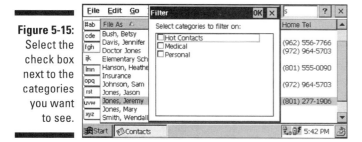

Figure 5-15: Select the check box next to the categories you want to see.

Customizing the Columns

You may find that the columns that appear in the Contacts window are not exactly the ones you want. If your list contains mostly personal addresses, for example, you probably don't care for the Company and Work Tel columns.

To specify which columns appear in the Contacts window, choose Tools⇨ Customize Columns. The Customize Columns dialog box appears (see Figure 5-16). The Customize Columns dialog box enables you to specify which columns appear in the Contacts window.

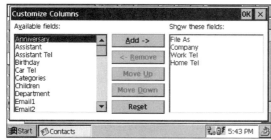

Figure 5-16: You can specify which columns appear in the Contacts window.

The Show these fields column lists the names of the columns that the contact card displays. You can remove columns from the list by highlighting the desired column name and tapping the Remove button; the selected column moves to the Available fields list and it no longer appears on the contact card. Table 5-2 gives you an overview of the results you get when you select each button in the Customize Columns dialog box.

Table 5-2	Buttons for Customizing the Contacts Window
Tap This Button	*If You Want To*
Add	Take a column listed in the Available fields list and add it to the Show these fields list so that it will display on your list of contacts.
Remove	Take a column listed in the Show these fields list and place it in the Available fields list. This column will not display when you view your list of contacts.
Move Up	Move a column so that it displays before the column listed above it.
Move Down	Move a column so that it displays after the column listed below it.
Reset	Reset the columns back to the original Windows CE default settings.

You will probably notice that the Show these fields column does not list a field called *Name*. The File As field contains the names of your contacts. So if you want to move the column of contact names, you need to move the File As field.

Changing the Default Options

The Contacts program has been set up to use a default value of United States for the Country field and 206 for the Area Code field when you create your contacts. If you want to change these values, you need to use the Options dialog box, displayed in Figure 5-17. Choose <u>T</u>ools⇨<u>O</u>ptions to see this dialog box.

To change the default country, tap the down-arrow button next to the Country field and select the appropriate country. If you want to change the area code, type the area code in the Area Code field. Doing so changes the default area code for the Contacts program and leaves the system information alone.

Figure 5-17:
Indicate the country and area code you want to use as a default when creating contact cards.

 You can also modify the fonts that the Contacts program uses for displaying information by tapping the Choose Font button. Doing so displays the Font dialog box, where you can select the font type and size for all text that the Contacts program displays.

Removing a Contact

You don't have to purchase a new address book to revise your contacts. Windows CE makes removing unwanted contacts from your Contact list easy.

To delete a contact, follow these steps:

1. Locate the contact in the contact list.

2. Tap the contact to highlight it.

 3. Tap the Delete button in the toolbar at the top of the screen.

The Delete button resembles a giant X. When you tap it, a message box appears to ask you to verify your selection (see Figure 5-18).

Figure 5-18:
To delete the selected contact, tap the OK button.

 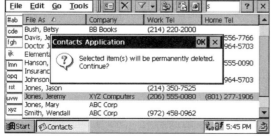

You can also delete a contact by choosing Edit⇨Delete Item. Or you can press Ctrl+D to delete the selected contact, in case you prefer to use the keyboard.

Sending E-Mail to a Contact

Have you ever looked at your list of contacts and suddenly remembered you wanted to send an e-mail message to one of the people on the list? The Contacts program makes this step easy by enabling you to tap one button to open a new message page in the Inbox program, where you can compose the message that you want to send. To do this, follow these steps:

1. **In the contacts list, highlight the name of the contact to whom you want to send a message.**

   Hopefully, you have already specified an e-mail address for the selected contact. After all, the Contacts program needs to know where you want to send the message. If you haven't specified an e-mail address for the selected contact, you must manually type the address on the message.

2. **Tap the e-mail button on the toolbar.**

   This opens up a New Message window, where you can compose the message that you want to send. If the contact information includes an e-mail address, that address is listed in the To field at the top of the screen. Otherwise, you need to type the address so that Inbox knows where to send the completed message.

3. **Type the message and tap the Send button.**

   For more information about sending e-mail messages, see Chapter 17.

Sharing Contacts with Other CE Devices

You can use the Contacts program to share contacts with another CE device, as long as both CE devices have an infrared port. The infrared port looks sort of like a black mirror on your CE device. If you are unsure whether your CE device has an infrared port, refer to the hardware documentation that came with the CE device.

To share contacts with another CE device, follow these steps:

1. **Make sure that both CE devices are turned on and the Contacts program is running on each CE device.**

2. Place the CE devices so that the infrared ports line up.

The ports need to be within about three feet of each other with nothing blocking the view. Because infrared ports use light beams to transfer data, they can't transfer information unless they have a good view of each other.

3. On the first CE device (the one with the information), highlight the contacts you want to send to the other CE device.

To select multiple contacts, hold down the Ctrl key on the keyboard and tap the contacts you want to highlight.

4. Choose File⇨Send.

A message box indicates that the CE device is looking for another CE device.

5. On the other CE device, choose File⇨Receive.

When the CE devices make contact with each other, the information is transferred from the first CE device to the second CE device.

Some types of fluorescent lighting can interfere with the data transfer. If you have problems transferring data, try moving the CE devices to another location.

Make sure that nothing blocks the infrared ports. If they cannot see each other, the CE devices can't transfer data.

Transferring Information between Your CE Device and a Personal Computer

If you currently use your personal computer to maintain your contact list, you probably do not want to retype everything onto your new CE device. If you use Microsoft Schedule+ 7.0 or Microsoft Outlook under either Windows 95 or Windows NT 4.0, you don't have to.

Windows CE has been designed so that you can copy all of the contact information from your personal computer onto your CE device. You can also turn around and copy the contact information on your CE device back into Schedule+ or Outlook. This process of making sure that both the CE device and the personal computer contain the same personal contact information is called *synchronizing*.

To synchronize your CE device with your personal computer, you need to have a few things:

- ✔ A data cable connected between your CE device and the personal computer
- ✔ Windows CE Services running on your personal computer
- ✔ Microsoft Schedule+ 7.0 or Microsoft Outlook on your personal computer

You need to keep a few things in mind when you transfer contact information between your CE device and Microsoft Schedule+.

- ✔ Unfortunately, Schedule+ does not offer all the information fields that are available in the Contacts program on your CE device. You cannot transfer the following fields of information into Schedule+:
  - Middle
  - Mr/Mrs/Dr
  - Suffix
  - Car Tel
  - Children
  - Email2
  - Email3
  - Home Fax
  - Web Page
- ✔ A few information fields in Schedule+ are not available in the Contacts program. You cannot copy the information in these fields to your CE device:
  - User2
  - User3
  - User4
- ✔ Two fields change names when you transfer from a CE device to a personal computer. The Email1 field on your CE device becomes the User1 field in Schedule+, and the Work Fax field on your CE device becomes the Fax field in Schedule+.

For more detailed information about synchronizing your CE device and your personal computer, see Chapter 12.

Chapter 6

Working with Documents in Pocket Word

. . . .

. . . .

*H*ave you ever dreamed of being able to take minutes at a meeting and instantly have the minutes transferred to your personal computer without totally retyping them? Or maybe — like me — you've sat in the waiting room at a doctor's office wishing you could be working on the proposal for the presentation you have to give the next day.

Windows CE devices save precious time with a standard feature that sets them off from the competition: word processing capabilities. The word processing program available on your CE device, called Microsoft Pocket Word, very closely resembles other versions of Microsoft Word. If you're an avid Microsoft Word user, however, you'll quickly find that Pocket Word lacks several of the bells and whistles that come with Microsoft Word.

In this chapter, you discover how to unleash the powers of Pocket Word. You find out how to create new documents, work with documents that you've created on your CE device, and transfer documents back to your personal computer. I also show you how to use the Pocket Word formatting options to add some pizzazz to each document.

Locating Pocket Word

Before you can create memos, work on a proposal, or type a letter to your sister, you need to locate Pocket Word on your CE device. On most CE devices, you can find the Pocket Word icon on your Windows CE desktop. The icon looks like a piece of paper with a large W sitting on top of it. Double-tap the icon to display Pocket Word.

If you cannot find the Pocket Word program icon on your desktop, don't despair. You can locate it by following these simple steps:

1. **Tap the Start button (in the lower-left corner of the screen).**

   When you tap the Start button, a pop-up menu that contains various options appears.

2. **Tap the Programs option.**

   Selecting this option opens another menu containing a list of the programs and other menus on your CE device.

3. **Tap the Office option.**

   You see a third menu containing more programs, as illustrated in Figure 6-1.

Figure 6-1: Tap the Start button and then find the Pocket Word program in the pop-up menus.

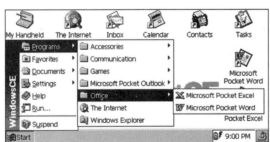

4. **Tap the Microsoft Pocket Word option on the menu to display the Pocket Word program, shown in Figure 6-2.**

You can work on Microsoft Word documents that you copy to your CE device from your personal computer. You find out more later in this chapter, in the section "Converting a Microsoft Word Document."

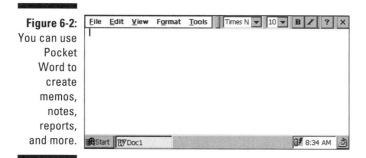

Figure 6-2:
You can use Pocket Word to create memos, notes, reports, and more.

Creating a New Document

Pocket Word provides two different methods for creating a new document. You can either design your document from scratch by starting with a blank screen, or you can use a template and create the document. You can get pointers on each method in the following sections.

Starting with a blank document

When you start Pocket Word, the program automatically opens a new, blank document. You can begin to create your document and then save it when you're finished.

If you've already opened a document and want to create a new document, choose File⇨New. A blank, unnamed document appears, ready for your information.

Using a template

Have you ever needed to create a letter but forgotten how to format one? If so, you are in luck. Pocket Word comes with templates that you can use to create different documents such as letters and meeting notes. When you use a template, the information it contains is placed directly into your document so you have a starting point. You can then modify the information until you have the document designed the way you want it.

If you don't find the type of template you want to use, you can create one and save it for future uses. In fact, you can save any document as a template. For more information about saving templates, refer to the next section in this chapter.

Follow these steps to open a template for the document that you want to create:

1. **Choose File⇨New⇨Document from Template.**

   As shown in Figure 6-3, Pocket Word displays the Template dialog box, which contains the templates that you currently have on your CE device.

Figure 6-3:
The template dialog box lists the available document templates.

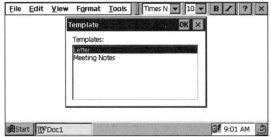

You only see the templates that are sitting in the Templates folder. This folder is located within the Office folder, which sits inside the Program Files folder. If you have created other templates, you need to make sure that they're sitting in this folder so that you can select them.

2. **Double-tap the name of the template that you want to use.**

   For example, if you want to create a letter, double-tap the Letter option. As shown in Figure 6-4, Pocket Word places a copy of the selected template in your document.

3. **Enter the appropriate information in your document.**

Figure 6-4:
You can use templates to create documents.

You will probably want to replace almost all the text that is copied by the template, especially the places where you see the ⟨ and ⟩ characters. These characters indicate the type of information that you should type in the field. To replace the information, highlight it and type the correct information.

Saving Your Document

When you create a new document or modify an existing document, you need to save it so that you can access it again at another time. When you save a document that you created by using Microsoft Pocket Word, Windows CE places a copy of the document in the folder that you specify. This process is essentially the same as placing a copy of a memo in a file cabinet at your office. You locate the file where you want to store the document, and then you place the file in the folder.

If a document is very large, save it often as you work on it. An unexpected dead battery or wrong key combination can wipe out your efforts. By saving your document often, you ensure that you don't lose your work or your most recent changes if something goes wrong.

Depending on the document that you have open, the process that occurs when you save the document varies. If you have never saved the document, Windows CE needs to gather some information from you before you save the document. On the other hand, if you've worked on the document in the past, you hardly even notice Windows CE doing anything when you save the document.

Saving a document for the first time

When you save a document for the first time, Pocket Word needs to know the name that you want to give the document and the location where you would like to place the document.

You must name the document so that Windows CE can distinguish among the different documents on your CE device. The document name should identify the information that the document contains so that you can quickly locate it later.

To save a document for the first time, you specify information describing the document in the Save As dialog box. To do so, follow these steps:

1. Choose File⇨Save.

When you select the Save option, the Save As dialog box appears, as shown in Figure 6-5.

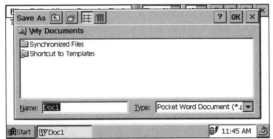

Figure 6-5:
Use the
Save As
dialog box
to name
your
document
and specify
its location.

If you have not previously saved a document, the Save As dialog box appears when you select the Save option. For a previously saved document, Pocket Word simply saves the file without displaying the Save As dialog box.

2. In the folder list, tap the folder in which you want to save your document.

When you save a document using Pocket Word, Windows CE assumes that you want to place it in the My Documents folder. This may not always be the location where you want to place it, however. If the icon for the folder you want is in the folder list, double-tap the folder to open it.

If an icon is not displayed for the folder you want to save your document in, you can tap the Previous Folder button. The Previous Folder button looks like a folder with an up arrow on it. When you tap the Previous Folder button, the parent folder opens. You can continue tapping this button or folder icons until you locate the desired location for the document.

3. Type a name for the document in the Name field.

Use a name that indicates what the document is about — for example, **Memo1**, if you're creating a memo. You can type something even more descriptive like **Office Memo**, for a memo to the folks at the office.

4. In the Type field, tap the down-arrow button and highlight the format in which you want to save the file. Table 6-1 outlines the five different file type options available in the Type field.

5. Tap the OK button to save the new document.

Table 6-1	Pocket Word File Formats
Format	*When to Use It*
Pocket Word Document (*.pwd)	When the document includes formatting that you've applied using Pocket Word. If you transfer this document to your personal computer, it is converted to a .DOC file format for use with Microsoft Word. You can only share these documents with other Windows CE 2.0 devices; CE 1.0 devices cannot open them.
Rich Text Document (*.rtf)	When you plan to use the file on your personal computer in a word processing program that does not use .DOC files. Rich Text Formatting (RTF) is a standard document format recognized by most all word processing programs. By saving as an .RTF file, you preserve the formatting in your document when you open your document is another word processing program.
Plain Text Document (*.txt)	When you want to use the document with a program that cannot read a .PWD or .RTF file. If you select the Plain Text Document format, Pocket Word saves only the text of the document. Any formatting that you may have applied to the document, such as special fonts, is not saved.
Pocket Word 1.0 Document	When you plan to give the document to someone who uses a Windows CE 1.0 device. Otherwise, the CE 1.0 user will not be able to open the document.
Pocket Word Template (*.pwt)	When you want to save your document as a template to be used to create other similar documents within Pocket Word.

You can save a document in another way: Press the Ctrl key and the S key simultaneously on the keyboard. Just another pointer for all you keyboard fanatics.

Windows CE allows each filename to be a total of 255 characters long. This length includes the period and the three-character extension that is added to each Pocket Word document to identify its file type. So basically, each filename can be 251 characters long. The filename can include any characters and numbers, with the exception of these: /, ?, : *, ", <, >, and |.

You may find that you want to store your document in a folder that does not exist on your CE device. Fortunately, Pocket Word lets you quickly create the folder while you are saving the document. To create a new folder for a document, open the folder where you want to place the new folder. Then tap the New Folder button in the toolbar at the top of the Save As dialog box. The New Folder button looks like a folder with a starburst behind it.

When you tap the New folder button, a folder icon appears in the folder listing with the name New Folder highlighted, as shown in Figure 6-6. To name the folder, type a name for the folder, and then press the Enter key. After you create the folder, you can specify the name for the document and then tap the OK button.

Figure 6-6:
Type the name of the new folder in the box.

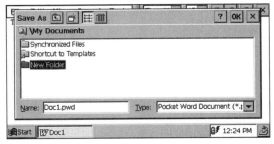

Saving a document that you previously saved

As I mention earlier in the chapter, you should save your documents often. If you've saved your document previously, saving the document again and again is really quite easy. Choose File➪Save. As long as the document you are saving has been previously saved, Windows CE saves the document immediately so that you can continue to work.

Saving a document with a new name

How often have you placed a document in one folder and later moved it to another folder? Pocket Word enables you to do the same thing. You may find that after you have saved a document, you want to save it in another location or give it another name. You can accomplish all this stuff by choosing File➪Save As.

When you select the Save As option, the Save As dialog box appears on-screen (refer to Figure 6-5). The current name of the document appears in the Name field. To change the name, type a new name in the Name field and tap the OK button.

To save the document with the same name but in a different folder, locate the folder in which you want to save the document and double-tap the associated icon to open that folder. If the folder doesn't appear in the listing, tap the Previous Folder icon to close the current folder and open the folder above it.

When you use the Save As option, the previous document remains with the same name and in the same location. The Save As option creates a new copy of the original document that contains any new changes that you've made.

You can also use the Save As option to save the document with a new file format, by selecting a different option in the Type field in the Save As dialog box.

If you want to get rid of the original document, you need to use the Windows CE Explorer to delete the document. For more information, see Chapter 9.

Keep in mind that Windows CE allows you to have multiple documents with the same name in a folder, as long as each one has a different three-character extension (such as .TXT for a text document and .PWD for a Pocket Word Document).

Closing a Document

Windows CE lets you have several documents open at a time. For each document you open, a button appears on the taskbar. The number you can open varies based on the amount of memory you have available and the size of each document. For the sake of convenience, I suggest not opening more than three documents at a time. Having too many windows open at the same time can be cumbersome.

When you get tired of working on a document, you can close it so that it doesn't stay open and use up memory on your CE device. To close a document, simply tap the X button in the upper-right corner of the screen. If you have only one document open in Pocket Word, the Pocket Word program also closes when you tap the X button. If you still have other documents open, the current document closes, and Pocket Word displays the last document that you worked on.

You can also close a document by choosing File➪Close. The Close option produces exactly the same result as the X button.

If you have not previously saved the document, a message window asks if you want to save the document before closing. To save it, tap the Yes button. If you messed up the document or just decided you don't want it, tap the No button, and Windows CE discards the document.

Opening an Existing Document

After you save a document in a folder under Windows CE, you can open it again at any time. You may want to open and revise it, or just read it again. To open a document, you need to choose File⇨Open. When you select the Open option, the Open dialog box appears, as shown in Figure 6-7.

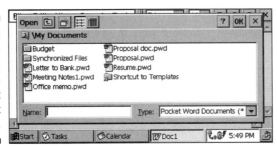

Figure 6-7: Use the Open dialog box to open a document in Pocket Word.

Pocket Word assumes that you want to open a file from the My Documents folder. If the document you want to open is located in another folder, tap the Previous Folder button to close the My Documents folder and open the folder above it. When you find the folder that contains the document you want to open, tap the folder.

You can also open a document from Windows CE Explorer by double-tapping the document's icon. If you double-tap an icon for a Pocket Word document, the document automatically opens in Pocket Word.

Pocket Word remembers the last four documents that you worked on. To see what you last worked on, or last opened and viewed, choose File⇨Recent Files, as shown in Figure 6-8. You see a list of the last four Pocket Word documents that you opened. Use the stylus to tap the document that you want to select, or type the number next to the document's name.

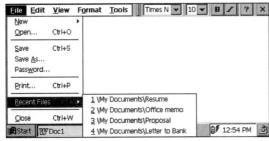

Figure 6-8: Pocket Word helps you remember what you did yesterday.

If you still cannot locate the document you are looking for, try checking the Recent folder. This folder appears when you select the Documents option on the Start menu. For more information, see to Chapter 2.

Finding the Toolbar Buttons

Pocket Word comes with several useful buttons that you can use to format your document. These buttons are all located on the command bar at the top of the screen. Table 6-2 describes the purpose of each button. Remember, if you cannot see all the buttons, tap the double vertical bar (commonly referred to as the *slider*) to move the button toolbar so all the buttons are displayed, as shown in Figure 6-9. To see the menus again, tap the Menu button again.

Menu button

Double vertical bar

Figure 6-9:
Don't forget to look for the hidden Pocket Word buttons.

Table 6-2	Those Elusive Pocket Word Buttons
Tap This Button	*If You Want To*
Times N ▼	Change the font type of the text.
10 ▼	Change the size of the selected text.
B	Bold the selected text or the text you are going to type.
I	Italicize the selected text or the text you are going to type.

(continued)

Table 6-2 *(continued)*

Tap This Button	If You Want To
U	Underline the selected text or the text you are going to type.
(left-justify icon)	Left-justify the selected text or the text you are going to type.
(center icon)	Center the selected text or the text you are going to type within the margins.
(right-justify icon)	Right-justify the selected text or the text you are going to type.
(bulleted list icon)	Create a bulleted list of items.
(numbered list icon)	Create a numbered list of items.
(spell check icon)	Check the spelling of the document.
(zoom icon)	Zoom in on the document so that you can read the text better. Each time you tap the button, Pocket Word adjusts the zooming level; it zooms to 50%, 75%, 100%, 125%, and 150% of the actual size of the text on the screen.

When you tap a button, the formatting is applied to any text that you type. If you want to change something that you have already typed, select the text on the screen and then tap the desired button.

Locating Text

Sooner or later, you will want to locate a specific word or phrase within a document. You may just want to read the text surrounding a word or phrase, or you may need to correct a misspelled word.

You can use either the Find or the Replace option to locate text within your document. The Find option searches for the text and then highlights the text when it locates it. The Replace option searches for the specified text, highlights it, and then replaces it with the text in the Replace With field.

Finding specific text

Follow these steps to search for specific text in your document:

1. Choose Edit⇨Find or press Ctrl+F.

The Find dialog box appears, as shown in Figure 6-10.

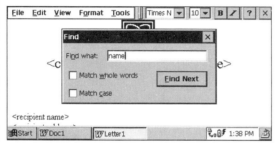

Figure 6-10:
Use the
Find dialog
box to
locate
specific text
within your
document.

2. Type the text you want to look for in the Find what field.

You can type more than one word or only a portion of a word in the field.

Select the Match whole words option to have Pocket Word find only whole occurrences of the text you enter in the Find what field. For example, if you enter **is** in the Find what field and select the Match whole words option, Pocket Word does not stop on words that contain *is,* such as *this* and *Miss.*

Select the Match case option to have Pocket Word find only words that match both the characters and the case of the text you enter in the Find what field. For example, if you enter **Is** in the Find what field and select the Match case option, Pocket Word stops on *Is* but does not stop on *is.*

3. Tap the Find Next button.

Pocket Word searches the document from the current cursor location to the end of the document. It stops when it locates the first occurrence of the text that you entered in the Find what field. When Pocket Word locates the matching text, it highlights the text (see Figure 6-11).

To have Pocket Word find another occurrence of the text that you typed in the Find what field, tap the Find Next button. Or if you have closed the dialog box, you can press Ctrl+F4.

Figure 6-11:
Pocket
Word
locates the
specified
text and
highlights it.

Replacing text

Have you ever misspelled the same word again and again throughout a document? You could use the Find option to search for the word you want to modify and then manually enter the correct spelling. But that is the long and tedious method.

When you need to replace text, use the Replace option. To search for and replace a word or phrase, follow these steps:

1. Choose Edit⊏>Replace or press Ctrl+H.

The Replace dialog box appears, as shown in Figure 6-12.

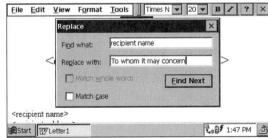

Figure 6-12:
Use the
Replace
dialog box
to locate
and replace
a specific
word or
phrase.

2. Type the text that you want to replace in the Find what field.

You can type more than one word or only a portion of a word.

3. Type the text with which you want to replace the specified text in the Replace with field.

4. Tap the Find Next button.

Pocket Word searches the document from the current cursor location to the end of the document. It stops when it locates the first occurrence of the text that you typed in the Find what field. When Pocket Word locates the matching text, it highlights the text, and the Find/Replace dialog box appears, as shown in Figure 6-13.

Figure 6-13:
Pocket
Word
verifies that
you really
want to
replace
the text.

5. **To replace the highlighted text, tap the <u>R</u>eplace button.**

   If you don't want to replace this text, tap the Find Next button, and Pocket Word searches through the document for the next occurrence of the text.

If you are confident that you want to change every location of the text specified in the Find what field, you can tap the Replace All button. Pocket Word replaces all the remaining locations of the text without prompting you first.

Moving Text

After you finish writing a letter to Grandma, you may decide that you want to move the paragraph asking her for a loan to follow the paragraph telling her how much you enjoyed snuggling with that quilt she spent six months knitting. This task is a piece of cake if you write the letter in Pocket Word.

To move items around in a document in Pocket Word, you use the Cut and Paste options, located on the Edit menu.

To move text, simply highlight the text on the screen and choose <u>E</u>dit⇨<u>Cut</u>. Then move the cursor to the location within the document where you want to move the text and choose <u>E</u>dit⇨<u>P</u>aste.

Looking for a diversion?

Very few of us can go through the day without some kind of diversion to break up the monotony. You may call mom on the phone, jog three miles, or take a long lunch and go shopping.

For those of you who have used previous versions of Windows, you have probably, on at least one occasion, found your escape in a game of Solitaire. Well, I have good news: Windows CE also comes with a version of Solitaire.

You can find the Solitaire program by choosing Programs➪Games➪Solitaire from the Start menu.

The game of Solitaire on a Windows CE device follows the age-old rules of Solitaire, except that you will find it difficult to cheat because Windows CE deals the cards. The object of the game is for you to get all the cards stacked into four suit piles in order from ace to king.

To move cards on-screen, simply touch the stylus to a card and drag the card across the screen to the location where you want it to appear. To deal the cards from the deck, you just need to double-tap the top of the deck.

Just remember, if you are playing Solitaire during a business presentation, simply tap the Solitaire button on the taskbar if the boss walks by. That minimizes Solitaire so that you look like you're hard at work.

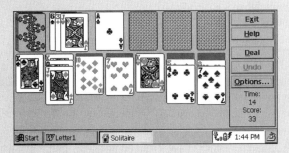

You can cut and paste any portion of a document, even pictures. You can even paste the text into another document, as long as you open that document and then find the desired location for the text before pasting.

You can also paste the text into another Windows CE program, as long as that program has a Paste option. Simply open the program in which you want to paste the text and use the Paste option.

Whenever you cut or copy something within Pocket Word, or any other Windows CE program, Windows CE places the information in an invisible location called the *Clipboard*. The Clipboard can contain only one selection at a time. So if you cut something that you want to paste somewhere else, be sure to paste it before copying or cutting anything else.

Selecting text with Windows CE

If you have used a previous version of Windows, you probably know that you can *select,* or highlight, text in many ways. In previous versions of Windows, one of the easiest ways to select text is to use your faithful mouse.

Well, as I am sure you have figured out, Windows CE does not come equipped with a mouse. You have a stylus instead. The following table describes the easiest ways to select text in Windows CE.

To Select This Item	Do This
Any amount of adjacent text	Drag the stylus across the text.
A word	Double-tap the word.
A paragraph	Tap three times somewhere in the middle of the paragraph.
The whole document	Choose Edit⇨Select All.
A picture	Tap the picture.

Copying Text

Have you ever typed a line of text that was so profound that you wanted to repeat it again in your document? Okay, maybe you're not a poet, but I'm sure that you have written, or will someday write, something that you would like to copy and use in another location.

You copy text in Pocket Word just about the same way as you move text. To copy the selected text in Pocket Word, you choose Edit⇨Copy to copy text to the Clipboard and then choose Edit⇨Paste to place the text in its new location.

You can copy and paste any portion of a document, even pictures. You can paste into the current document, another document, or even in the middle of a document in another program (as long as that program has a Paste option).

The Clipboard can contain only one selection at a time. So make sure that you paste whatever you copy before you cut or copy something else; otherwise, you lose the information that you first copied.

Formatting Text

Unless you have been hiding in some dark room for the last few years, you have probably noticed that almost every type of document you see — memos, letters, reports, notes, and so on — uses different fonts, font sizes, and styles.

Using a variety of font types, sizes, and styles helps to make a document more appealing to its readers. For example, if you look at the layout of this book, you will notice that the main headings for each section are in a larger and bolder font than the subordinate headings so that the main headings are easy to spot as you thumb through the book.

With Windows CE, you can change the text formatting while you are creating a document. You can select a new font type, change the size of the current font, or apply font styles, such as bold and italic.

Selecting a different font

You can add variety to your documents by using more than one font. For example, you may want to use one font for the headings or the address information at the top of a letter and a different font for the body of the document.

To change the font you are using in a document, you use the Font drop-down list box, which is located just to the left of the Font Size drop-down list box (see Figure 6-14).

Figure 6-14:
The Font
drop-down
list box
displays the
fonts you
can select.

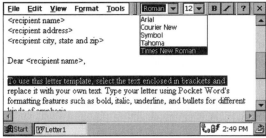

To format text with a different font as you enter the text into a document, tap the down-arrow button next to the Font drop-down list box and then tap the name of the font you want to use. Any text that you type from that location on appears in the new font, until you change the font selection again.

To change the font of a block of text that you have already entered into a document, select the text and then tap a font in the Font drop-down list box.

All Pocket Word documents use the same font when you first open them. To change the font throughout an entire document, choose Edit⇨Select All. Then select a font from the Font drop-down list box. All text you enter into the document uses the font you select.

Windows CE comes with only a few fonts. You can, however, copy fonts from your personal computer to Windows CE by using the Windows CE Services program under Windows 95 or Windows NT 4.0. For more information, see Chapter 11. **Remember:** Each font you add to your CE device takes up some of the device's memory.

Changing the font size

One way to make something stand out in your document is to change the size of the font. For example, you should normally use a larger font for the headings than for the text, so that readers can quickly spot the headings.

To change the size of a font, tap the down-arrow button next to the Font Size drop-down list box and highlight the number that corresponds to the appropriate font size. The Font Size drop-down list box is located at the top of the screen, between the Font Type drop-down list box and the Bold button, as shown in Figure 6-15.

Figure 6-15:
The drop-down list box displays the font sizes you can select for the current font.

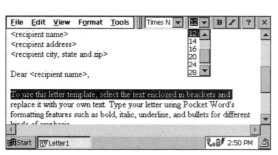

When you change the font size in the middle of a document, any text that you type from that location on appears in the new font size. You can change the font size for a block of text by highlighting the text and then selecting the new font size in the Font Size drop-down list box.

Modifying the font style

Probably the easiest way to make text stand out in a document is to change the font style. See Table 6-3 for descriptions of the three font style buttons.

Table 6-3	Font Style Buttons
Button	**Description**
B	Makes the text appear in a bold font.
I	Makes the text appear in an italicized font.
U	Underlines the text.

To change the style of a font, tap one or more of the font style buttons and start typing. All the text that you type appears in the selected font style until you deselect the style by again tapping the corresponding button or buttons.

To change the font style for a block of text that you have already entered into a document, select the text and then tap the appropriate font style buttons.

Doing it all with the Font dialog box

If you like to do everything in one place, then the Font dialog box, shown in Figure 6-16, may be the solution for you. Here, you can change everything about the way the font looks, including changing the color of the font (a useful feature if you want to print the document on a color printer).

Figure 6-16:
Use the
Font dialog
box to
specify the
default
formatting
for the
document.

The changes you make in the Font dialog box are applied to whatever text you have selected in Pocket Word. As you make changes, you can even see a preview of the changes in the Preview section of the dialog box.

If you want to change the default font information for documents that you open in Pocket Word, make the appropriate changes in the Font dialog box and then tap the Set as Default button. By doing this, each new document you open will use these new text formatting options.

If you tap the Apply Default button, your current default settings are applied to the selected text.

Formatting a Paragraph

You are probably going to find that you don't want all of the paragraphs in your document to look the same. For example, you may want to indent the first paragraph on the page, or center another paragraph. You can perform all the formatting for your paragraph in the Paragraph dialog box, as shown in Figure 6-17. This dialog box displays when you choose Format➪Paragraph.

Figure 6-17:
Use the
Paragraph
dialog box
to set the
indentation
for the
paragraph.

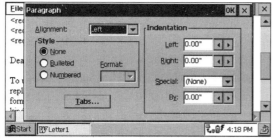

The Paragraph dialog box has three sections: Alignment, Style, and Indentation. The first two sections provide options that you can also accomplish using the buttons on the command bar, but you can only specify indentation settings on the Paragraph dialog box, as I outline in Table 6-4.

Table 6-4	Setting Indentations
Use This Field	*If You Want To*
Left	Indent the text a certain amount from the left margin of the page. Either type a value in the field or tap the left- and right-arrow buttons to set the indentation.
Right	Indent the text a certain amount from the right margin of the page. Either type a value in the field or tap the left- and right-arrow buttons to set the indentation.
Special	Set special indenting for the first line of the paragraph. If you select First line, only the first line of the paragraph is indented. If you select Hanging, the first line of text hangs out in the left margin based on the value you specify in the By field.

To select the alignment for the paragraph, simply tap the down-arrow button next to the Alignment field and select the type of alignment you want.

Creating Lists

Do you have a list of items that you want to add to your document? People commonly refer to a list of items as either a *numbered list* or a *bulleted list,* depending on how the list is created. Pocket Word allows you to create both numbered and bulleted lists.

 If you are creating a list of steps or listing items that need to remain in a specific order, you usually use a numbered list. You can create a numbered list by simply tapping the Numbered List button.

A *bullet* is a small circle that is placed to the left of each item in the list. The bullet informs readers that the items are listed in no particular order.

Creating lists is quite simple in Pocket Word. The following steps show how easy it is to create a bulleted list of items:

 1. To start a bulleted list, tap the Bullets button.

A bullet appears on the left side of the screen, and the paragraph is indented, as indicated by the position of the cursor.

2. Type a word, such as Apple, **and press the Enter key.**

A bullet appears in the left margin for the next item in the bulleted list.

3. **Type another word, such as** Banana, **and press the Enter key.**

   Again, another bullet appears at the beginning of the next line of text.

4. **Type another word, such as** Orange, **and press the Enter key.**

   You now have a list of three bulleted items, with a bullet on the next blank line of text, as shown in Figure 6-18.

5. **Tap the Bullets button again.**

   The Bullets button no longer looks as if it's pressed down. The fourth bullet is removed, and now the text that you type will have normal formatting.

Figure 6-18:
When you turn on the Bullets option, a new bullet appears each time you press the Enter key.

To place bullets next to a block of paragraphs, select the block of text and then tap the Bullets button. You can use the same steps I outline in the preceding paragraphs to create a numbered list — just tap the Numbered List button instead of the Bullets button.

You can also choose Format➪Paragraph and create the bulleted and numbered lists using the Style section of the Paragraph dialog box. This option is useful if you want to create a numbered list that has a format other than 1, 2, 3 (such as A, B, C). You specify the format for the numbered list by tapping the down-arrow button next to the Format field and selecting the desired format.

Outlining Your Document

You may have created a few outlines back in high school. As you may remember, you are supposed to list the topics that you want to discuss and then take each topic and write a series of paragraphs that cover that information.

You can view your documents in Outline view in Pocket Word. You may find this view handy for viewing long documents. If you open a document in Outline view, you see only the headings. You can then locate and open the section of the document that contains the information you want to view.

You can also use the Outline view to take notes for a meeting. In fact, the Meeting Notes template that comes with Pocket Word is designed to be used in Outline view.

Viewing the outline of a document

Pocket Word usually displays documents in Normal view. To switch to Outline view, choose View⇨Outline. The text appears indented based on its heading level (see Figure 6-19).

Figure 6-19:
Outline
view is
useful for
viewing a
large
document.

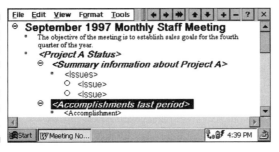

When you look at your document in Outline view, you find a small symbol in the left margin next to each paragraph. These symbols can provide valuable information if you know how to interpret them. Table 6-5 offers an overview of each symbol that Pocket Word uses.

Table 6-5	Interpreting the Outline Symbols
This Symbol	*Indicates That*
○	This text is a heading, but it does not have any body text or subheadings under it.
⊖	This text is a heading and the corresponding body text and subheadings are currently displayed on-screen. A heading with this symbol is considered to be *expanded* because you can read the associated body text. Tap this symbol to collapse the text.

This Symbol	Indicates That
▫	This text is a heading but the corresponding body text and subheadings do not appear on the screen. A heading with this symbol is considered to be *collapsed* because you cannot read the associated body text. Tap this symbol to expand the text.
⊕	This text is body text.

Working in Outline view

For some types of documents, you may find that it is easier to work in Outline view than in Normal view. For example, if you want to write the main topics of a proposal first and then go back and expand on each topic later, you should use Outline view.

If you have worked in Outline view before, you may have noticed a bunch of funny arrow buttons on a toolbar near the top of the screen. You can use these buttons to help you move information around easily while in Outline view. See Table 6-6 for a brief description of each button. To use any of the buttons, you need to select the text that you want to change before you tap the button.

Table 6-6	Outline Buttons on the Toolbar
Button	**Purpose**
←	Moves the current text up one heading level.
→	Moves the current text down one heading level.
⇒	Changes the current text to the body text level.
↑	Moves the currently selected text (and all the body text and subheadings) above the heading that precedes it.
↓	Moves the currently selected text (and all the body text and subheadings) below the heading that follows it.
+	Displays the body text and subheadings for the currently selected heading.
−	Hides the body text and subheadings for the currently selected heading.

Where does Pocket Word find the heading levels?

If you have ever used Outline view in Microsoft Word for Windows, you may be aware that the heading levels used with Outline view correspond to the styles you use in your document. If you create a document in Outline view, Pocket Word uses nine heading level styles and one body text style. If you open a document that you created in Normal view and display it in Outline view, Pocket Word assumes that the parts of the text that use a font size or style that differs from the font size or style used by the rest of the text are headings. So these lines of text appear at a higher level than the rest of the text in the document.

You use the drop-down list box that sits between the – button and the ? button to indicate which heading levels you want to view (see Figure 6-20). To view the entire document, select the All Levels option. If you want to view only a portion of the document, such as the headers, select a heading level, such as Level 2.

Figure 6-20:
Use the drop-down list box to specify the amount of information you want to see.

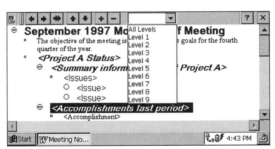

Converting a Microsoft Word Document

The fact that you can transfer most Microsoft Word documents to a CE device that runs Windows CE is reason enough to use Windows CE. But, unfortunately, the more complex the formatting is in your Microsoft Word document, the more you lose during the conversion.

Because Pocket Word is a scaled-down version of Word for Windows, it doesn't provide many of the fancy formatting features that you may often use in Word for Windows. Table 6-7 outlines some of the common formatting features and explains what happens when you convert the document to Windows CE.

Table 6-7	Lost Formatting for Pocket Word
Word for Windows Formatting Option	**Result in Pocket Word**
Fonts	Text appears in the closest font available in Pocket Word.
Font color	Text appears in the closest shade of gray on monochrome screens.
Tabs, alignment, bullets, numbering, and indentation	Text appears as in Word for Windows.
OLE objects	If possible, OLE objects are converted to pictures and left in the document.
Tables	Because Pocket Word does not support tables, the cells are separated by tabs.
Columns, index, and table of contents	The text appears in the document, but some of the formatting is usually lost.
Numbering and fields	The text appears in the document, but some of the formatting is usually lost.
Headers, footers, footnotes, annotations, revisions, style sheets, borders, and shading	All these items are removed from the document.

Keep in mind that when these formatting options are removed from the document during the conversion to Pocket Word, they are not added back when you convert the document back to Word for Windows. Therefore, if you copy the same document back to your personal computer, you may want to place it in a different location so that you do not overwrite the original; otherwise, you may find yourself forced to do a lot of reformatting.

For more information about copying documents from your personal computer to your CE device, refer to Chapter 11.

Printing Documents

You are probably going to have times when you want the capability to print your documents directly from your CE device. This is possible if you have the printer connected to the serial port on your CE device (the port you use to connect to your personal computer) or if you are able to send stuff to your printer using the infrared port (if the printer has an infrared port to receive the stuff).

To print out your document, choose File⇨Print to display the Print dialog box, shown in Figure 6-21. Table 6-8 describes the information you can specify on the Print dialog box.

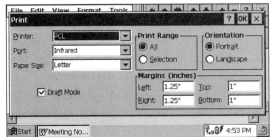

Figure 6-21:
You can print out your document using your CE device.

Table 6-8	Fields for Printing Tasks
In This Field	*Indicate*
Printer	The type of printer to which you are sending the information. PCL represents a standard type of HP printer.
Port	The port you are going to use to send the information to the printer. If the printer has an infrared port, you can use the infrared port on your CE device to send the information to the printer. Otherwise, you need to connect a serial printer cable between your printer and your CE device.
Paper Size	The size of paper on which you are printing. Letter size is the most common paper size for printers. It refers to an 8^1/$_2$-x-11-inch piece of paper.
Draft Mode	The check box if you want to print the information in draft mode on your printer. This option normally prints the information faster, but does not look as nice as the nondraft mode.
Print Range	The amount of information you want to print. Select the All radio button to print the entire document, or the Selection radio button to print only the text you have highlighted.
Orientation	The way the information should be printed on the page. To orient it vertically, select the Portrait radio button; otherwise, select the Landscape radio button to orient it horizontally on the paper.
Left Margin	The amount of space that should be left blank on the left side of the paper.
Right Margin	The amount of space that should be left blank on the right side of the paper.

In This Field	Indicate
Top Margin	The amount of space that should be left blank on the top of the paper.
Bottom Margin	The amount of space that should be left blank on the bottom of the paper.

If you can't print from your CE device, you need to use the Windows CE Services program on your personal computer to print a file. To do so, select the file on your personal computer and choose File⇨Print. For more information about working with the Windows CE Services on your personal computer, see Part III.

Checking Your Spelling

If you are at all like me, no matter how well you spell, you always tend to mistype something. Luckily, Pocket Word knows how to double-check your spelling. Whenever you want to check the spelling of your document, tap the Spelling button, and Pocket Word will check it out. If a misspelling is encountered, Pocket Word displays the word in a box so that you can correct it, as shown in Figure 6-22.

Figure 6-22:
When an unrecognized word is located, you have the opportunity to correct the spelling.

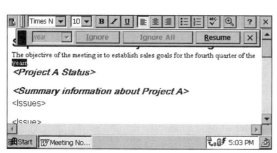

You have basically five choices when this happens:

- ✔ Tap the Ignore button to keep the word in the document as is (if you know this word occurs several times, you may want to select the Ignore All button).
- ✔ Accept the spelling suggestion in the drop-down list box.

✔ Tap the down-arrow button next to the drop-down list box and select a new spelling option.

✔ Type the correct spelling for the word in the drop-down list box.

✔ Tap the Add button to place the word in the spelling dictionary so that Pocket Word will know how it should be spelled next time around.

Password-Protecting Your Document

If you have sensitive documents that you want to make sure no one else can read, you may want to consider password-protecting those documents. By doing this, the only way another person can open the document is if the person knows the password that you assigned to the document.

Be careful with setting passwords. If you set a password and then forget it, you will not be able to open the document. If you use passwords, make sure you can easily remember them. On the other hand, you want to make sure they're not too easy for someone else to guess, or setting a password doesn't do you any good.

To set a password for the current document, choose File➪Password to display the Password dialog shown in Figure 6-23. Simply type the desired password in the Password field and again in the Verify Password field. As you type your password, Pocket Word displays asterisks in place of the characters you type in each field. This prevents someone from looking over your shoulder and seeing your password. Tap the OK button, and the password is attached to the document.

Figure 6-23:
You see asterisks as you type the password in each field.

You can remove the password by coming back to the Password dialog box and deleting the password characters from each field. Remember, however, that you can only do this after opening the document.

Chapter 7

Crunching Numbers in Pocket Excel

. . . .

. . . .

Spreadsheet programs are among the most popular types of software used on personal computers. You can use a spreadsheet to keep track of all types of data, such as hours worked, travel expenses, and monthly budgets. And by placing the data in a series of rows and columns, you can easily manipulate the data in various ways.

To keep up with the popular trend, Windows CE provides Pocket Excel, a scaled-down version of Microsoft Excel, the spreadsheet powerhouse that runs on personal computers. Pocket Excel provides many of the same capabilities found in its bigger sibling. You can even open an Excel spreadsheet in Pocket Excel.

This chapter explains how to use Pocket Excel. I tell you how to create worksheets, use formulas, and format your worksheets. I even help you sort out the difference between the terms *spreadsheet*, *worksheet*, and *workbook*.

Locating Pocket Excel

 To calculate expenses, create a timesheet, or manage other types of data, you must first locate Pocket Excel. The icon for Pocket Excel sits on the Windows CE desktop on most CE devices. The icon looks like a piece of paper with a large X on top of it. To display Pocket Excel, locate the Pocket Excel icon and then use your stylus to double-tap it.

If you can't find the Pocket Excel icon sitting on your desktop, don't despair; you should be able to locate it by following these simple steps:

1. **Tap the Start button (in the lower-left corner of the screen).**

   When you tap the Start button, a pop-up menu that contains various options appears.

2. **Tap the Programs option.**

   Selecting this option opens another menu containing a list of the programs and other menus on your CE device.

3. **Tap the Office option.**

   You see a third menu containing more programs, as shown in Figure 7-1.

Figure 7-1: Find Pocket Excel on the pop-up menus when you tap the Start button.

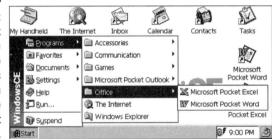

4. **Tap the Microsoft Pocket Excel option on the menu to display the Pocket Excel program, shown in Figure 7-2.**

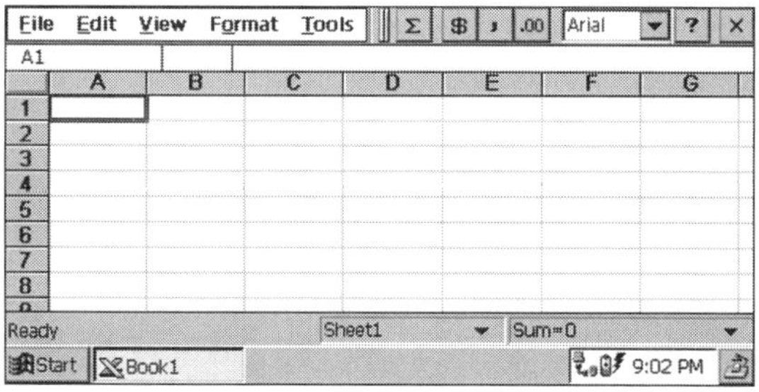

Figure 7-2:
Use Pocket
Excel to
create
worksheets.

If you have used other spreadsheet programs, you will probably quickly notice that Pocket Excel uses two terms not found in many spreadsheet programs: *workbook* and *worksheet*. The *workbook* is what both Pocket Excel and Microsoft Excel for Windows call the file where you store your data. Within each workbook, you can have several related pages called *worksheets*. You place the data on a worksheet. That is, you lay out your spreadsheet on a worksheet. If you have a complex spreadsheet, you may use multiple worksheets to create it. After you create all your worksheets, the workbook is the location where you store them. In other words, the workbook is the container for the individual worksheets; and the worksheet is where you create your spreadsheet.

See the section "Opening a Microsoft Excel Workbook" later in this chapter, to find out how you can use Pocket Excel to work on Excel documents from your personal computer.

Creating a New Workbook

Microsoft Pocket Excel provides two methods for creating a new workbook. You can either design your workbook from scratch using a blank workbook, or you can choose a template similar to the workbook you want to create and then make the changes necessary to produce the desired result.

Using a blank document

When you first open Pocket Excel, a new, blank workbook appears. If you are ready to create a new spreadsheet, you can enter your information and then save the completed workbook.

If you already have one workbook open, you can create a new workbook by choosing File⇨New. When you select the New option, a blank, unnamed workbook appears. You can see a button on the taskbar for the new worksheet you just opened.

You can also create a new workbook by pressing Ctrl+N.

You have probably noticed by now that each worksheet in Pocket Excel looks like a big grid. Series of horizontal and vertical lines divide the screen, and small little boxes, or *cells,* appear between all these lines.

If you look closely, you can see that the cells are lined up in rows and columns on-screen. Pocket Excel provides labels for each row so that you can easily identify individual cells. The first cell on the spreadsheet is in column A and row 1, so it is called cell A1. The cell under it is cell A2, and the cell on the right side of it is cell B1.

By using this type of grid system to keep track of cells, you can easily manipulate the data in a worksheet by stating that you want to add all of the values in column A or row 2, for example.

Using a template

Templates provide the capability to create a workbook without starting from scratch. When you use a template, you start with something that resembles the workbook you want to create and then make the desired modifications to produce the workbook you want. When you open a template, all the information in that template is copied directly into your workbook.

If you do not find the type of template you want to use, you can create one and save it for future uses. In fact, you can save any workbook as a template. For more information about saving templates, refer to the section "Saving a workbook for the first time" later in this chapter.

Follow these steps to open up a Pocket Excel template:

1. **Choose File⇨New⇨Workbook from Template.**

   As shown in Figure 7-3, Pocket Excel displays the Template dialog box, which contains the templates that you currently have on your CE device.

Figure 7-3:
Select the
template
you want to
use to
create your
worksheet.

You will see only the templates that are sitting in the Templates folder. This folder is located within the Office folder, which sits inside the Program Files folder. If you create other templates, you need to make sure they are sitting in this folder so that you can select them.

2. Double-tap the name of the desired template.

A copy of the selected template is placed in your document, as shown in Figure 7-4.

3. Enter the appropriate information on your worksheet.

Figure 7-4:
Everything
in the
selected
template is
copied
into your
worksheet.

Opening an Existing Workbook

After you save a workbook, you may need to open and revise it or just read it again. To open a workbook, choose File➪Open. The Open dialog box appears (see Figure 7-5).

Figure 7-5:
Use the
Open dialog
box to
locate a
workbook
that you
want to
open.

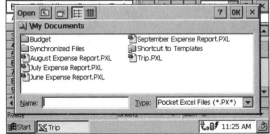

 Pocket Excel assumes that you want to open a workbook from the My Documents folder. If the workbook is located in another folder, tap the Previous Folder button and open the folder above the My Documents folder. After you find the correct workbook, double-tap it to open it. For more information on files and folders, refer to Chapter 9.

 You can also open a workbook from the Windows CE Explorer or from anywhere you see an icon for a Pocket Excel workbook. If you double-tap an icon for a Pocket Excel workbook, Pocket Excel automatically opens that workbook.

Opening the Workbook that You Worked On Last

What happens if you forget the name of the workbook that you worked on yesterday? If that hasn't happened to you yet, don't worry — it will. Fortunately, Pocket Excel remembers the last four workbooks that you worked on.

To see what you last worked on — or at least opened and viewed last — open the File menu and tap the Recent Files option. You see a list of the last workbooks that were opened on your CE device using Pocket Excel. To select one of these workbooks, tap the workbook name with the stylus, or type the number next to the workbook name.

Adding Data to a Worksheet

Opening a workbook doesn't do you much good if you don't know how to add data to it. Although you can add multiple types of data — such as dates, percentages, and fractions — to a worksheet, data comes in just two different categories: constants and formulas.

Working with constants

In Pocket Excel, all text, numbers, dates, times, currency, and percentages are considered to be *constants* (values that remain unchanged on the worksheet). When you enter a constant into a cell, it remains there until you replace it.

Pocket Word does recognize the difference between certain kinds of data. Therefore, you must use specific rules to enter specific kinds of values.

Adding text

To ensure that Pocket Excel treats text as text, format the cell as text. See "Formatting Cells" later in this chapter to find out how to format cells. You can enter as many as 255 characters in one cell. Although you normally see only the number of characters that fit in that cell's on-screen width, you may see more if the cell to the right is empty. Pocket Excel automatically left-justifies text within the cells.

Entering numbers

Pocket Excel assumes that all the numeric values are positive, unless you indicate that they aren't. To indicate that a value is negative, type a minus sign in front of the number or place the entire number within parentheses.

Pocket Excel right-justifies numbers within the cells. Pocket Excel stores the numeric values with as many as 15 digits of precision, even if fewer than 15 appear on-screen. This arrangement means that Pocket Excel keeps track of a total 15 digits on the left and right side of the decimal point.

Adding dates and times

You can enter times by a 12-hour or 24-hour (commonly referred to as military time) clock. If you enter time by the 12-hour clock, type **am** or **pm** after the time. For example, type **4:00 pm** to represent 4:00 in the afternoon. To enter time for the 24-hour clock, type the desired time with a colon between the hour and minutes value, such as **15:35**.

You can enter dates by using either the / or the - (hyphen) character to separate the date. For example, you can type either **4/14/97** or **4-14-97** for April 14, 1997. You can also use three-character abbreviations, such as **Apr**, to represent the months. You can also enter a date and time in the same cell by placing a space between the two values.

Dealing with currency

 Pocket Excel provides the capability to quickly format a cell for currency by selecting the desired cell and then tapping the Currency button on the toolbar. The Currency button is the one with the dollar sign on it.

After you format the cell for currency values, you need to type the currency amount in the cell, and the dollar sign appears next to the value.

The default number of decimal places for currency values is 2, but you can reformat the cell to display as many as 15 decimal places. Pocket Excel assumes that all the currency values are positive, unless you indicate otherwise. To indicate that a value is negative, type a minus sign in front of the currency value or place the entire value within parentheses.

Just like numeric values, currency values are right-justified within the cell, with the dollar sign left-justified in the cell.

Inserting percentages

You can enter a percentage in a cell in many different ways. The most common way to enter a percentage is to type a numeric value followed by the percent sign, such as **4%**. If you format the cell as a percentage, you can also enter the value as a decimal value, such as **0.67**, or as a formula that represents the percentage, such as **3/4**. For more information about formatting the cell, refer to "Formatting Cells" later in this chapter.

Using formulas

Formulas are basically any combination of operators, cell references, Pocket Excel functions, and names. For example, 5+6 is a formula, as is =SUM(A3:A7). You can use formulas to manipulate and analyze the data that you add to the worksheet.

You can use the normal mathematical operators as well as approximately 100 functions that come with Pocket Excel to create formulas.

To insert a function in a cell, you need to select it in the Insert Function dialog box, shown in Figure 7-6. The Insert Function dialog box appears when you choose Tools⇨Insert Function.

Figure 7-6:
The Insert
Function
dialog box
provides
approx-
imately 100
functions.

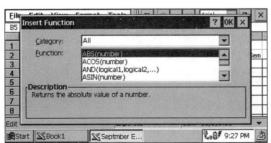

Highlight the function you want in the Function drop-down list box. Then tap the OK button to paste the function into the formula bar.

To limit the list of functions in the Function drop-down list box, you can specify that only a particular type of function appears in the box by using the Category field. Tap the down-arrow button next to the Category field to display the Category drop-down list box and then select the type of function you want. The functions are divided into categories based on the type of results they produce, such as Financial, Date and Time, and Statistical.

Resizing Rows and Columns

When you look at a worksheet, you notice that all the cells on the sheet are evenly sized. This consistency is okay for some worksheets, but quite often you probably want to resize the cells on the screen so that you can read the contents of the cells better. For example, you may have one column that contains the descriptions for another column of numeric values. You can size the description column to be wider so that you can see the contents of each cell.

Dragging rows and columns

The quick and easy way to resize a row or column is to tap one of the lines that separate the column and row headings, hold the stylus down, and drag the line until the row or column is the size you want. When you tap one of the lines, your cursor turns into a double-headed arrow, indicating that you can now drag the line to the size you want, as shown in Figure 7-7.

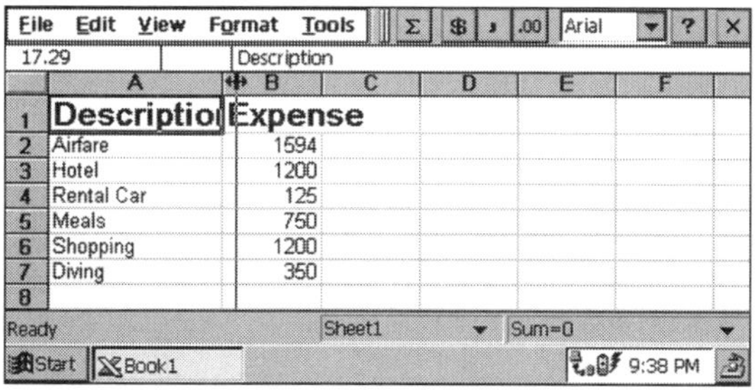

Figure 7-7:
The double-headed arrow indicates that you can change the size of the row or column.

File	Edit	View	Format	Tools		Σ	$	,	.00	Arial	▼	?	×

17.29			Description				
	A	B	C	D	E	F	
1	**Description**	**Expense**					
2	Airfare	1594					
3	Hotel	1200					
4	Rental Car	125					
5	Meals	750					
6	Shopping	1200					
7	Diving	350					
8							

Ready		Sheet1	▼	Sum=0	▼
Start	Book1			9:38 PM	

Another easy way to resize the column is to simply double-tap the line that separates the column. Pocket Word resizes the entire column so that it is wide enough for the largest cell in the column.

Using the formatting options

The Format menu provides some additional options for setting the size of rows and columns on your worksheet. These options are available by tapping either the Row or Column option on the Format menu.

If you want to be more exact about the sizing that you use for a column or row, you can choose either Format⇨Row⇨Height or Format⇨Column⇨Width to specify the exact size for the column or row.

The default size of each cell in the worksheet is 9 characters wide and 12.75 points high. A *point* is a unit of measurement that describes the height of characters.

To change either the row height or the column width, choose the corresponding option on the Format menu. Enter the size in the Column Width dialog box that appears and then tap the OK button (see Figure 7-8).

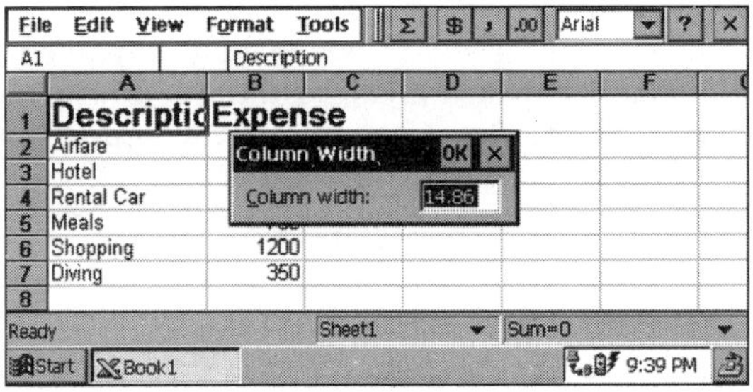

Figure 7-8:
In the
Column
Width
dialog box,
type the
column
width you
want.

File	Edit	View	Format	Tools	Σ	$	,	.00	Arial	▼	?	X

A1		Description				
	A	B	C	D	E	F
1	**Descriptic**	**Expense**				
2	Airfare	Column Width	OK X			
3	Hotel					
4	Rental Car	Column width:	14.86			
5	Meals					
6	Shopping	1200				
7	Diving	350				
8						

Ready   Sheet1 ▼   Sum=0 ▼

Start   Book1   9:39 PM

You can even hide a row or column that you don't want to appear on the worksheet. If you need to compute the results of some data but only want the results to appear on the worksheet, not the data, you can hide the row or column in which the data lies, by choosing Format⇨Row⇨Hide or Format⇨Column⇨Hide. To view the column again, select the Unhide option.

Adding and Removing Cells

It may sound a little crazy to add more cells to a worksheet; after all, the worksheet appears to have an endless number of rows and columns. Sometimes, however, you may want to add another value or row of values or remove some values from the middle of the worksheet after you have already added data to the worksheet.

In case you were wondering about the maximum size of a worksheet, I thought I would point out that a Pocket Excel worksheet can have a maximum of 16,384 rows and 256 columns.

Adding cells

You can insert new cells into a worksheet at any location by following these steps:

1. **Choose Format⇨Insert Cells to display the Insert Cells dialog box, shown in Figure 7-9.**

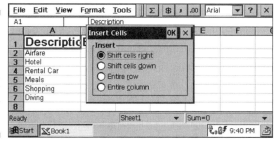

Figure 7-9:
Use the
Insert Cells
dialog box
to add new
cells to your
worksheet.

2. **Select the radio button that indicates how you want the new cell added to the worksheet.**

   Table 7-1 describes the options available in the Insert Cells dialog box. When new cells are added, the surrounding cells move to make room for the new cells. For example, if you select the Shift cells right option in the Insert Cells dialog box, all the cells in the row to the right of the new cell move over one column. So if you add a new cell at location B2, the cell labeled B2 becomes C2, and C2 becomes D2, and so on.

3. **Tap the OK button to insert the cell as specified.**

Table 7-1	Inserting Cells
Option	**Result**
Shift cells right	All other cells in the row to the right of the new cell shift to the right one column.
Shift cells down	All other cells in the column shift down one row.
Entire row	A new row is added, and all rows below shift down one row.
Entire column	A new column is added, and all columns to the right shift over one column.

Removing cells

You can remove cells from any location in a worksheet by following these simple steps:

1. **Choose Format⇨Delete Cells to display the Delete Cells dialog box, shown in Figure 7-10.**

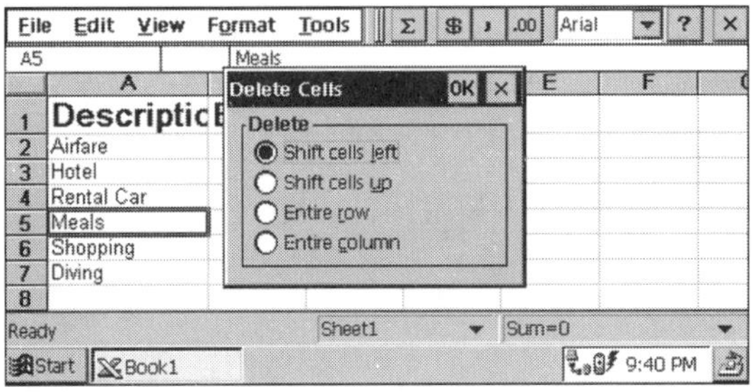

Figure 7-10:
Use the
Delete Cells
dialog box
to remove
individual
cells or
entire
rows and
columns.

2. **Select the radio button that indicates how you want the cell removed from the worksheet.**

   Table 7-2 describes the options in the Delete Cells dialog box. Before you delete the cells, you need to determine what will happen to the cells around the one you plan to remove. If you select the Shift cells left option in the Delete Cells dialog box, all the cells in the row to the right of the deleted cell move left one column. So if you delete the cell at location B2, the cell labeled C2 becomes B2, and the cell labeled D2 becomes C2, and so on.

3. Tap the OK button to delete the cell as specified.

Table 7-2	Deleting Cells
Option	*Result*
Shift cells left	All other cells in the row to the right of the deleted cell shift to the left one column.
Shift cells up	All other cells in the column shift up one row.
Entire row	The current row is deleted, and all rows below shift up one row.
Entire column	The current column is deleted, and all columns to the right shift over to the left one column.

Moving Data on the Worksheet

You may find that you want to reorganize data after you place the data on the worksheet. Pocket Excel lets you copy the data from one or more cells and place it in another location within the worksheet. You can even place it in another worksheet or workbook.

To move data around in a worksheet, you need to use the Cut and Paste options on the Edit menu. To move the data, highlight the cells on the screen and then choose Edit⇨Cut. Then move the cursor to the location within the worksheet (or another worksheet) where you want to place the data and choose Edit⇨Paste. If you are pasting multiple cells of data, you need to place the cursor in the first upper-left cell in which you want to paste the data.

Instead of moving the data within the worksheet, you may want to copy the data and paste a copy of it in another location. To copy the data, select the cells you want to copy on the screen and then choose Edit⇨Copy. Then select the cell (in any workbook) where you want to paste the copied data and choose Edit⇨Paste.

Whenever you cut or copy something within Pocket Excel, or any other Windows CE program, the copied information is placed in an invisible location called the Clipboard. The Clipboard can hold only one selection at a time. So if you cut something that you want to paste somewhere else, make sure that you paste it before copying or cutting something else; otherwise, you may lose the information.

TIP

You can also press Ctrl+X to cut the data, or Ctrl+C to copy, and then Ctrl+V to paste the data in the desired location.

Formatting Cells

In Pocket Excel, you can apply different types of formatting to each cell. By formatting values in cells, you can ensure, for example, that Pocket Excel treats the value in a particular cell as a percentage.

You can also specify how the data appears in the cell by selecting the desired font characteristics, such as font size and font style. Or you can add borders to the cell to make it stand out on the worksheet.

All these cell formatting options are available in the Format Cells dialog box. The Format Cells dialog box appears when you choose Format➪Cells.

Indicating the category of data

You use the Number tab of the Format Cells dialog box, shown in Figure 7-11, to indicate the type of data that the selected cell contains. For example, if you assign a category of Percentage to a cell, Pocket Excel treats the value in that cell as a percentage.

Figure 7-11:
Use the
Number tab
to specify
the type of
value in
the cell.

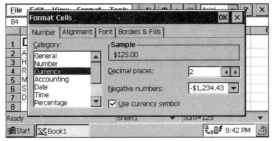

To specify the category for the cell, highlight the desired value in the Category list box. When you select the category, a sample of the first cell in the selected range appears in the Sample section.

Each category type offers different options that appear on the right side of the dialog box. For example, if you select Number, you can select three more options. In the Decimal places field, use the left- and right-arrow buttons to specify the number of decimal places that you want to display. Then in the

Negative numbers field, select either the value with the minus sign or the value surrounded with parentheses to indicate how negative values should be displayed. Finally, if you want a comma to separate every three digits of a number (such as 5,434), select the box next to the Use 1000 separator field. While you change the options for the cell, look at the Sample section to see how the cell will look.

Specifying cell alignment

Pocket Excel always formats certain types of data in certain ways. For example, by default, text is always left-justified in the cell, and numeric values are right-justified.

You may decide that you want to specify your own alignment for the data in cells. To do this, you use the Alignment tab on the Format Cells dialog box, as shown in Figure 7-12. You can select the horizontal and vertical alignment of the data in the cell by tapping the desired options.

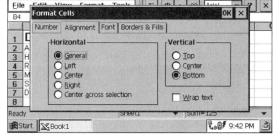

Figure 7-12: Use the Alignment tab to specify the horizontal and vertical spacing of cell data.

Indicating font values

You can make text in certain cells stand out on the screen by changing the font values for those cells. To change font values, tap the Font tab on the Format Cells dialog box, as shown in Figure 7-13.

As you make selections on this tab, the Preview section illustrates how the font selections will look in the cell. For the Font, Size, and Color drop-down list boxes, tap the down-arrow button and highlight the desired selections. In the Style section, tap the box next to the desired font styles.

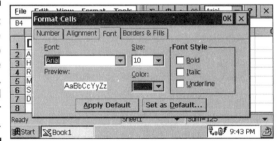

Figure 7-13:
Use the
Font tab to
select the
font type,
size, and
style for
the cell.

Selecting borders and fills

Of course, no worksheet would be complete without some borders and even a little background color. You can select the borders on the Borders & Fills tab of the Format Cells dialog box, shown in Figure 7-14. Tap the boxes for the types of borders you want.

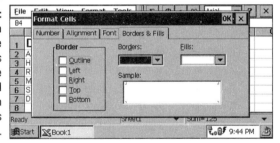

Figure 7-14:
You can
create
borders
around the
selected
cells with
the Borders
& Fills tab.

Selecting the Outline option is the same as selecting all four of the other Border options (Left, Right, Top, Bottom). So if you want borders around the entire cell, select the Outline option.

The Fills option is probably only useful if you are using Pocket Excel on a CE device with a color monitor, or if you plan to copy the worksheet over to a personal computer so that you can use it with Microsoft Excel. Anyhow, if desired, you can specify the color of the selected cell of the worksheet.

Quickly Summing Data

 The AutoSum button enables you to quickly sum the numeric values in a row, column, or even a series of rows and columns. The following steps show how you can easily sum numeric values within your worksheet:

1. In the first cell of the worksheet, enter a numeric value, such as 3.

The first cell in a worksheet is always labeled A1. To place a value in that cell, tap the cell with the stylus and then type the desired value. Whatever you enter appears in the formula bar under the standard toolbar, as shown in Figure 7-15. To move the value to the cell, press Enter or tap the check mark button next to the formula bar.

Formula bar

Figure 7-15:
The formula
bar is
where all
data entry
occurs
for the
worksheet.

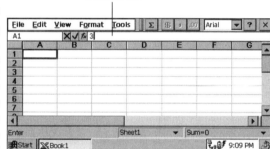

2. In the cell labeled A2, enter a numeric value, such as 4.

Cell A2 is located directly under the first cell.

3. In the cell labeled A3, enter a numeric value, such as 5.

4. Tap the cell labeled A4 to select it.

The cell should be highlighted on-screen.

5. Tap the AutoSum button.

When you tap the AutoSum button, the formula =SUM(A1:A3) appears in the formula bar. Tap the check mark button to place the formula in cell A4.

The following tips are important to keep in mind when you work with formulas and the AutoSum button:

✔ Whenever a cell contains a formula, the results of the formula appear in the cell while you view the worksheet. To see the actual formula in the formula bar, tap the cell to select it.

- ✔ If you tap the AutoSum button and it doesn't display the desired range of cells, you can drag the stylus across the cells to select them. Or you can enter the appropriate cells in the formula bar.

- ✔ You can use a colon in the formula to indicate a range of cells. For example, a formula that says =SUM(A1:A3) and one that says =SUM(A1, A2, A3) both do the same thing; they add the values in cells A1 through A3.

Automatically Filling Cells with Data

If you want to copy data from some cells to other cells or insert a series of data in certain cells, you can use the Fill dialog box, shown in Figure 7-16. The Fill dialog box appears when you choose Edit⇨Fill.

Figure 7-16:
Add related data to a series of cells in the Fill dialog box.

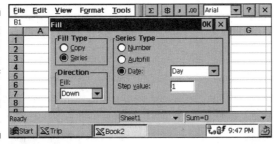

Copying data

Copying data from cells within a worksheet is one of the most common uses for the Fill option. The following steps illustrate how to copy data from cells:

1. **Highlight the cells that contain the data you want to copy.**

   You cannot select more than one row or one column. To select a row or a column, tap its heading.

2. **Extend the selected cells to include the location where you want the cells to be copied.**

   To select more cells, hold down the Shift key and select the new cells. If you are moving the data to a new row or column, tap the heading.

3. **Choose Edit⇨Fill.**

   The Fill dialog box appears.

4. **Select the Copy option in the Fill Type section.**

5. **Select the direction that you want to fill the cells in the Fill drop-down list.**

   Depending on the cells you've selected, you can fill either Down, Up, Left, or Right. For example, if you select the Down option, the top row will be used to fill the other selected rows. Select Right to fill all rows with data in farthest left row.

6. **Tap the OK button to copy the data.**

   Pocket Excel copies the selected data into the specified cells.

Inserting a series of data

You can use the Fill option to add a series of data to the selected cells of your worksheet. A *series* is data that is arranged in some logical order. For example, the days of the week, when listed in order, are a series. In Pocket Excel, you can have a series of numbers, a series of text that is followed by a number (such as session1), or a series of dates. The following steps illustrate how to create a series of data:

1. **Type the first value of the desired series in a cell.**

   Make sure that the cell is at the beginning of where you want your series to be located.

2. **Highlight the cell where you typed the data.**

   You can select one cell or an entire row or column. To select a row or a column, tap its heading.

3. **Extend the selected cells to include the cells where you want the series to be located.**

   To select more cells, hold down the Shift key and select the new cells. If you are inserting the series into a new row or column, tap the row or column heading.

4. **Choose Edit⇨Fill.**

   The Fill dialog box appears.

5. **Select the Series option in the Fill Type section.**

6. **In the Series Type section, select the type of series that you want to create.**

   Select Number to create a series of numbers. Enter the amount that the number should be incremented by in the Step value field. For example, to display every other number, enter **2**.

Select Autofill to create a series of values that is based on the contents of the first cell. The first cell must contain a day of the week, a month (you can use a three-character abbreviation or spell it out), or text followed by a number, such as **Session1**.

Select Date to create a series of dates. Select a value in the drop-down list box indicating whether you want a day, month, or year for the date. Remember to type a value in the Step value field that indicates the increment value for the date. For example, to increase by one day, enter **1**.

7. Tap the OK button to create the series.

The selected series is created in the specified cells.

Locating Desired Data

You can use two different tools to locate data within your workbook. The Find option searches for the data and then highlights the data. The Replace option searches for the specified data and then replaces it with the data in the Replace With field.

Finding text

If you want to search for specific data, you can use the Find option. Follow these steps to look for some data in a worksheet using the Find option.

1. Choose Edit⇨Find/Replace.

The Find dialog box appears, as shown in Figure 7-17.

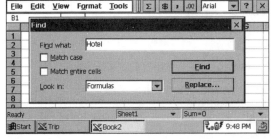

Figure 7-17: Locate specific data with the Find dialog box.

2. Type the data that you want to look for in the Fi<u>n</u>d what field.

You can type either all the data or just a portion of it, up to a maximum of 255 characters.

3. Tap the Find button.

Pocket Excel searches the document from the current cursor location to the end of the worksheet. It stops when it locates the first occurrence of the text that you entered in the Find what field. When Pocket Excel locates the matching data, it highlights the data on the screen, as shown in Figure 7-18.

Figure 7-18:
Pocket
Excel
locates the
specified
data and
highlights it
on the
screen.

| File Edit View Format Tools | Σ | $ | , | .00 | Arial | ▼ | ? | × |
| A3 | | Hotel | | | | | | |

	A	B	C	D	E	F
1	**Description**	**Expense**				
2	Airfare	1594				
3	Hotel	1200				
4	Rental Car	125				
5	Meals	750				
6	Shopping	1200				
7	Diving	350				
8						

| Ready | | Sheet1 ▼ | Sum=125 | ▼ |
| Start | Trip | Book2 | 9:50 PM |

If you have multiple cells selected on the screen when you select the Find option, Pocket Excel searches only in the cells you've selected.

When you work with the Find/Replace option, these three tips help simplify the process of locating information, especially when you're searching a large document:

✔ To have Pocket Excel find another occurrence of the data that you typed in the Find what field, choose Edit⇨Find Next.

✔ Select the Match entire cells option to have Pocket Excel locate only the cells that contain an exact match to the text you enter in the Find what field. If you enter **153.34** in the Find what field and select the Match entire cells option, Pocket Excel does not stop at cells that contain any characters in addition to the ones in the Find what field. Pocket Excel, for example, does not match a cell that contains 2153.34.

✔ If you select the Match case option, Pocket Excel locates only cells that match both the characters and the case of the text you enter in the Find what field. For example, if you enter **Is** in the Find what field and select the Match case option, Pocket Excel stops on the word *Is* but not the word *is*.

✔ If you to avoid looking at the formulas, select the Values option in the Look in drop-down list box. To check everything in the worksheet, make sure this field contains the value Formulas.

You can also use the keyboard for the Find/Replace and Find Next options. To display the Find dialog box, press the Ctrl and F keys simultaneously. To perform a Find Next option, press the Ctrl and 4 keys simultaneously. The keyboard options are useful when you don't have your stylus in your hand.

Replacing text

Have you ever misspelled a word throughout a spreadsheet? You can use the Find/Replace option to search for a misspelled word and replace it with the correctly spelled word. To replace text in a worksheet, follow these steps:

1. **Choose Edit⇨Find/Replace.**

2. **Tap the Replace button to display the Replace dialog box.**

   The Replace dialog box, shown in Figure 7-19, lets you specify the data to be placed in the location where Pocket Excel finds the data.

Figure 7-19:
Use the Replace dialog box to replace data within your worksheet.

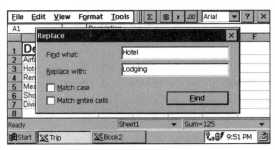

3. **In the Find what field, type the data that you want to replace.**

4. **In the Replace with field, type the data with which you want to replace the specified data.**

   Type the desired replacement data in this field. Pocket Excel places the exact text that you type in the location that you specified.

5. **Tap the Find button.**

   Pocket Excel searches the worksheet from the current cursor location to the end of the document. It stops when it locates the first occurrence of the data that you entered in the Find what field. When Pocket Excel locates the matching text, it highlights the text, and the Find/Replace dialog box appears, as shown in Figure 7-20.

Figure 7-20:
Pocket
Excel
locates
the data
and
confirms
that you
really
want to
replace it.

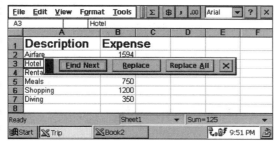

6. To replace the highlighted data, tap the Replace button.

If you don't want to replace the data, tap the Find Next button, and Pocket Excel searches through the document for the next appearance of the data.

If you are confident that you want to change every location of the data specified in the Find what field, you can tap the Replace All button and have Pocket Excel replace all the remaining locations of the text without prompting you first.

Sorting Data

Sooner or later, you are probably going to have a list of items in a worksheet that you want to sort. You may, for example, have a list of the employees that attended the training seminar. By using the Sort option in Pocket Excel, you can sort the list by first name and even by last name (as long as you place each name in a different column). Perform these steps to sort your Pocket Excel data:

1. Highlight the data in your worksheet that you want to sort.

Pocket Excel only sorts data in columns; it does not allow you to sort by rows.

2. Choose Tools⇨Sort to display the Sort dialog box.

On the Sort dialog box, shown in Figure 7-21, you indicate the column you want to sort the data by and the order you want to sort in (ascending or descending). You can even sort by a second or third column, by specifying the necessary sorting column on this dialog box. For example, if the first column has last names, and the second column has first names, sorting by the first column and then the second column will place Smith, Albert before Smith, Debbie.

3. In the Sort by field, select the column that you want to use to sort the data.

Figure 7-21:
You need to select the column that you want to use to sort the data.

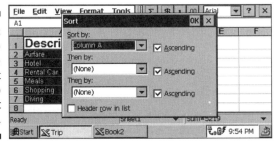

Performing quick calculations

Obviously, worksheets serve a valuable function, but sometimes you just yearn for a calculator.

Well, you are in luck. You don't need to dig through those drawers to locate your trusty calculator; Windows CE provides one for you. Now you can have the best of both worlds — create elaborate spreadsheets and figure out the cost of two gallons of milk.

You can find the Calculator program by choosing Programs⇨Accessories⇨Calculator from the Start menu.

The Calculator program is similar to an adding machine; on the left side of the screen, it keeps a running total of the calculations that you have performed. The totals remain in the list box until you choose Edit⇨Clear Paper Tape.

To use the Calculator program, you can enter the values on the keyboard or tap the desired buttons on the screen. Obviously, not all the buttons on the display are available on the keyboard, but you can find the buttons you use most often.

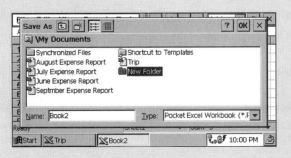

4. If the Ascending check box has a check mark, the data will be sorted in ascending order (smallest to largest, or A to Z). To sort in descending order, tap the box to remove the check mark.

5. If you want to sort by another column, select the desired column in the Then by field.

Pocket Excel allows you to sort data using up to three different columns. When you select multiple columns, it uses the first column first (the one specified in the Sort by field) and then sorts using the values in the next column.

6. Tap the OK button to close the Sort dialog box and sort the data.

If the first row of the data you selected is the header row, you probably don't want those headings sorted with the data. To make sure this doesn't happen, simply select the check box Header row in list. Remember, if this check box is selected, the first row of values will not be sorted.

Working with Different Worksheets

Microsoft created workbooks to provide a more convenient way of linking together different worksheets. In Pocket Excel, each workbook can contain several related worksheets. For example, within a workbook titled Budget, you can have a separate budget worksheet for each month of the year.

When you open a specific workbook, Pocket Excel opens all the worksheets contained in the workbook. The worksheets are initially arranged in the order that they were added to the workbook. You can, however, rearrange them, as well as rename, remove, and add worksheets.

Most of the options for worksheets are available in the Modify Sheets dialog box, shown in Figure 7-22. This dialog box appears when you choose Format⇨Sheet⇨Modify Sheets.

Figure 7-22:
The Modify
Sheets
dialog box
lists all the
current
worksheets
in your
workbook.

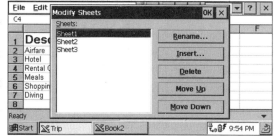

Viewing a different worksheet

Having access to different worksheets doesn't do you much good if you can view only the first one that appears. To view another worksheet within the currently displayed workbook, choose Format➪Sheet➪Modify Sheets to display the Modify Sheets dialog box. Then highlight the desired worksheet and tap the OK button in the upper-right corner of the dialog box.

You can also view a different worksheet by tapping the down-arrow button next to the worksheet name at the bottom of the screen. On the menu that appears (see Figure 7-23), tap the name of the desired worksheet.

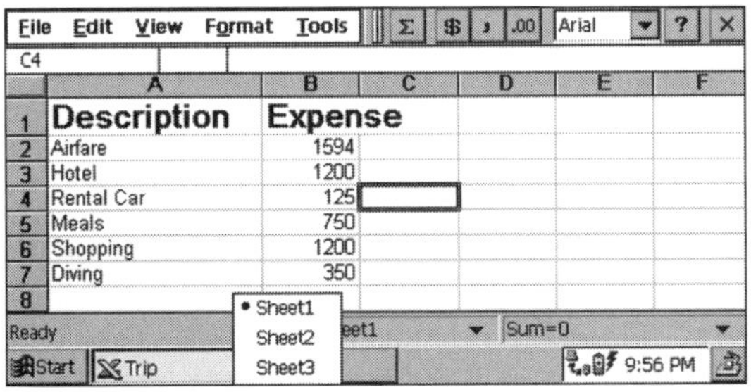

Figure 7-23:
Use the
menu to
select the
worksheet
you want
to view.

Changing the name of a worksheet

You may want to apply more creative names to each worksheet than those that Pocket Excel assigns. After all, Pocket Excel uses such lifeless names as Sheet1, Sheet2, and Sheet3. Modifying the name of a worksheet is easy. Just follow these steps:

1. Choose Format➪Sheet➪Modify Sheets.

The Modify Sheets dialog box appears.

2. Highlight the name of the worksheet that you want to rename.

Tap the name with the stylus.

3. Tap the Rename button.

The Rename Sheet dialog box appears, as shown in Figure 7-24.

4. Type the new name for the worksheet in the Sheet name field.

You can assign a name of as many as 31 characters in length.

5. Tap the OK button at the top of the Rename Sheet dialog box to change the name.

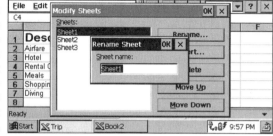

Figure 7-24:
Enter the
new name
for a
worksheet
in the
Rename
Sheet
dialog box.

Adding a new worksheet

Pocket Excel automatically creates three worksheets for each workbook.
You can follow these steps when you want to add worksheets to a
workbook:

1. **Choose Format⇨Sheet⇨Modify Sheets.**

   The Modify Sheets dialog box appears.

2. **In the Modify Sheets dialog box, tap the Insert button.**

   The Insert Sheet dialog box appears, as shown in Figure 7-25.

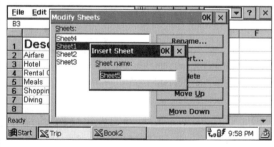

Figure 7-25:
Name the
new
worksheet
before it is
added
to the
workbook.

3. **Enter a name for the worksheet in the Sheet name field.**

   You don't have to name the worksheet; if you don't enter a name,
   Pocket Excel uses the name that appears in the field. You can assign a
   name with as many as 31 characters to the worksheet.

4. **Tap the OK button at the top of the Insert Sheet window to add the
   sheet to the list in the Modify Sheets dialog box.**

You can also quickly add a new worksheet by choosing Format⇨Sheet⇨ Insert. This adds a new worksheet, but you are not given the opportunity to name it. If you don't care what it is named, this is the fastest way to add a new worksheet to your workbook.

Getting rid of a worksheet

You can remove a worksheet by using the Modify Sheets dialog box. Highlight the desired screen and tap the Delete button. A confirmation message appears, asking you to verify your selection (see Figure 7-26). To remove the worksheet, tap the Yes button; to keep it, tap the No button.

Figure 7-26: Pocket Excel verifies your selection before removing a worksheet.

Reordering the worksheets

You can also use the Modify Sheets dialog box to change the order of the worksheets within the workbook. To move a worksheet, highlight the worksheet and tap either the Move Up button or the Move Down button. Repeat the process until the worksheets are listed in the order you want.

Closing a Workbook

You can have several Pocket Excel workbooks open at the same time. The number you can open varies based on the amount of memory you have available and the size of each workbook. I suggest that you don't open more than three workbooks at a time. Having too much open makes working difficult.

When you get tired of working on a workbook, you can close it so that it does not eat your CE device's memory. To close a workbook, tap the X button in the top-right corner of the screen. If you have only one workbook open in Pocket Excel, Pocket Excel also closes itself when you tap the X button. If you still have other workbooks open, the current workbook closes, and Pocket Excel displays the last workbook that you worked on.

You can also close a workbook by choosing File⇨Close.

If you have not previously saved the document, a message window asks whether you want to save the workbook before closing it. To save it, tap the Yes button. If you messed up the workbook or just decide that you don't want it, tap the No button to have Pocket Excel discard the workbook.

Saving a Workbook

Whenever you create a new workbook or modify an existing one, you need to save it in order to be able to access it again at another time. When you save a workbook that you've created using Microsoft Pocket Excel, Windows CE places a copy of the workbook in the folder that you specify.

Save the workbook not only when you finish working on it but also while you are working on it. By saving it periodically, you help to ensure that you don't lose your work if something goes wrong with your CE device.

Saving a workbook for the first time

When you save a workbook for the first time, you need to name the workbook and specify the location where you want to store it in the Save As dialog box.

To save a workbook for the first time, follow these steps:

1. **Choose File⇨Save.**

   The Save As dialog box appears (see Figure 7-27). The Save As dialog box appears only if you have not previously saved the workbook.

2. **Tap the folder in which you want to save the workbook.**

   Whenever you save a workbook using Pocket Excel, Windows CE assumes that you want to place it in the My Documents folder. If this is not where you want to place it, look in the folder list for the appropriate folder and double-tap its icon to open it.

Figure 7-27:
Indicate the
name of
your
workbook
and its
location in
the Save As
dialog box.

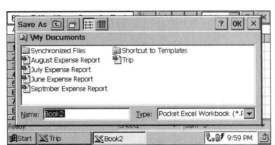

 If you can't find an icon for the folder where you want to store the workbook, tap the Previous Folder button. The Previous Folder button looks like a folder with an up arrow on it. When you tap the icon, the current folder is closed and the parent folder, or the folder above the current folder, is opened.

3. Enter a name for the document in the Name field.

You can assign any name to the workbook. Just remember to use a name that indicates the kind of information that the workbook contains. Don't worry about typing a file extension in this field. Pocket Excel adds one automatically based on the selection in the Type field.

4. In the Type field, tap the down-arrow button and highlight the format in which you want to save the file. The Type field gives you three different file type options, as I outline in Table 7-3.

5. Tap the OK button to save the new workbook.

Table 7-3	Pocket Excel File Formats
Format	*When to Use It*
Pocket Excel Document (*.pxl)	When the document includes formatting that you've applied using Pocket Excel. If you transfer this workbook to your personal computer, it will be converted to an .XLS file format for use with Microsoft Excel. You can share these workbooks with other Windows CE 2.0 devices, but CE 1.0 devices cannot open them.
Pocket Excel 1.0 Document (*.pxl)	When you plan to give the workbook to someone who uses a Windows CE 1.0 device. Otherwise, he or she will not be able to open the workbook. Any formatting that is not available in Pocket Excel 1.0 will not be saved in the workbook.

Format	When to Use It
Pocket Excel Template (*.pxt)	When you have created a workbook that you would like to use as a template. You should place the file in the Windows/Templates folder so that you can easily select it by choosing File➪New➪Workbook from Template.

You can also save a document by pressing the Ctrl and S keys simultaneously. Just another pointer for all you keyboard fanatics.

A filename can be 255 characters long. This length includes the period and the three-character extension that is added to each Pocket Excel document to identify its file type. So basically, each filename can be 251 characters long. These characters don't count as part of the 251: / ? : * " < > | (and they can't be used to name a workbook).

Saving a workbook that you previously saved

You should periodically save a workbook that you are working on. You never know when you may run out of battery power or when some other un-planned event may occur that causes you to lose power.

To save a workbook, choose File➪Save or press Ctrl+S.

Saving a workbook with a new name

After you save a workbook, you may want to save it in another location or give it another name by choosing File➪Save As.

When you choose the Save As option, the Save As dialog box appears on the screen, as shown in Figure 7-28. The current name of the workbook appears in the Name field. To change the name, type a new name in the Name field and tap the OK button.

To save the workbook with the same name but in a different folder, locate the desired folder in the folder listing and double-tap its icon to open it. If the folder does not appear in the listing, tap the Previous Folder icon to close the current folder and open the folder above it.

When you use the Save As option, the original workbook remains with the same name and in the same location.

You can also use the Save As option to save the workbook with a new file format by selecting a different option in the Type field.

Remember, if you want to get rid of the original workbook, you need to use the Windows CE Explorer and delete it. For more information, see Chapter 9.

Figure 7-28:
Use the
Save As
dialog box
to change
the name
of your
document
and/or
specify
a new
location.

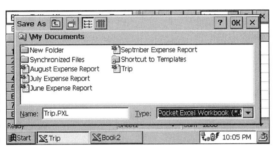

Opening a Microsoft Excel Workbook

One of the big advantages of owning a device that runs Windows CE is the fact that you can transfer most Microsoft Excel workbooks to your CE device. But, unfortunately, the more complex the formatting is in your Microsoft Excel workbook, the more you lose during the conversion.

When you convert a Microsoft Excel workbook to a Pocket Excel workbook, the file extension changes from .XLS to .PXL. When you convert the workbook back to your personal computer, the extension changes back to .XLS.

Because Pocket Excel is a scaled-down version of Microsoft Excel, several of the fancy formatting features in Windows 95 are not available on Pocket Excel. Table 7-4 outlines some of the common formatting features and explains what happens when you copy a spreadsheet to Pocket Excel.

Don't be too concerned with the information presented in Table 7-4. Use it as a reference if you want to determine why something was not converted in your workbook. Just keep in mind that most of the fancy features that are used in Microsoft Excel to make your spreadsheet more appealing can't be converted to Pocket Excel.

Table 7-4	Lost Formatting When Converting from Excel to Pocket Excel
Excel Formatting Option	*Result in Pocket Excel*
Fonts	All fonts that are not available on your CE device are matched to the closest available font.
Font color	Any colored fonts are converted to the closest shade of gray on monochrome screens.
Formats	Custom number formats are displayed using the closest number format that is supported by Pocket Excel.
Formula	All formulas that are not supported by Pocket Excel are removed from the spreadsheet. If your Microsoft Excel spreadsheet contains a formula that is an array of values or contains an array argument, the formula is converted to a value.
Functions	All functions that are not supported by Pocket Excel are removed from the spreadsheet, and the value of the function appears in the corresponding cell.
Names	All names that reference other workbooks, arrays, formulas, or intersection ranges are replaced with the value #NAME?, indicating that the name could not be converted.
Objects	All types of objects are removed.
Pictures	All pictures are removed during conversion.
Pivot table data	All data is converted to values.
Sheets	All chart sheets, dialog sheets, and Excel 4.0 macro sheets are replaced with blank worksheets.
Text boxes	All text boxes are removed.
VBA modules	All VBA modules are replaced with a blank worksheet.

Keep in mind that when these options are removed or changed in the workbook during the conversion to Pocket Excel, they are not added back in when you convert it back to Excel. Therefore, if you decide to copy the same workbook back to your personal computer, you may want to place it in a different location so that you do not overwrite the original. Otherwise, you may find yourself forced to do a great deal of reformatting to make the workbook look like the original on your personal computer.

For more information about copying documents from your personal computer to your CE device, refer to Chapter 11.

Printing Worksheets

Sooner or later you're going to want to print a worksheet directly from your CE device. This is actually possible, if you have one of two things: either the printer is connected to the serial port on your CE device (the port you use to connect to your personal computer) or you are able to send stuff to your printer using the infrared port (that is, if the printer has an infrared port to receive the stuff).

Before you actually select the Print option, you need to indicate the part of the worksheet that you want to print. To do this, highlight the part of the worksheet you want to print and choose File➪Print Area➪Set Print Area. Now you are ready to select the Print option.

If you have the capability to print from your CE device, choose File➪Print to display the Print dialog box, as shown in Figure 7-29. For descriptions of all the information that you can specify on the Print dialog box, see Table 6-9 in Chapter 6.

If you can't print from your CE device, you need to use the Windows CE Services program on your personal computer to print a file. To do so, select the file on your personal computer and choose File➪Print. For more information about working with the Windows CE Services on your personal computer, see Part III.

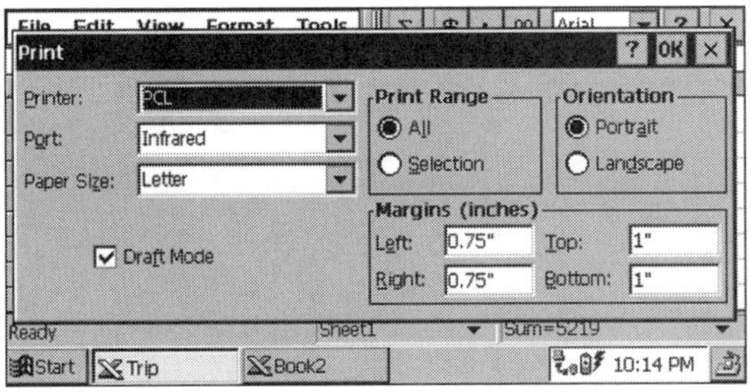

Figure 7-29:
You can print out your document using your CE device.

[Print dialog box showing: Printer: PCL, Port: Infrared, Paper Size: Letter, Draft Mode checked, Print Range: All selected / Selection, Orientation: Portrait selected / Landscape, Margins (inches): Left: 0.75", Right: 0.75", Top: 1", Bottom: 1"]

Chapter 8

Delivering a Presentation with Pocket PowerPoint

- -

In This Chapter

▶ Locating Pocket PowerPoint on your CE device

▶ Opening a presentation

▶ Modifying the way you view the presentation

▶ Specifying settings and saving your presentation

▶ Delivering a presentation from your Windows CE device

▶ Installing Pocket PowerPoint on your CE device

- -

*O*ne of the most exciting additions to Windows CE 2.0 is Pocket PowerPoint. If you have used Microsoft PowerPoint on your personal computer, you probably already know that it provides capabilities for creating professional-quality slide shows to accompany your presentations or demonstrations. Pocket PowerPoint enables you to take this concept a step further; by using this program, you no longer need to lug around a laptop computer just so you can deliver your presentation. Instead, you can store everything you need on your CE device and deliver the presentation all from the palm of your hand.

Unfortunately, Pocket PowerPoint does not provide the tools necessary for creating your presentation. You still must rely on Microsoft PowerPoint running on a personal computer to create your presentation. But after you create the presentation, you can use Pocket PowerPoint on your CE device to review and even present it without the need for bulky equipment. You can even display your presentation on a VGA monitor from your CE device. With Pocket PowerPoint, you also can accomplish such tasks as reordering slides and adding a title slide.

In this chapter, I show you how easy it is to work with a PowerPoint presentation. You find out how to open the desired presentation, set up the presentation mode, reorder the slides, and deliver the presentation. And if you can't find Pocket PowerPoint on your CE device, turn to this chapter to find out how to go about installing the software.

Locating Pocket PowerPoint

Before you can work with a PowerPoint presentation that you've copied onto your CE device, you must locate Pocket PowerPoint. The icon for Pocket PowerPoint sits on the Windows CE desktop on most CE devices. To display Pocket PowerPoint, locate the Pocket PowerPoint icon and then use your stylus to double-tap it.

Note: If you can't find Pocket PowerPoint on your CE device, it probably was not loaded on your device with the Windows CE operating system. Not all CE devices come with Pocket PowerPoint preinstalled. If you don't find it, check out the section "Installing Pocket PowerPoint," later in this chapter, for information about installing Pocket PowerPoint on your CE device.

Before you install the Pocket PowerPoint software, however, look for it on the Start menu by following these steps:

1. **Tap the Start button (in the lower-left corner of the screen).**

   When you tap the Start button, a pop-up menu containing various options appears.

2. **Tap the Programs option.**

   This option opens another menu containing a list of the programs and other menus on your CE device.

3. **Tap the Office option.**

   You see a third menu containing more programs, as shown in Figure 8-1.

4. **Tap the Microsoft Pocket PowerPoint option on the menu to display the Pocket PowerPoint program.**

   When Pocket PowerPoint opens, you are immediately prompted for the name of the presentation that you want to view. See the next section, "Opening a PowerPoint Presentation," to find out how to open the desired slide presentation.

Figure 8-1:
Look for
Pocket
PowerPoint
on the pop-
up menus
available
from the
Start
button.

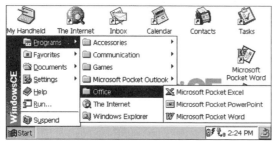

Opening a PowerPoint Presentation

Whenever you run Pocket PowerPoint, it immediately wants to know which presentation you want to open. This may seem a little odd, seeing as how you can open other programs, such as Pocket Word or Pocket Excel, and they give you a blank page on which you can type. Because you can't create a presentation in Pocket PowerPoint, the program immediately asks you to specify which presentation you want to work with, as shown in Figure 8-2.

Figure 8-2:
You need to
locate the
presentation
that you
want to
open.

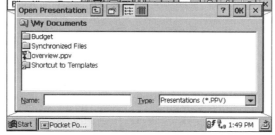

 Pocket PowerPoint assumes that you want to open a presentation in the My Documents folder. If the presentation you want is located in another folder, tap the Previous Folder button and open the folder above the My Documents folder. After you find the correct presentation, double-tap to open it.

 You can also open a presentation from the Windows CE Explorer or from anywhere you see an icon for a Pocket PowerPoint presentation. If you double-tap an icon for a Pocket PowerPoint presentation, Pocket PowerPoint automatically opens that presentation.

Deciphering the Pocket PowerPoint buttons

Pocket PowerPoint provides a bunch of cool buttons that can be really useful, if you know what they do. Keep in mind that these buttons may not be available on every screen. The following table provides a helpful overview of these buttons.

Tap This Button	If You Want To
	View the slide show in presentation mode.
	Look at the slides in slide mode. In this mode, you do things like zoom in or reorder slides.
	View both the slide and the associated notes.
	Sort the slides into the order in which you want them to appear in the presentation. You can even hide some slides that you do not want to see.
	Show the previous slide.
	Show the next slide.
	Zoom in on the slides and notes.
	Make annotations on the slides during the presentation. When this button is selected, you can draw on the slide with the stylus.

TIP

While in Pocket PowerPoint, if you ever want to open a different presentation, simply choose File➪Open and then select the name of the presentation that you want to open.

Working with the Slides

In Pocket PowerPoint, or actually any version of PowerPoint, each page of the presentation is commonly referred to as a *slide*. In Pocket PowerPoint, you can do a few things to change the way your slides fit together into a presentation, such as adding a title slide or reordering the slides. I cover these topics in the following sections.

Creating a title slide

The only slide you can add to any Pocket PowerPoint presentation is a title slide. Creating this slide for your presentation is similar to signing your name on your painting. Complete the following steps to design the title slide using the Title Slide dialog box:

1. **Choose Tools⇨Title Slide to display the Title Slide dialog box.**

   Figure 8-3 shows the Title Slide dialog box, in which you specify the text that you want to display on the title slide.

Figure 8-3:
Indicate the
text you
want to
display on
the first
(title) slide
of the
presentation.

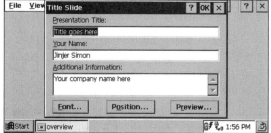

2. **Type a title for your presentation in the Presentation Title field.**

   If you type more characters than can be placed on the presentation title line, some of the text is placed on the next line. The number of characters that can fit on each line is based on the font size you've selected.

3. **Type your name in the Your Name field.**

   Actually, Windows CE automatically grabs the name of the person who is set up as the owner of the device and places it in the Your Name field. If this is not your name, or at least the name you want to display, make the desired corrections. The name in this field is the one that shows up on the title slide, so if you don't want to take credit, simply type someone else's name.

4. **Add any other information you want in the Additional Information field.**

   If you specified a company name when you set up your CE device, that name is placed in this field; otherwise, Pocket PowerPoint places the text *Your company name here,* suggesting that you type your company name in the field. This field actually can contain any information that you want to display on the screen. If you don't want any information in this field, make sure that you remove any text that may exist in the field.

5. **After you enter the desired information for your title slide, tap the OK button to save your slide and have it added to the beginning of the presentation.**

Or if you want to change the look or location of the text, you can tap the Font and Position buttons to make changes for the entire slide. I describe the use of these buttons in the following sections.

If you do not want to display a value for any one of the fields in the Title Slide dialog box, simply remove the text from the field and leave it blank.

Changing the way the text looks on the title slide

You can change the following characteristics of the text that appears on the title slide: the font, the size of the characters, the color of the characters, and the font style. You make these font changes in the Font dialog box, shown in Figure 8-4. The Font dialog box displays when you tap the Font button in the Title Slide dialog box. Keep in mind that when you make these changes, they are applied to all the text on your title slide. Table 8-1 explains the font changes that you can make to the text on the title slide.

Table 8-1	Cool Font Changes for the Title Slide
Use This Option	*If You Want the Characters to Be*
Font	Displayed in a different font. Simply tap the down-arrow button next to the field and select the desired font.
Size	A different size. Tap the down-arrow button next to the field and select the desired font size.
Color	Displayed in a different color when you show the title slide on a color monitor. To change the font color, tap the down-arrow button and select the desired color.
Bold	Displayed in a bold font. Tap the check box next to the field to select this option.
Italic	Displayed in italics. Tap the check box next to the field to select this option.
Underline	Underlined on the title slide. Tap the check box next to the field to select this option.

The Preview section of the Font dialog box shows a sample of your font selections. As you make any changes, they are reflected in this section.

Figure 8-4:
Use the Font dialog box to indicate how the characters should look on your title slide.

Moving the text to another location on the title slide

Not only can you specify how the text looks, but you can also indicate where it is placed on the title slide. For example, you may want to right-justify the text and place it in the middle of the screen. You use the Position dialog box, shown in Figure 8-5, to indicate the desired position and alignment of the text for your title slide. To open the Position dialog box, tap the Position button in the Title Slide dialog box.

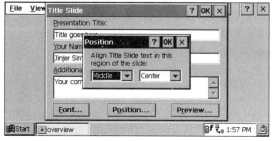

Figure 8-5:
Indicate the region of the slide where you want to place the block of text.

In the Position dialog box, you see two drop-down list boxes that you can use to indicate your desired position and alignment for the text on the title slide. You need to select a value from each list box when specifying the text location on the slide. The left-hand drop-down list box contains the position values Top, Middle, and Bottom; the right one has the alignment values Left, Center, and Right. Table 8-2 simplifies the selection process by indicating what happens when you select different combinations.

Table 8-2	Positioning the Title Slide Text	
Position Option	*Alignment Option*	*Places the Text*
Top	Left	In the upper-left corner of the slide
Top	Center	In the top center of the slide
Top	Right	In the upper-right corner of the slide
Middle	Left	In the left middle section of the slide
Middle	Center	Smack-dab in the middle of the slide
Middle	Right	In the right middle section of the slide
Bottom	Left	In the lower-left corner of the slide
Bottom	Center	In the bottom center of the slide
Bottom	Right	In the lower-right corner of the slide

Previewing the layout of the slide

At any time during the creation of the title slide, you can get a preview of how it looks by tapping the Preview button in the Title Slide dialog box. When you tap the Preview button, a sample of your title page temporarily displays on the screen so that you can make sure that the font and position settings are appropriate.

Quickly reordering the slides

Sooner or later, you will need to change the order of the slides in your presentation. The boss may not like the order in which you are delivering the information, or you may just want to move things around, but no matter what the reason, reordering the slides is easy to do with Pocket PowerPoint.

To change the order of your slides, perform the following steps:

1. **Tap the Slide Sorter button on the toolbar to display the Slide Sorter dialog box.**

   Figure 8-6 shows the Slide Sorter dialog box, which you use to indicate the exact order of the slides in your presentation. The Change Order list box shows the current order of the slides in your presentation.

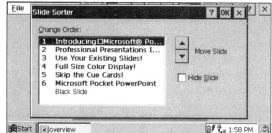

Figure 8-6:
You can
quickly
change the
order of the
slides
in your
presentation.

If you've added a title slide to the presentation, it appears as the first slide in the list. You can't move the title slide; it must remain the first slide in the presentation.

2. **To move a slide, tap the desired slide to highlight it and then tap either the up-arrow button or the down-arrow button until the slide is listed in the desired location.**

If you no longer want to use a particular slide in the presentation, you can hide the slide. The slide remains as part of the PowerPoint file, but it does not display during the presentation. To hide a slide, tap the slide name to highlight it and then tap the Hide Slide check box. When a slide is hidden, it does not have a number in the Change Order list box.

3. **After you have the slides in the desired order, tap the OK button to close the Slide Sorter dialog box.**

Reviewing the notes for each slide

Whenever a presentation is created in Microsoft PowerPoint, you can add notes about each slide. You can use these notes during the presentation to help you describe each slide. You can check out the notes for each slide by tapping the Notes button on the toolbar. Figure 8-7 shows the notes for a sample presentation.

If you have a difficult time reading the text, tap the Font button, and the text will be enlarged to make it easier to read on your Windows CE device.

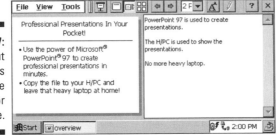

Figure 8-7: Check out the notes that you've created for each slide.

Specifying the Settings for Your Presentation

Before you can display your slide presentation from your Windows CE device, you need to specify how you want to display it. For example, you need to tell Windows CE whether you want to display it on the screen of your device or on an external VGA monitor so that you can show it to several people simultaneously. You also should specify whether you want the slides to advance manually or automatically.

You specify all this information in the Set Up Show dialog box, shown in Figure 8-8. To open the Set Up Show dialog box, choose Tools➪Set Up Show.

Figure 8-8: Select the type of monitor you plan to use for displaying the presentation.

Indicate how you want to display the slide show in the list box labeled View Show on. If you have a VGA card installed in your PC Card slot, you have two selections in this list box: Built in LCD and VGA Device. If you want to show your presentation on the external monitor, select the VGA Device option.

If you want to manually advance through the slides in your presentation by tapping the left- and right-arrow buttons, select the Manually radio button. The Automatically every radio button is useful if you intend to set up a presentation that you want to run unattended. Make sure that you indicate how long Pocket PowerPoint should wait between slides by typing a value in the seconds field.

You can even make sure the presentation repeats by selecting the Repeat continuously check box. Keep in mind, this option is available only if you select the option to advance automatically through your slides.

Saving the Presentation

Whenever you make any type of modification to your presentation, such as changing the order of the slides or adding a new title page, you need to save the changes so that they will be there the next time you open the file. You can either save the presentation with the same name, or you may decide that you want to save it with a different name so that the original presentation remains intact.

To save the presentation after making any type of changes simply choose File⇨Save.

If you want to save the presentation with a different name or put it in a different folder, choose File⇨Save As to display the Save Presentation As dialog box, shown in Figure 8-9.

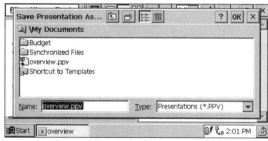

Figure 8-9:
Indicate the name and folder location for the presentation.

The current name of the presentation appears in the Name field. To change the name, type a new name in the Name field and tap the OK button.

To save the presentation with the same name but in a different folder, locate the desired folder in the folder listing and double-tap its icon to open it. If the folder does not appear in the listing, tap the Previous Folder icon to close the current folder and open the folder above it.

Remember, when you use the Save As option, the original presentation remains with the same name and in the same location. If you want to get rid of the original presentation, you need to use the Windows CE Explorer and delete the file. For more information, see Chapter 9.

Delivering Your Presentation

When you're ready to deliver your presentation, simply tap the View Show button on the toolbar. When you tap this button, you either see your presentation on your Windows CE device, as shown in Figure 8-10, or on the external VGA monitor, depending on the settings you selected in the Set Up Show dialog box.

Figure 8-10:
Your presentation displays on the full screen with buttons for annotating and changing slides.

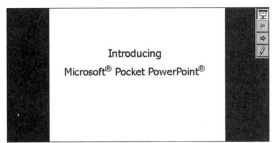

Introducing
Microsoft® Pocket PowerPoint®

Making annotations during your presentation

No matter how detailed you make the slides in your presentation, you are probably going to find a time when you need to emphasize something. The easiest way to do this is to use your stylus to draw right on the slide. To do this, simply tap the Draw button (the icon that looks like a pencil) and then use your stylus to circle, underline, or even draw pictures on the slide. If you are using a VGA monitor to display your presentation, your annotations show up on the VGA monitor, too.

Keep in mind, the stuff you draw does not get placed on the slide permanently. It is only there while you are viewing the slide. Also, if you are in the automatic presentation mode, this option is not available.

Switching slides

If you have ever used any type of presentation software, you know that presentations normally consist of a series of slides, or screens, containing various information. When you view a presentation, you can see only one page at a time, so you need to scroll or move through the slides one at a time.

If you do not have your presentation set up to advance through the slides automatically, you need to use the left- and right-arrow buttons to change slides. Remember, you tap the right-arrow button to view the next slide or tap the left-arrow button to view the previous slide.

When you are finished viewing the presentation, tap the View Show button again and you'll be back in the normal Pocket PowerPoint mode. When you do this, the show is no longer displayed on the external monitor (if you were using one).

Exiting the presentation mode

After you put Pocket PowerPoint into the presentation mode, it remains in that mode until you indicate that it should switch. To switch back to the slide viewing mode, tap the View Show button again.

If you are viewing the presentation on an external monitor, it will no longer display information when you tap the View Show button.

Installing Pocket PowerPoint

If you find that you do not have Pocket PowerPoint installed on your CE device, you need to install it from your personal computer. To install it, you must locate the Windows CE Services 2.0 CD that came either with your new CE device or with the upgrade you purchased for your device. The following steps tell you how to quickly install Pocket PowerPoint onto your CE device.

You must install Microsoft Windows CE Services on your personal computer before you can run the Pocket PowerPoint installation. The Windows CE Services installation sets up the communication between your personal computer and the CE device. For more information on installation, refer to Chapter 10.

1. **Run the Setup.exe program on the Windows CE Services 2.0 CD.**

   If your CD-ROM drive is d:, you need to select the Run option on the Start menu and then type **d:\setup.exe** in the Open field. When you select this option, the Windows CE Services 2.0 setup screen displays.

2. **Select the Optional Components option.**

   This option displays an Explorer window containing folder icons for each of the optional Windows CE components that can be installed. Keep in mind that the actual size of the icons in the Explorer window varies depending on the settings on your personal computer.

3. **Click the Setup Microsoft Pocket PowerPoint Version 1.0 folder to open it.**

   You see icons for the different files in the folder.

4. **Click the Setup icon to display the Pocket PowerPoint installation program, shown in Figure 8-11.**

Figure 8-11:
The installation for Pocket PowerPoint takes you through a series of different dialog boxes.

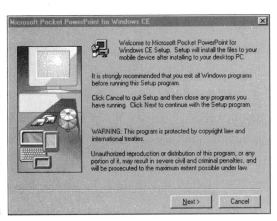

5. **In the first dialog box, click the Next button to start the installation process.**

   This standard dialog box normally appears when you install any new software on your personal computer. It reminds you not to run any other programs on your personal computer during the installation process.

6. **In the Software License Agreement dialog box, click the Yes button to continue the setup process.**

   This dialog box contains the entire license agreement that Microsoft has created for the Pocket PowerPoint software, as shown in Figure 8-12. By clicking the Yes button, you are stating that you agree to adhere to the terms outlined in the license agreement.

Figure 8-12:
You must
agree to all
this legal
stuff before
you can
continue
installing
Pocket
PowerPoint.

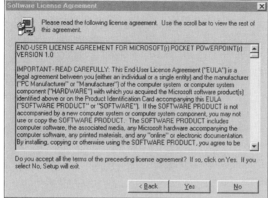

7. **Type your name in the Name text box and press the tab key. Type your company name (optional) in the Company text box and then click the Next button (see Figure 8-13).**

Figure 8-13:
You must
type a name
in the
Name field,
but the
Company
entry is
optional.

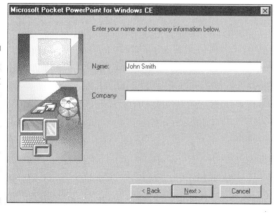

8. **In the Select Destination dialog box, make sure that the folder where the setup program wants to install the Pocket PowerPoint information on your personal computer is the right one. If so, click the Next button.**

The setup program needs to install some files on your desktop computer before placing the Pocket PowerPoint files on your CE device. It automatically defaults to a folder where other Windows CE program information is stored on your personal computer, as shown in Figure 8-14.

When you tap the Next button, the setup program copies all the necessary files to your personal computer.

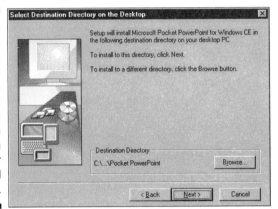

Figure 8-14:
The setup
program
places all
Windows
CE program
stuff in one
common
location
on your
personal
computer.

9. **When you get the Pending Application Install window, connect your CE device and your personal computer and then click the OK button.**

   This window indicates that all files have been installed on your personal computer and are ready to be installed on your CE device. When you connect your CE device to the personal computer, the setup process is completed by copying the Pocket PowerPoint files onto your CE device. For more information about connecting the two machines, refer to Chapter 10.

Chapter 9

Managing Your Files

. . . .

In This Chapter

▶ Locating files

▶ Determining file types

▶ Viewing file properties

▶ Creating new files and folders

▶ Removing and renaming files and folders

▶ Changing the location of a file

▶ Working with added storage on PC Cards

▶ Sharing files with another CE device or a personal computer

. . . .

*F*iguring out how to organize your files is probably one of the most difficult tasks you must perform in order to use your CE device. To help you deal with that horrible syndrome of the lost file (I know, I was there yesterday), Windows CE comes with its own type of file management system that you can tailor to fit your likes and dislikes.

This chapter explains how to use the various file management features available with Windows CE. I discuss the basics of using Windows CE Explorer to perform file management tasks, such as viewing the contents of folders, creating new files, and moving and deleting files. I also talk about how to locate files and folders on PC storage cards and how to share files with other Windows CE devices.

Locating Files

Imagine the ideally organized office in which all important and even not-so-important documents are filed in easy-to-find folders in a file cabinet. If you want a document, you just pull open the appropriate drawer in the file cabinet, open the appropriate folder, and remove the document. It may seem like I am describing an unrealistic dream scenario, but the file management system that Windows CE uses resembles the one in the ideally organized office.

 The Windows CE file cabinet is called Windows CE Explorer; this program provides access to all the folders on your CE device. You can use two methods to open the main drawer of the Windows CE Explorer. The easiest method is to double-tap the corresponding icon on the desktop. If you are using a handheld PC, the icon is named My Handheld PC and resembles a handheld PC with a stylus pointing at it. If you don't like that option or if you just like to be different, choose <u>P</u>rograms⇨Windows Explorer from the Start menu.

When you select an option that opens the Windows CE Explorer, the main folder is opened on your CE device (see Figure 9-1). This folder is named My Handheld PC, which explains the origin of the icon's name. (Or perhaps the icon name came first.) It contains all the folders and files on your CE device.

Figure 9-1:
Windows
CE Explorer
enables you
to view the
contents of
your CE
device.

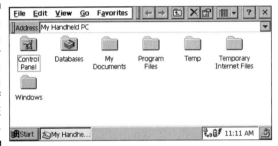

When you look inside the My Handheld PC folder, you probably see at least five other folders. (You may see more if you have created some folders of your own.) Each of these folders contains a specific type of file, as outlined in Table 9-1.

Table 9-1	Figuring Out the My Handheld PC Folder
Folder	*Purpose*
🖳	The Control Panel folder contains all the stuff you need to control the settings for your CE device. You also can open this folder by tapping the Settings option in the Start menu. For information about the contents of the Control Panel folder, see Chapter 19.

Folder	Purpose
	The Databases folder maintains the database files used by the programs that run under Windows CE. A *database* is essentially a complex file that keeps track of related pieces of information. Windows CE maintains a database in this folder that contains all the contacts you have set up by using the Contacts program. You should leave this folder alone; if you mess with one of the database files in this folder, your Windows CE programs may not work properly.
My Documents	The My Documents folder is a generic folder that is the home for all your documents. By default, each time you create a document in a program, Windows CE stores the document in this folder. If all your documents are in one location, they should be easy for you to locate. If you use this folder for documents, you may want to create additional folders to sort the documents into groups.
Program Files	The Program Files folder contains additional folders that hold all the programs on your CE device, with the exception of the system programs. When you add a new program to your CE device, Windows CE creates a folder for the program files used by the new program in the Program Files folder.
Temp	Windows CE uses the Temp folder to temporarily store files.
Temporary Internet Files	The Temporary Internet Files folder is where Windows CE temporarily stores stuff that you view on the Internet.
Windows	The Windows folder contains all the files and programs that are required to make Windows CE work properly. Try to avoid making changes to the files in this folder; Windows CE uses them to keep your CE device running efficiently.

If you seem to be running out of storage space on your CE device, check the Temp and Temporary Internet Files folders. If all programs are closed on your CE device, you can delete anything that is sitting in these folders.

Changing the way you view folder contents

You can view the contents of a folder in Windows CE Explorer in many ways. You can change the way you view a folder's contents by using the different options available on the View menu or by selecting one of the three view options available when you tap the View drop-down list box on the toolbar, as shown in Figure 9-2. Table 9-2 describes the results of selecting one of the three view options.

Figure 9-2:
You can select how the folder contents appear on the screen.

Table 9-2	Windows CE Explorer View Options
Select This Option	**If You Want To**
Large Icons	View the contents of the folder by using large icons. You can quickly see what is in the folder, although you can't see everything on-screen at the same time if the folder contains several items.
Small Icons	View the contents of the folder by using small icons. You can see more icons on-screen at the same time than you can if you use large icons.
Details	View the details about each item in the folder, including the name of the item, its size, its type, and the date and time when it was last modified.

When you view the details of the folder, you may find that the columns that display the information are not wide enough. You can adjust the width of a column by touching the stylus to the separator line next to the column name, and then dragging the line to the size you want. You can also double-tap the separator line and Windows CE Explorer will size the column to fit the longest entry in the column.

Keep in mind that Windows CE does not save your view settings within Windows CE Explorer. In other words, the folder's contents appear in large icons every time you run the Windows CE Explorer.

Within any view, you can sort the items either by name or by file type. To sort by name, choose View⇨Arrange By Name. To sort by file type, choose View⇨Arrange By Type.

If you are viewing the contents of the folder in Detail mode, you can also sort the contents of the folder by tapping the column heading. The first time you tap, the contents are sorted in ascending order (A to Z). Tap again to sort in descending order (Z to A).

If you have added an item to this folder since opening the Windows CE Explorer, you may need to refresh the screen before the new item appears in the list. To refresh the list, choose View⇨Refresh.

Windows CE Explorer lets you hide certain system files so that you do not accidentally delete them. To hide system files, choose View⇨Options to display the Options dialog box, shown in Figure 9-3. Then select Hide hidden files and files with the following extensions: .DLL and .CPL. This option is automatically set for you as the default so that you don't get confused when you find a bunch of system files that Windows CE needs in order to run properly.

If you select the Hide file extensions check box, you will not see the three-character extensions that identify the file type to the system.

Figure 9-3:
Use the
Options
dialog box
to hide
system
files.

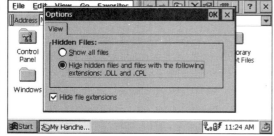

Looking inside a folder

You cannot look at an item in a folder in your real-life file cabinet without locating and opening the folder. The same holds true on your CE device — if you want to see which programs or documents are in a particular folder, you need to open the folder in question.

To open a folder in Windows CE Explorer, you simply double-tap the folder's icon.

When you open a folder, the folder's name appears in the bar under the toolbar. This bar is commonly called an *address bar*. For those of you who come from a DOS background, the banner basically contains the path. The *path* is just a computer nerd term that indicates the names of the folders that are currently open. For example, in Figure 9-4 the path bar says \Program Files\Games. Because Games is the last folder name listed, it is the folder that appears on the screen.

Address bar

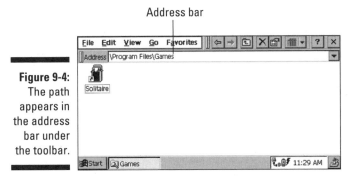

Figure 9-4:
The path appears in the address bar under the toolbar.

Keep in mind that after you open a folder that is within the main folder — that is, within the My Handheld PC folder on a handheld PC — the name of the main folder (My Handheld PC) does not appear in the path.

 To close the current folder and view the contents of the previous folder, you can tap the Previous Folder icon on the toolbar. The Previous Folder button resembles a folder with an arrow on it. You can keep closing folders and displaying the previous folder contents until you get back to the Desktop folder.

Working with Folders

In keeping with its office theme, Windows CE uses files and folders to deal with everything that is stored on your CE device. A *folder* is a place to store related files, just as you store related pieces of paper in a folder on your desk. For example, Windows CE comes with a folder called My Documents, in which you can place documents you create on your CE device. The word *file* is a general term that refers to each item on your CE device, such as a program, a word processing document, or a spreadsheet. You use the Windows CE Explorer to deal with the different files and folders that you have on your CE device.

If you are one of those old-timers who started using computers when DOS was the only operating system, you may be comforted to know that *folder* is just another name for *directory.*

When you see an icon that resembles a folder, double-tap the icon, and the folder opens and reveals its contents — usually a bunch of files. A folder can also contain other folders. In fact, Windows CE lays out the entire storage area of your CE device by using a series of folders within folders. The main folder on your CE device is named to identify your device type, such as My Handheld PC on a handheld PC. This main folder contains all other folders and files on your CE device.

The following sections describe several interesting things that you can do with folders and files.

Creating a new folder

Hopefully, you are not content using the folders that come with Windows CE. After all, you should organize your own stuff. The more folders you use to organize your files, the more easily you can locate your files later.

Creating a new folder under Windows CE is almost as easy as picking up a new folder and writing a name on it. To create a new folder, you choose File➪New Folder. To create a new folder called Budget within the My Documents folder, follow these steps.

1. **Open the Start menu and choose Programs➪Windows Explorer.**

   You can also tap the My Handheld PC icon on your desktop to display Windows CE Explorer.

2. **Double-tap the My Documents icon to display the current contents of the My Documents folder.**

   Before you create a folder, you always need to open the folder where you want the new folder to reside.

3. **Choose File➪New Folder.**

   A new folder icon appears with the name New Folder highlighted (see Figure 9-5).

4. Type a new name for the folder.

Because the name of the folder is highlighted, you can simply start typing a name for the folder — for example, **Budget**.

5. Press the Enter key.

You can double-tap the folder to open it and begin adding files to it.

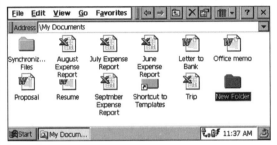

Figure 9-5:
You can add new folders to organize the related files on your CE device.

Renaming a folder or file

With Windows CE Explorer, you can easily modify the names of files and folders on your CE device. Tap the item to highlight it and then choose File⇒Rename. Explorer draws a box around the name and places the cursor at the end of the name. If you want to replace the entire name, start typing, and the new name appears in the box. If you want to modify only a portion of the name, use the arrow keys to move the cursor to the desired location in the name and then begin typing.

Use the Rename option to change the names of your personal document files only. Do not attempt to rename system or program files. If you avoid renaming any files in the Windows folder, where Windows CE stores the files it requires for the operating system, you should be OK. If you make changes to your system or program files, your CE device may not run properly.

Moving stuff around — Cut, copy, and paste

Not too many of us are content to leave things where we first put them. You know how it is — the plant looks just fine in the corner until you buy new drapes. Then you need to move the plant into the kitchen.

Well, lucky for you, you have plenty of ways to move items around on your CE device. You can move a file, a folder full of files, or several files and folders all at the same time, as long as you move them to the same folder.

You can use the Cut, Copy, and Paste options on the Edit menu of Windows CE Explorer to move and copy any files and folders that are not read-only. (You can find out more about making files read-only in the section "Viewing file properties," later in this chapter.) For example, to move the January, February, and March budget spreadsheets inside your Budget folder, follow these steps:

1. **Locate and highlight the files that you want to move.**

   If you select multiple files, as shown in Figure 9-6, you can move them at the same time. If the files are located next to each other, you can select them by tapping the first file, holding down the Shift key, and then tapping the last item. If the items are not next to each other, hold down the Ctrl key while you tap the files you want to select.

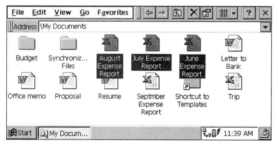

Figure 9-6:
You can
select
multiple
files.

2. **Choose Edit⇨Cut.**

   Explorer copies the files into the CE device's storage closet, commonly referred to as the Clipboard. The selected file icons appear grayed-out on-screen to remind you that you just cut them.

   If you select the Copy option rather than the Cut option, the items you select remain in the original folder.

3. **Open the folder where you want to put the files.**

   If you want to put the files in a folder that is in the current folder, double-tap the folder icon to open it; otherwise, tap the Previous Folder button and find the correct folder.

4. **Choose Edit⇨Paste.**

   Windows CE copies the stored items out of the Clipboard and into your folder.

You can use the drag-and-drop method to move items into a folder whose icon sits on the screen. Simply touch the stylus to the item you want to move and drag the item to the new folder.

Deleting a folder or file

With Windows CE Explorer, you can quickly remove unwanted folders or files. Simply tap the item to highlight it and then tap the Delete button on the toolbar. The Delete button resembles a big X. You can also delete a selected item by choosing File➪Delete.

When you delete an item, Windows CE verifies your selection by displaying an alert box, as shown in Figure 9-7. This way, Windows CE makes sure that you really want to delete the item you selected. If you are sure that you want to delete the item, tap the Yes button, and Windows CE moves the item to the Recycle Bin to await trash pickup. If you tap the No button, the item remains unaffected in the same location. Refer to Chapter 2, for more information about the Recycle Bin.

Figure 9-7:
Before
deleting
an item,
Windows CE
verifies
your
selection.

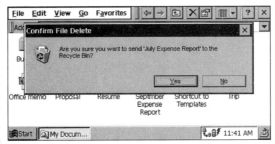

You can restore an item to its original location as long as you have not emptied the Recycle Bin. After you empty the Recycle Bin, however, its contents are gone forever. After all, you don't expect to be able to find something after it has been hauled to the city dump, do you?

If you delete a shortcut off the Windows CE desktop or from any location on your CE device, Windows CE deletes only the shortcut; the original program remains intact in the appropriate folder. Remember, you can tell a shortcut icon from the original program icon by the small arrow in the lower-left corner of the shortcut icon. Almost all the icons sitting on your desktop, with the exception of the My Handheld PC and the Recycle Bin icons, are shortcuts.

If you want to remove a program from your CE device, use the Remove Programs option from the Control Panel, as I describe in Chapter 19.

Do not delete files from the Windows folder. If you remove the wrong files, your CE device will not run properly.

Rescuing a deleted file

Before you pull out too much hair over that report you accidentally deleted, you should know that you can retrieve it if the file is still waiting in the Recycle Bin. Simply follow these steps:

1. **Open the Recycle Bin by double-tapping the Recycle Bin icon on your desktop.**

   The Recycle Bin window appears (see Figure 9-8).

Figure 9-8:
Double-tap the Recycle Bin icon to see the contents of the Recycle Bin.

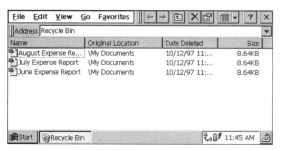

2. **Highlight the file you want to undelete.**

3. **Choose File⇨Restore.**

   The file is placed into its original folder location and is essentially as good as new.

To get the full scoop on the Recycle Bin, check out Chapter 2.

Determining file types

As I am sure you have already determined, your CE device contains many different types of files. Many of the types of files are just program files that are required to make a specific program work properly under Windows CE.

You may be able to determine a file's type by examining the file's icon or by viewing the file's properties.

All files have icons that represent them in Windows CE Explorer. Table 9-3 describes several standard icons that are used to indicate specific types of files.

Table 9-3	Common File Icons
Icon	*Always Indicates*
	A folder that contains other files and possibly even other folders.
	A document that was created in Pocket Word and saved as a Pocket Word document.
	A document that was created in Pocket Excel and saved as a Pocket Excel workbook.
	A file that contains only text. If it was created in Pocket Word, it does not have any of the formatting options you may have used, such as bold, italics, or font size changes.
	A Pocket PowerPoint presentation.
	A database file. These files are used with programs, such as the Contacts program, to maintain the data that you add to the program.
	A help file. These help files provide extra information about a specific topic.
	A bitmap graphics file. If this file is copied to your personal computer, it is converted to a .BMP file.
	A sound file. These types of files contain the different sounds, such as the beep when it is time for an appointment, that you may hear on your CE device.
	A favorite Internet site. This file contains the information that Pocket Internet Explorer needs to locate your favorite site.

Files with .EXE extensions are program files. The .EXE extension is an abbreviation for *executable,* which refers to a file that is actually a program. If you double-tap the icon for the EXE file, the specified program opens on your CE device.

Working with Files on a PC Card

Most CE devices come with a slot in which you can add different types of PCMCIA cards, commonly referred to as PC Cards. You can use a PC Card slot to add features, such as a modem or a storage card, to your CE device. If you insert a storage card into your CE device, you see a folder called Storage Card in the My Handheld PC folder when you open Windows CE Explorer (see Figure 9-9).

Figure 9-9:
A folder is
added
so that
you can
manage the
files on a
PC Card
used for
storage.

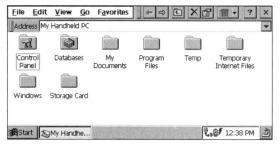

Although the storage card is not a permanent fixture in your CE device, Windows CE treats it as just another folder on the CE device. You may want to think of a storage card as essentially an expensive floppy disk for your CE device.

You can copy and move files between the card and your CE device. To copy files from either location, highlight the files in Windows CE Explorer and choose Edit➪Copy. Then locate the new spot for the file and choose Edit➪Paste. To move files, use the Cut option rather than the Copy option.

Do not remove a storage card while your CE device is turned on. If you pull out a card with your CE device turned on, you may lose some of your data or even ruin the card (and believe me, they are not cheap enough to just throw away). Before removing a card, make sure that the files from the card are all closed within Windows CE. Then turn off the CE device and remove the card.

Because each CE device is designed differently, there is no exact science when it comes to removing the PC Cards from a CE device. For information about removing the card from your CE device, refer to the hardware documentation that came with your CE device.

Sharing Files with Another CE Device

You can share files on your CE device with someone else who has a Windows CE device as long as both devices have an infrared port.

The infrared port looks sort of like a black mirror. To determine whether a CE device has an infrared port, refer to the hardware documentation that came with the CE device.

You perform the following steps to transfer files between two CE devices:

1. **Make sure that both CE devices are turned on and Windows CE Explorer is running on each unit.**

2. **Place the CE devices so that the infrared ports are lined up.**

   The ports need to be within about three feet of each other, with nothing blocking the view. Because infrared ports use light beams to transfer data, they cannot transfer information if the ports do not have a good view of each other.

3. **On the first CE device (the one with the information), highlight the file you want to send to the other CE device.**

   Windows CE allows you to send only one file at a time using the infrared port. If you have multiple files that you want to copy to the other CE device, you need to repeat these steps for each file.

4. **Choose File▷Send To▷Infrared Recipient.**

   An alert box indicates that the CE device is looking for another CE device.

5. **On the other CE device, choose File▷Receive.**

   When the CE devices make contact with each other, the file is transferred from the first CE device to the second CE device.

Some types of fluorescent lighting can interfere with the data transfer. If you have problems transferring data, try moving the CE devices to another location.

The infrared ports use light beams to send information back and forth. You need to make sure that the infrared ports are not blocked by anything. If the ports cannot see each other, the CE devices cannot transfer data.

Part III
Interfacing with Your Personal Computer

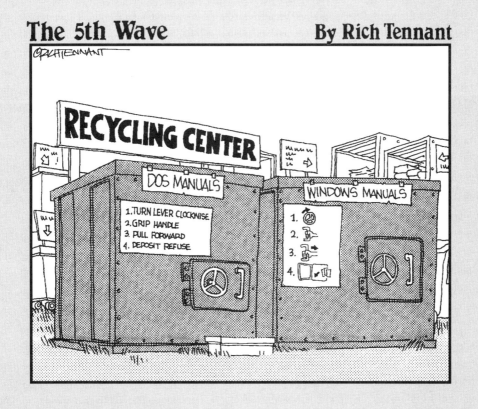

In this part . . .

You don't have to look too long at your CE device to realize that it's missing some common desktop computer features, such as a floppy drive, a CD-ROM drive, or other methods for loading new software programs. Fortunately, Windows CE does have a way of loading new software programs, backing up the contents of the CE device, and synchronizing appointments, tasks, and contacts with a desktop computer. To perform these tasks, you need to *interface,* or connect your CE device to a personal computer.

This part covers everything you need to know to interface with a personal computer and then tells you in a step-by-step fashion how to back up your CE device, load new software, and even synchronize all appointments, tasks, and contacts.

Chapter 10

Installing the Windows CE Services

. . . .

In This Chapter

▶ Figuring out what's required to connect Windows CE to your personal computer

▶ Installing the personal computer programs you need

▶ Connecting the interface cable

. . . .

*O*ne of the biggest advantages of selecting a CE device over other types of handheld devices (commonly referred to as PDAs — personal digital assistants) is the capability to easily interface with a personal computer running either Windows 95 or Windows NT 4.0. Whew! OK, I know that was a mouthful — so what exactly does it all mean?

To be as plain and simple as possible, you can connect your CE device to any personal computer that is running Windows 95 or Windows NT 4.0. After you connect to the personal computer, you can do all kinds of cool stuff. For example, you can copy a Microsoft Word document from your personal computer and place it on your CE device.

This chapter explains how to set up the connection between Windows CE and your personal computer, including how to connect the serial cable between your CE device and your personal computer and how to install the necessary software on your personal computer.

Figuring Out When to Connect

By connecting your CE device to a personal computer, you can move all kinds of information back and forth between the two machines. The personal computer and the CE device can become partners in the effort to make sure that you can accomplish your various tasks. Here is a list of the different things you can do when you interface your CE device with a personal computer:

✔ Install new programs on your CE device.

✔ Back up your CE device in case something goes wrong.

✔ Restore a backup after something has gone wrong on your CE device.

✔ Copy files between the two machines.

✔ Install new fonts on your CE device.

✔ Make sure that appointments, tasks, messages, and certain files match on both machines.

Understanding the Requirements for Connecting

Before you can interface your CE device with your personal computer, you must complete a few tasks. Unfortunately, you're kind of stuck if you don't have a personal computer that runs either Windows 95 or Windows NT 4.0. The Windows CE Services CD-ROM that comes with your CE device or with your Windows CE 2.0 update runs only on Windows 95 or Windows NT 4.0.

If you have a personal computer but are unsure whether your computer is running Windows 95 or Windows NT 4.0, the quickest way to find out is to look for the Start button at the bottom of the screen. If you do not have a Start button at the bottom of your screen, chances are you are running an older version of Windows. You can purchase a copy of Windows 95 or Windows NT 4.0 from any computer software store.

To interface your CE device with your personal computer, you must install the Windows CE Services program on your personal computer. (You can find that program on the Windows CE Services CD.) You need the Windows CE Services to perform the interface tasks, such as backing up your CE device, or synchronizing appointments and tasks. If you have not already installed the program on your computer, see the section "Running the Windows CE Services Install Program" later in this chapter for step-by-step instructions on setting up the program.

Finally, you need a serial interface cable to connect your CE device to the personal computer. If you didn't receive one of these cables with your CE device, contact your CE device manufacturer for information about how to purchase one.

Connecting the Interface Cable

The only way to connect a CE device to a personal computer is with the serial interface cable. When the cable is connected, you can copy data files and programs to and from your CE device.

This interface cable should have been packaged with your CE device when you purchased it. If you are not sure which cable it is, refer to the hardware documentation that came with your CE device. Some CE devices may not have been shipped with the cable; if this is the case with yours, you can obtain the cable by contacting your CE device's manufacturer.

You connect the cable to a serial port on the back of your computer. You can recognize the correct serial port because it has nine little pins poking out of it, as shown in Figure 10-1. If you only have a 25-pin serial port available on your computer, you need to locate an adapter to convert the cable so you can plug it into a 25-pin port. You should be able to purchase a 9-pin to 25-pin adapter at any computer store.

Figure 10-1:
A 9-pin
serial port.

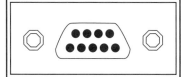

You connect the other end of the interface cable to the *data interface port* on your CE device. This port may be covered with a small door, which you need to open in order to plug in the cable. This port is where data is sent from your CE device to the personal computer. If you are using a docking station with your CE device, you probably need to plug the cable into the docking station. To determine the exact location for the cable, refer to the hardware documentation that came with your CE device.

You need to make sure that you properly attach the cable anytime you intend to interface your CE device with your personal computer. If the cable is not properly connected, the two units can't interact.

Running the Windows CE Services Install Program

Before you can interface your CE device with your personal computer, you must install the stuff on the Windows CE Services CD-ROM. You will probably only have to go through this process one time. If you decide to interface with another personal computer, however, you will need to repeat this installation process on that personal computer, too. For example, you may decide you want to interface with both a home computer and an office computer.

If you purchased a new Windows CE 2.0 device, the Windows CE Services CD-ROM should have been in the box with your CE device. If you had your CE device upgraded to Windows CE 2.0, you should have received the CD-ROM with the upgrade.

Remove the CD-ROM from the case and place it in the CD-ROM drive on the personal computer where you intend to create the interface with your CE device. Remember, the computer must be running Windows 95 or Windows NT 4.0, or the programs will not install properly. The Windows CE Services CD-ROM setup program should appear automatically, as shown in Figure 10-2.

If the Windows CE Services CD-ROM setup screen does not load automatically when you insert the CD-ROM into your computer, you need to run the Windows CE Services CD-ROM setup program manually. To do this, click the Run option in the Start menu to display the Run dialog box. Type **d:\setup** in the Open text box, as shown in Figure 10-3, to run the setup program on the CD-ROM. If your CD-ROM drive has been assigned a drive letter other than D, such as drive E:, type that drive letter instead of D.

Figure 10-2:
You can install the different options needed to run Windows CE Services on your personal computer.

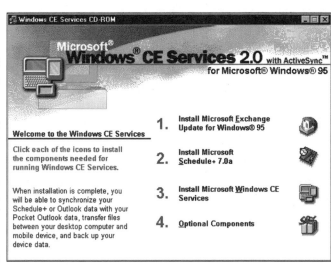

Figure 10-3:
Specify the
location of
the setup
program
and click
the OK
button.

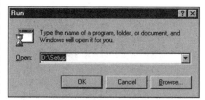

In the Windows CE Services setup screen, you see four options under Windows 95 and three options under Windows NT 4.0, as outlined in Table 10-1. Each option loads programs that are related to the different options that are available using the Windows CE Services program. Because of the requirements of each setup option, the setup program is designed to have you run each installation separately. When you run the Windows CE Services CD-ROM setup program, it checks your system to see whether you need to install each option. If an option appears grayed out on the setup screen, you do not need to install that option on your personal computer.

Table 10-1	The Windows CE Services Options
Option	*Purpose*
Microsoft Exchange Update for Windows 95	This option updates the version of Microsoft Exchange on your personal computer if the version is 4.0.410.59 or earlier. You can find the version number by running Microsoft Exchange and choosing Help⇨About. If you do not have Microsoft Exchange loaded or the version number is higher than 4.0.410.59, don't run this installation option. Also, if you are running a non-U.S. English version of Windows 95, don't run this installation option. Keep in mind that the installation program is checking for these conditions, as well. If you are running Windows NT 4.0, this option doesn't appear on the CE device setup screen.
	When you select this installation option, you get a series of screens that walk you through the installation process.

(continued)

Table 10-1 *(continued)*

Option	Purpose
Microsoft Schedule+ 7.0a	This option installs Microsoft Schedule+ 7.0a if you do not already have Version 7.0a of Microsoft Schedule+ installed on your personal computer. If you are running Microsoft Outlook on your personal computer, this option is marked as already installed or not required.
	When you select this installation option, you get a series of screens that walk you through the installation process.
Microsoft Windows CE Services	This option installs all the files required to run the Windows CE Services program. If you want to interface your CE device with your personal computer, you must run this installation option. For specific information about this option, refer to the section "Installing Microsoft Windows CE Services" later in this chapter.
Optional Components	This option provides several program options that you can install. The options available here vary depending on your specific CE device. For example, some devices come with Pocket PowerPoint as an option here, while it is already installed on other devices. You also can install options for interfacing your CE device with your personal computer using either an infrared or LAN (local area network) connection.

Installing Microsoft Windows CE Services

The Install Microsoft Windows CE Services option on the Windows CE Services setup screen installs all the Windows CE Services program files on your personal computer. If you don't install this program, your CE device can't interface with your personal computer.

Follow these steps to install Windows CE Services on your personal computer.

1. Click the Install Microsoft Windows CE Services icon.

This is the second button from the bottom (number 2 for Windows NT, and number 3 for Windows 95) on the Windows CE Services setup screen. It resembles a personal computer sitting behind a CE device.

2. In the first dialog box of the Microsoft Windows CE Services Setup, click the Next button to start the installation process.

This standard dialog box normally appears when you install any new software on your computer. It reminds you not to run any other programs on your computer while installing this program.

3. In the Microsoft Windows CE Services License Agreement dialog box, click the Yes button to continue the setup process.

This dialog box contains the entire license agreement that Microsoft has created for the Windows CE Services software, as shown in Figure 10-4. By clicking the Yes button, you are stating that you agree to adhere to the terms outlined in the license agreement.

Figure 10-4:
You must agree to the legal stuff before you continue the installation.

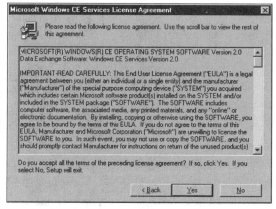

4. Type your name in the Name text box and press the Tab key. Type your company name (optional) in the Company text box and then click the Next button (see Figure 10-5).

Figure 10-5:
You must type a name in the Name field, but the Company entry is optional.

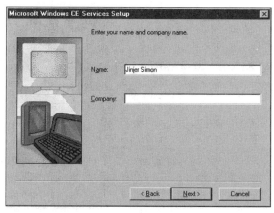

5. **In the Windows CE Services Setup dialog box, select the Typical button and make sure that the folder where the setup program wants to install the software is the right one. If so, click the Next button.**

The Windows CE Services Setup dialog box (see Figure 10-6) enables you to select the type of installation you want: Typical or Custom. I recommend that you select the Typical installation option to ensure that the proper files get placed on your personal computer.

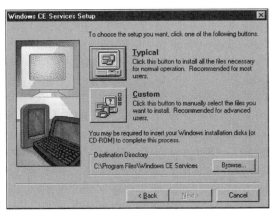

Figure 10-6: Select the Typical option to ensure that everything runs properly on your computer.

If for some reason you do not like the location where the setup program intends to place Windows CE Services, you can change the location by clicking the Browse button and then specifying a new location in the Choose Directory dialog box.

When you click the Next button, the setup program starts copying the necessary files to your personal computer. You see a status window indicating the progress.

6. **When you see the Setup Complete dialog box, shown in Figure 10-7, click the Finish button and connect your CE device to the personal computer.**

The setup program creates the connection between your CE device and personal computer.

Figure 10-7:
Now is the
time to
connect
your CE
device
to the
computer.

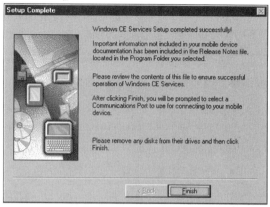

7. In the Get Connected window, make sure that your CE device and personal computer are connected properly and click the Start button.

This window reminds you that you need to connect your CE device to your personal computer.

8. When your personal computer and CE device get connected properly, you see the information in the Get Connected window, shown in Figure 10-8.

Figure 10-8:
Wait for
your
personal
computer to
connect to
your CE
device.

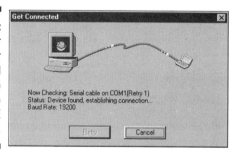

9. On the New Mobile Device Detected window, click the New Partnership button.

The New Mobile Device Detected window, shown in Figure 10-9, appears anytime you make a connection and the personal computer does not recognize the CE device.

Figure 10-9:
Select
the New
Partnership
option so
you can set
up the
relationship
between
your CE
device
and your
personal
computer.

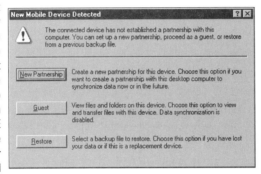

If you are installing the Windows CE Services to work with a device you have used on this machine in the past, you may want to click the Restore button. The only drawback is that this option causes the last backup to be copied onto your CE device; if you don't want that done, click the New Partnership button.

10. **If you see the Multiple Partnership Synchronization window, shown in Figure 10-10, the setup program has determined that you have synchronized your CE device with another computer. Click the Single button if you no longer want to synchronize with the other computer, or the Multiple button to synchronize with both computers.**

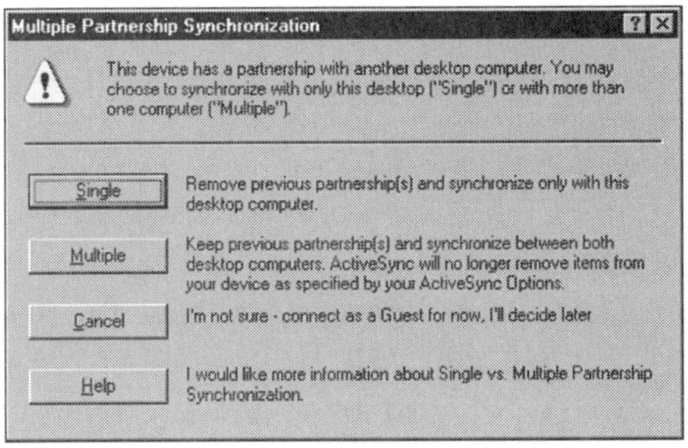

Figure 10-10:
Indicate
whether you
want to
synchronize
with more
than one
computer.

11. **In the first dialog box of the New Partnership wizard, click the Next button to start the process of creating the partnership between your personal computer and your CE device.**

12. **In the next dialog box of the New Partnership wizard, shown in Figure 10-11, specify the name you want to use to identify your CE device in the Device Name text box.**

    This name identifies your CE device when you connect to your personal computer. You can see this device name when you look at your folders and drives within Windows Explorer. It is not necessary to type a value in the Device Description field. The Device Description field can be useful if you are planning to connect multiple CE devices to your personal computer, because you can type something that identifies each CE device.

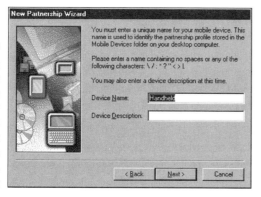

Figure 10-11:
Indicate
how you
want your
CE device
identified in
the Device
Name field.

13. **In the third dialog box of the New Partnership wizard, click the Next button.**

    This screen simply tells you that it has created a connection for your CE device with the name you specified on the previous dialog box.

14. **In the fourth dialog box of the New Partnership wizard, specify the type of synchronization you want and then click the Next button.**

    Make sure that you have the Enable synchronization option selected, as shown in Figure 10-12. Otherwise, your CE device and your personal computer will not synchronize the message, task, calendar, and file information that you specify. You can also indicate whether you want the machines to automatically synchronize when connecting and when the synchronization data is out of date. The first check box option, Automatically synchronize upon connecting, is probably adequate.

Keep in mind that after you set up the Windows CE Services program, you can change these options at any time within the Windows CE Services program.

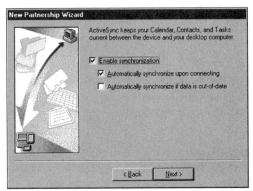

Figure 10-12:
Decide
when you
want to
synchronize
information
between
your CE
device
and your
personal
computer.

15. **In the final dialog box of the New Partnership wizard, click the Finish button to close the dialog box and connect to your CE device.**

You are ready to perform the various Windows CE Services options, such as copying files, backing up, restoring, and synchronizing. I discuss these options in Chapters 11 through 14.

Chapter 11

A Tour of Windows CE Services

*O*ne tool that you will definitely want to master is Windows CE Services. By using this program on your personal computer, you can form an alliance between your personal computer and your CE device. By connecting the two units, you can move information between your personal computer and your CE device.

This chapter explains how to use Windows CE Services on your personal computer to connect to your CE device and look for files, copy files, and even print files from your CE device. This tool can be especially valuable when you have a proposal you created on your CE device that you would like to give to a customer. Or you may have a monthly budget on your personal computer that you need to copy to your CE device so that you can work on it after dinner.

Running Windows CE Services

 Windows CE Services is the key to being able to transfer any type of information between your CE device and a personal computer. This program comes on a CD-ROM with your CE device (or with the Windows CE 2.0

upgrade you got for your CE device). Windows CE Services must be installed on your personal computer under Windows 95 or Windows NT 4.0; if you have not installed it yet, refer to Chapter 10.

Depending on how Windows CE Services was installed on your computer, you will probably find either its icon sitting on your desktop or a shortcut option on the Start menu called Mobile Devices.

Before you run the Windows CE Services program on your personal computer, make sure that your CE device is properly connected to the computer. Remember, you use the serial interface cable to connect your CE device to the personal computer. When the Windows CE Services program starts, it immediately tries to establish a connection with your CE device. For more pointers on connecting your computer and your CE device, refer to Chapter 10.

If you have set up your CE device to connect to a LAN, you can connect to your personal computer using the LAN connection. This option requires having a network card installed in your CE device and the appropriate files loaded from the Optional Components of the Windows CE Services 2.0 setup CD-ROM (refer to Chapter 10). If your desktop computer has an infrared port, you can also connect to it using the infrared port; this option also requires that you load some additional files as part of the Windows CE Services setup.

During the connection process, messages are displayed on both your computer screen and on your CE device indicating the progress of the connection.

If you have problems connecting your CE device to your desktop computer, the CE device probably isn't properly connected to the computer. Verify that the serial interface cable is properly connected to both the CE device and the computer.

The relationship between Windows CE Services and Windows Explorer

One thing you may quickly notice is that when you have your personal computer connected to your CE device, the Windows Explorer program actually provides you with access to most of the features of the Windows CE Services program. In fact, Windows CE Services is actually just a specialized version of the Windows Explorer. You can use either program to perform almost all the functions that deal with interfacing with your CE device.

For consistency, I explain most of the options in the chapter using the Windows CE Services, with the exception of a couple that are easier to perform using Windows Explorer.

Exploring Your CE Device from Your Personal Computer

If you're a Microsoft Windows veteran, you will soon recognize that Windows CE Services very closely resembles the Explorer programs that run on other versions of the Windows operating system, such as Windows 95 and Windows NT 4.0. In fact, with all the different Explorer programs, trying to keep track of which one you use when can be confusing.

As with other Windows Explorer programs, you can use Windows CE Services to look at the files and folders on your CE device in several ways. For example, you can display the contents of the folder specified in the address bar using large icons, as shown in Figure 11-1.

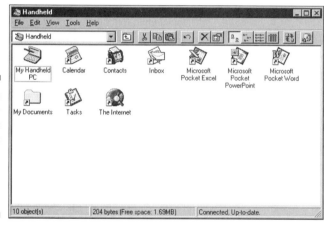

Figure 11-1:
Use
Windows
CE Services
to view the
folders and
files within
a folder.

Other view options are available on the View menu, shown in Figure 11-2. Or you can access the options by selecting one of the four buttons that I describe in Table 11-1.

Table 11-1	Windows CE Services Toolbar View Buttons
Click This Button	*To Do This*
	View the contents of the folder by using large icons. This way, you can quickly see what is in the folder; however, if you have several items, you will not be able to display everything on-screen at the same time and will need to use the scroll bars to look at the entire contents of the folder.

(continued)

Table 11-1 (continued)

Click This Button	To Do This
	View the contents of the folder by using small icons. Small icons look just like large icons, but the icons are smaller so you can get more on-screen at one time. Although these icons are more difficult to see, small icons are a better solution if you have a folder that contains several items.
	View a list of the files in the folder by using small icons and filenames.
	View the details about each item in the folder. This option displays information, such as the name of the item, its size, its file type, and the date and time when it was last modified.

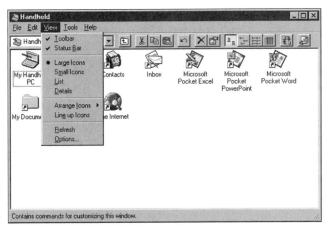

Figure 11-2: The View menu offers several options to customize the way you view things on your CE device.

After you decide how you want to view the information on your CE device, you can use the options on the View menu to arrange the order of the items in each folder:

✔ Within any view, you can sort items by name or file type. To sort by name, choose View➪Arrange Icons➪By Name. To sort by file type, choose View➪Arrange Icons➪By Type.

✔ If you have added an item to a particular folder since opening Windows CE Services, you may need to refresh the screen before the new item appears in the list. To refresh the list, choose View➪Refresh.

✔ You can hide certain system files so that you do not accidentally delete them. To hide the system files, choose View⇨Options to open the Options dialog box and tap the View tab, shown in Figure 11-3. Then select the Hide files of these types radio button to hide all files with the following extensions: .DLL, .SYS, .VXD, .386, and .DRV.

 ✔ You can also indicate whether the path for the current folder is displayed in the title bar (at the top of the window) and indicate whether you want to hide the file extensions for common file types.

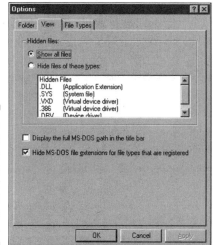

Figure 11-3:
Use the
Options
dialog box
to specify
which types
of files you
want to see.

You can ensure that the Windows CE Services uses only one window as you open different folders. To do this, choose View⇨Options to open the Options dialog box and tap the Folder tab. Select the radio button for the option called Browse folders by using a single window that changes as you open each folder radio button.

Moving Stuff Between Your Personal Computer and Your CE Device

One of the most useful features of connecting your personal computer and your CE device is the capability to copy documents back and forth. If you have a proposal that you just wrote in Microsoft Word, for example, you may need to copy it to your CE device so that you can quickly haul the document to a meeting. After you connect your CE device to your personal computer, moving files between the two units is easy. You can use either the drag-and-drop method or the cut, copy, and paste method. Both methods enable you to quickly move stuff back and forth. You can find more information about these methods for moving documents back and forth in the following section.

Dragging and dropping files and folders

One of the fastest and easiest ways to move files between your personal computer and your CE device is to use the drag-and-drop method. To drag and drop the files, you use Windows Explorer, as I describe in the following steps:

1. **Open the Windows Explorer program.**

   To open this program, choose Programs⇨Windows Explorer from the Start menu.

2. **In Windows Explorer, locate the file you want to move to your CE device.**

   For this example, I selected the Proposal.doc file in the My Documents folder under Windows 95, as shown in Figure 11-4.

3. **In the tree-view list on the left side of the Explorer window, click the plus sign (+) next to the Mobile Devices folder to see the folders inside. Continue tapping the + next to each folder until you locate the folder on your Windows CE device where you want to place the file.**

   You need to open the Mobile Devices folder and select the name of your CE device that is connected to the personal computer. Then locate the folder where you want to place the file from your personal computer, as shown in Figure 11-4, where I selected the My Documents folder on my CE device. You only want to click the + next to each folder so that the folders are opened on the left side of the screen, but the right side of the screen does not change.

4. **Drag the file from the right side of the screen and drop it on top of the selected Windows CE folder.**

   To copy the file, position the mouse cursor over the file's icon in Windows Explorer, press and hold the left mouse button, drag the icon to the folder name in the tree-view list on the left side of the screen, and release the mouse button.

To move the file from your personal computer to your CE device, hold down the right mouse button while you drag the file. When you release the file, you see a menu with options to either Move here or Copy here; click the Move here option and the file is moved to your CE device.

Figure 11-4:
In the
Windows
Explorer
program,
locate the
file that you
want to
copy and
the folder
where you
want to
place
the file.

5. **Indicate whether you want the file placed in the Synchronized Files folder by selecting the appropriate radio button and then click the OK button.**

   The Synchronize File window, shown in Figure 11-5, provides you with the opportunity to place the file in the Synchronized Files folder. If you place the file in this folder, it will be synchronized with the copy of the file on your personal computer each time you synchronize the two units. For more information about synchronization, see Chapter 12.

   The Copy & Convert to mobile format window appears, indicating that Windows is copying and converting the file (see Figure 11-6).

Figure 11-5:
Indicate
whether
you
want to
synchronize
the files.

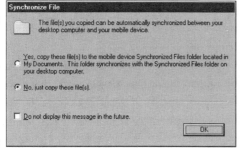

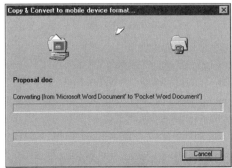

Figure 11-6:
You can
view the
progress as
the file is
copied
between
the two
machines.

Cutting, copying, and pasting files between locations

You can use the Cut, Copy, and Paste buttons, shown in Table 11-2, on the toolbar of both Windows CE Services and Windows Explorer to move and copy items from one location to another. This method is good for anyone who prefers to use buttons instead of the drag-and-drop method.

Table 11-2	Toolbar Move and Copy Buttons
Click This Button	**To Do This**
✂	Cut the existing file out of the existing folder. Remember, if you cut from your personal computer and paste on your CE device, the file or folder remains on your personal computer, too.
🗐	Copy the selected file.
📋	Paste the last file that was either cut or copied into the current folder.

To copy a file from your CE device and paste it onto your personal computer, follow these steps:

1. Open Windows Explorer on your personal computer.

You should be able to locate an option for the program on the Programs menu of the Start menu.

2. Open the folder that contains the file you want to copy and click the file's icon.

Click the icon with the mouse to select it. A black box appears around the name of the file, indicating that the file is selected, as shown in Figure 11-7.

Figure 11-7:
Highlight
the icon
that
corresponds
to the file
you want
to copy.

3. Click the Copy icon on the toolbar.

The Copy icon looks like two identical sheets of paper sitting one on top of the other.

4. Open the folder you want to place the file into.

5. Click the Paste button on the toolbar.

The window shown in Figure 11-8 appears, indicating that the selected file is being copied to the specified folder and converted from a Pocket Word file format (.PWD) to a Microsoft Word file format (.DOC).

Figure 11-8:
As long as
you have
automatic
conversion
selected,
the file is
quickly
converted
to the
appropriate
format as it
is copied.

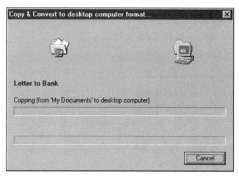

Dealing with Folders

Folders bring organization to your CE device by enabling you to group common files together in one location. With Windows CE Services, you can work with existing folders and create new folders on your CE device. You get the full scoop on folders in the following sections.

Adding a new folder

To use Windows CE Services to create a new folder, choose File⇨New Folder. A folder named New Folder appears, as shown in Figure 11-9. Type a name for the folder.

Figure 11-9:
You can add new folders to organize the related files on your CE device.

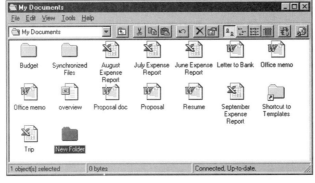

Renaming a folder or file

Suppose that when you name a file, you mistype the filename. Or maybe you decide to store different files in the folder and you want to change the folder name to reflect more accurately the contents of the folder. With Windows CE Services, you can easily modify the names of files and folders on your CE device from your personal computer.

In Windows CE Services, click the file or folder you want to rename and then choose File⇨Rename. A box appears around the name, and the cursor moves to the end of the item's name.

You can replace the entire name of the file or folder or change a portion of the name. If you want to replace the entire name of the item, simply start typing. The new name appears in the box. If you want to modify only a portion of the name, use the arrow keys to move the cursor within the name and then start typing.

Another easy way to rename the file or folder is to click the icon with the right mouse button; this displays a menu of options from which you can select the Rename option.

Use the Rename option to change the names of your personal document files only. Do not attempt to rename system or program files. Avoid renaming any files in the Windows directory — Windows CE stores the files it requires for the operating system there, and changes in this area can keep your CE device from running properly.

Printing Files

You have basically three ways to print files from your CE device:

- ✔ Using the infrared port to send the file to a printer with an infrared port.
- ✔ Connecting a printer to the serial port of your CE device.
- ✔ Copying the file to your personal computer and printing it using the appropriate program. For example, if you have a Pocket Word file, you use Windows CE Services to convert it to a Microsoft Word file and then open it up and print it from Microsoft Word. For information about copying files, refer to the section "Moving Stuff Between Your Personal Computer and Your CE Device," earlier in this chapter.

Keep in mind that the first two options can be accomplished within Pocket Word, Pocket Excel, Calendar, Contacts, Inbox, and Tasks. You can find out more about printing from these programs by referring to the corresponding chapters in this book.

Setting File Conversion Properties

If you have copied files between your computer and your CE device, you've probably noticed that besides copying each file, Windows CE Services also performs some type of data conversion. This conversion ensures that a file can be opened after it is copied to the personal computer or CE device. For example, when you copy Microsoft Word documents (.DOC files) to your CE device, the files are converted to Microsoft Pocket Word files (.PWD files).

To enable you to make some selections about the way files are converted, Windows CE Services provides the File Conversion option, located on the Tools menu. When you select this option, the File Conversion Properties dialog box appears, as shown in Figure 11-10.

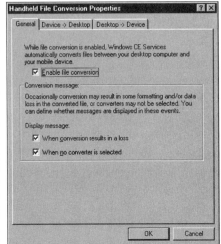

Figure 11-10:
Specify
whether
files
should be
automatically
converted
when you
copy them
between
your CE
device
and your
personal
computer.

The File Conversion Properties dialog box contains three tabs. You use the options on these tabs to customize your conversion settings. To view a different set of options, click the desired tab.

When you view many of the options within the Windows CE Services program, the name of the CE device you are connected to is automatically attached to the window name. For example, in Figure 11-10, the name of the dialog box is File Conversion Properties, but Windows CE Services tacks on the name Handheld (which is what my CE device is called) to the dialog box name. To reduce confusion, I just use the standard name, such as File Conversion Properties, to refer to each of these windows.

Setting general conversion options

When the File Conversion Properties dialog box appears, the General tab is visible. Although this tab has only three little check boxes, each one has an important purpose.

The Enable file conversion option indicates that whenever a file is copied between your CE device and your personal computer, the file is automatically converted based on the settings on the other two tabs. If this option is not selected, the file is copied onto the other unit but not converted. This option should only be turned off if you do not want any file conversion to occur when you copy files, but keep in mind that if the files are not converted, you can't open them after they are copied.

You can also have Windows CE Services display messages when specific conditions exist during the file conversion process. You can specify that a message appears when a data loss occurs during the file conversion process and also if a converter isn't specified for the type of file you are copying. You select the options to display these messages in the Conversion message section of the File Conversion Properties dialog box.

Indicating settings for copying to the personal computer

Although Windows CE has only a limited amount of file formats, I imagine you're aware that the number seems limitless on the personal computer. For example, Pocket Word can save documents in only four file formats (PWD, PWT, RTF, and TXT), yet Microsoft Word can save a file in several more formats.

On the Device -> Desktop tab of the File Conversion Properties dialog box, you need to indicate how each of the Windows CE file types should be converted when a file of that type is copied to your personal computer.

The following steps illustrate how you change the way a specific file type is converted when it is copied from your CE device to your personal computer:

1. **In the Mobile device convertible file types list, highlight the Windows CE file type that you plan to convert.**

   For example, maybe you want to convert a Pocket Word document to a rich text format (RTF) file so that you can read the document in a word processor other than Microsoft Word on your personal computer. In that case, highlight the Pocket Word Document option in the Mobile device convertible file types list.

2. **Click the Edit button.**

   When you click the Edit button, the Edit Conversion Settings window appears. The currently selected conversion type is specified in the Type field.

3. **Click the down-arrow button next to the Type field and highlight the file type to which you want the Windows CE file converted.**

   Continuing the example from the previous steps, you can specify that you want to convert the Pocket Word document to an RTF file. In that case, simply highlight the Rich Text Format (*.rtf) option in the Type field.

4. **Click the OK button to select the new format.**

You can modify the format conversions at any time by simply choosing Tools⇨File Conversion from Windows CE Services. When you change the conversion formats, the change does not affect any files that you have already copied to your computer. The setting only affects files that you copy to your personal computer after changing the setting.

Indicating settings for copying to your CE device

You can convert several types of files from your personal computer to be viewed on your CE device. To specify how these file types are to be converted, click the Desktop -> Device tab of the File Conversion Properties dialog box.

The file formats that can be converted for use on your CE device are listed in the Desktop computer convertible file types list. When you highlight one of these file types, the current conversion settings for the file format appear in the File conversion details section. You can change a format by highlighting it and then clicking the Edit button.

If you are using a word processor other than Microsoft Word on your personal computer, you probably can't save the documents as .DOC files (Microsoft Word file format). In that case, try saving the document as an .RTF file, commonly referred to as Rich Text Format. This standard file format can be read by most word processing programs. By using this file format, the file conversion option in Windows CE Services can then convert the .RTF file to a Pocket Word format of .PWD.

Keep in mind that Windows CE Services cannot convert a Microsoft Word or Microsoft Excel file that is password-protected. If you want to convert these files for use on your CE device, you must first remove the password protection from the file on your personal computer.

Chapter 12

Synchronizing Information

· ·

In This Chapter

▶ Understanding the synchronization process

▶ Performing a synchronization

▶ Setting the different synchronization options

· ·

*H*ave you ever set up your appointments for the next day, only to go home from the office and forget exactly what time you are expected to be in the office in the morning? With a CE device, you can copy all your appointments and your to-do list from either Microsoft Schedule+ or Microsoft Outlook to your CE device, and vice versa.

This chapter explains how to use Windows CE Services on your personal computer to synchronize the calendar and task information between your CE device and a personal computer. I also discuss how to set the different synchronization options.

Understanding Synchronization

If you have looked at any of the information that came with your CE device, or even just seen ads for CE devices, I'm sure you've heard mention of how easily you can synchronize with a personal computer. Isn't it nice how companies always mention all these benefits but never really take the time to explain them?

Well, to be totally honest, the concept of *synchronizing* two devices is rather simple: Essentially, all of the information on each unit is combined so that each unit not only has its current information, but also the information that was originally contained only on the other unit.

For example, suppose I ask you to list the five best Mexican restaurants in your town. I also ask your neighbor to do the same thing. If I wanted to synchronize the two lists, I would take your list of five names and combine it with your neighbor's list. If the combined list had any duplicates, I would remove the second copy of the item, leaving me with a list of favorite Mexican restaurants for your neighborhood.

When Windows CE Services synchronizes with your CE device, it performs the same steps I just described. The information on your CE device is combined with the information on your personal computer. Windows CE Services then copies the combined information to each unit. If any conflicts (such as two appointments scheduled at the same time) or duplicates are found, they are resolved using the current synchronization settings. For more information, check out the "Setting the Synchronization Options" section later in this chapter.

Windows CE allows you to synchronize the information outlined in Table 12-1.

Table 12-1	Synchronization Options
This Windows CE Option	*Synchronizes with This Personal Computer Option*
Calendar	All appointments and events are added to the calendar in Schedule+ or Outlook.
Tasks	All tasks become to-do items for Schedule+ and tasks for Outlook.
Contacts	All contact information is synchronized with the contacts in Schedule+ or Outlook.
Messages	All messages in the Inbox program are synchronized with the messages in Schedule+ or Outlook.
Files	Any files in the Synchronized Files folder are synchronized with files in the corresponding folder on your personal computer.

Only the files (programs, documents, sound files, and so on) in the Synchronized Files folder on your CE device can be synchronized with you personal computer.

Performing a Synchronization

You can synchronize task, calendar, and contact information between your CE device and your personal computer at any time by using Windows CE Services. All you have to do is click the Synchronize Now button on the toolbar.

To synchronize your CE device with your personal computer, click the Synchronize Now button, located on the toolbar of Windows CE Services. A window appears, indicating that Windows CE Services is merging all the contact, task, appointment, message, and selected file information from your CE device with the same information on your personal computer (see Figure 12-1).

Figure 12-1:
Windows
CE Services
notifies you
about the
status of
the synch-
ronization
process.

If this is the first time you have synchronized your CE device with this personal computer, or some of the settings have changed in your e-mail program, you may see the ActiveSync window, shown in Figure 12-2, during the synchronization process. If you see this window, click the Combine button to combine the information on your personal computer with the information on your CE device, remove the duplicates, and make sure that each unit has an identical list of items.

Figure 12-2:
The
Combine
option
ensures
that the
same
information
exists
on your
personal
computer
and your CE
device.

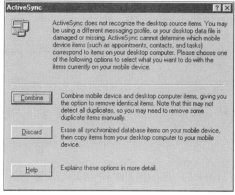

If for some reason you do not want to retain the contact, task, and calendar information on your CE device, you can select the Discard option, and Windows CE Services removes the information from your CE device and copies all the personal computer contact, task, and calendar information to your CE device. This option is useful when the information on your personal computer is more current than the information on your CE device.

Setting the Synchronization Options

Windows CE Services lets you customize your synchronization settings. For example, you may want to make sure that your CE device is synchronized with the personal computer every time the two units are connected. You can also indicate how Windows CE Services should resolve conflicts, such as two appointments scheduled at the same time.

You specify the synchronization options in the ActiveSync Options dialog box, shown in Figure 12-3. This dialog box appears whenever you choose Tools⇨ActiveSync Options within Windows CE Services.

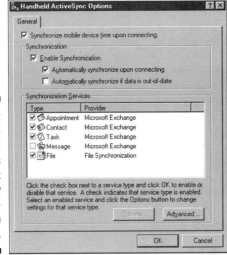

Figure 12-3:
Use the
ActiveSync
Options
dialog box
to specify
synchroni-
zation
settings.

Make sure that you select the appropriate check boxes in the Synchroniza-tion Services list to indicate the information that you want Windows CE Services to synchronize between your personal computer and your CE device. For example, if you only select the Appointment check box, the tasks, contacts, messages, and files will not be synchronized during the synchronization process.

You can make sure that the time setting on your CE device matches that of the computer by selecting the Synchronize mobile device time upon connecting option in the ActiveSync Options dialog box. The option is selected if a check mark appears in the check box next to the option. Of course, if you know that your computer does not keep the correct time, you probably want to make sure that this option is not selected.

Selecting automatic synchronization

If you are scheduling appointments and tasks on both your CE device and your personal computer, make sure that you synchronize the two units frequently to help ensure that you have not created conflicting appointments. The best way to make sure that your device gets synchronized frequently is to have Windows CE Services automatically synchronize the appointment, task, and contact information on your CE device and personal computer when you run the program. If you select this option, Windows CE Services automatically synchronizes the two units immediately after establishing a connection between your CE device and your personal computer.

To specify that the synchronization should occur whenever the device and computer are connected, you need to make sure that the Automatically synchronize upon connecting option is selected in the ActiveSync Options dialog box.

With automatic synchronization, you have to wait for the synchronization process to finish before you can use Windows CE Services to perform other tasks with your CE device. Of course, the more frequently you synchronize, the faster the process is.

You can also have a synchronization happen anytime you change something in your list, such as a contact if you have the Contacts selected to be synchronized. To do this, simply select the Automatically synchronize if data is out-of-date check box. Of course, this automatic synchronization happens only if the CE device is connected to your personal computer.

Resolving scheduling conflicts

Have you ever accidentally scheduled yourself to be in two places at the same time? Conflicting appointments, tasks, and contacts can exist on your CE device and your personal computer. When you have an appointment, task, or contact record that was modified on both your CE device and personal computer, and the two records don't match, Windows CE Services considers this situation a *conflict*.

To specify how to handle conflicts, you need to click the Advanced button in the ActiveSync Options dialog box to display the Advanced ActiveSync Options dialog box, shown in Figure 12-4.

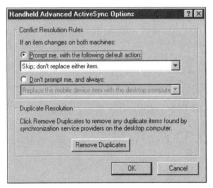

Figure 12-4:
Make sure
you specify
how to deal
with any
conflicts
that may
arise during
the synch-
ronization.

You can have Windows CE Services prompt you each time the synchronization encounters a conflict by selecting the Prompt me option. When you are
prompted during the synchronization process, you need to specify how to
handle each conflict that's encountered. If you select this option, you also
need to select one of the options in the drop-down list box to indicate the
default action for resolving conflicts, as outlined in Table 12-2.

If you want Windows CE Services to automatically resolve all the conflicts
that a synchronization encounters, select the Don't prompt me option. With
this choice too, you must select one of the options in the drop-down list box
to indicate how Windows CE Services should resolve all conflicts, as outlined in Table 12-2.

Table 12-2	Conflict Resolution Options
If You Want to Always	*Select This Drop-Down List Option*
Select the CE device item	Replace the desktop computer item with the mobile device item
Select the personal computer item	Replace the mobile device item with the desktop computer item
Keep both items	Skip, don't replace either item

Tweaking your synchronization selections

Windows CE Services also enables you to modify the setting for each type of
synchronization that is listed in the Synchronization Services list on the
ActiveSync Options dialog box. For example, you may only want to synchronize the tasks that need to be completed next week, or the appointments for
the next three weeks. To modify the options for any of the synchronization
types, you need to select the synchronization type and then click the
Options button, as I outline in the following steps:

1. **In the Synchronization Services section of the ActiveSync Options dialog box, highlight the synchronization type that you want to modify.**

   Keep in mind that the Options button remains grayed out (meaning you can't select it) if the check box next to the synchronization type is not selected.

2. **Click the Options button to display the appropriate dialog box for the synchronization type.**

   You see a File Synchronization Options dialog box, similar to the one in Figure 12-5. Each file is customized for the synchronization type you select.

Figure 12-5: Select the files that you want to have synch-ronized.

3. **Make the appropriate selections in the Files Synchronization Options dialog box.**

   For example, you can add files to the synchronization list by clicking the Add button and specifying the files you want to be synchronized. These files are added to the Synchronized Files folder on your personal computer and they are copied to your Windows CE device, if they do not already exist there. They are placed in the Synchronized Files folder under the My Documents folder on your Windows CE device. You can remove a file from the synchronization process at any time by highlighting the desired file and clicking the Remove button.

On the other hand, if you are viewing the Tasks Synchronization dialog box, you can specify the exact group of tasks that you want synchronized — for example, you can synchronize only the active tasks, tasks within a specific category, or even ones within a certain time frame.

4. **Click the OK button to save your selections and close the Files Synchronization Options dialog box.**

Checking the Synchronization Status

The Windows CE Services program keeps a log of the activity that occurs each time you synchronize your CE device with your personal computer. If you want to check to see exactly what happened during the last synchronization process, you can look at the ActiveSync Status dialog box, shown in Figure 12-6. You view this dialog box by choosing Tools➪ActiveSync Status.

This screen indicates the different Windows CE items that were synchronized with your personal computer and identifies the program or file location where the synchronization was made. For example, if you use Microsoft Outlook for your appointment scheduling, you should see that the appointments were synchronized with Microsoft Outlook, or the Microsoft Outlook profile that you used.

If you want to perform another synchronization, you can click the Synchronization Now button on the toolbar or choose Tools➪Synchronization Now.

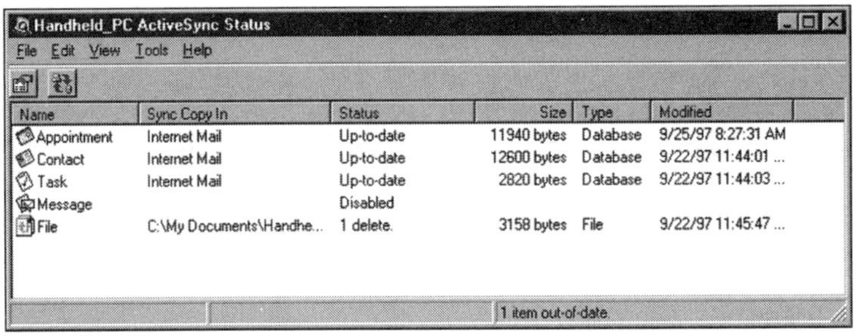

Figure 12-6:
See what happened the last time your CE device was synchronized with the personal computer.

Name	Sync Copy In	Status	Size	Type	Modified
Appointment	Internet Mail	Up-to-date	11940 bytes	Database	9/25/97 8:27:31 AM
Contact	Internet Mail	Up-to-date	12600 bytes	Database	9/22/97 11:44:01 ...
Task	Internet Mail	Up-to-date	2820 bytes	Database	9/22/97 11:44:03 ...
Message		Disabled			
File	C:\My Documents\Handhe...	1 delete.	3158 bytes	File	9/22/97 11:45:47 ...

Handheld_PC ActiveSync Status

File Edit View Tools Help

1 item out-of-date.

Chapter 13

Backing Up and Restoring Windows CE Information

In This Chapter

▶ Backing up your CE device

▶ Setting the backup options

▶ Restoring a backup

---

*H*ave you ever had an important paper that you wanted to keep, but someone in the family decided that the paper made a good gum wrapper? Or perhaps you did some spring cleaning of your own and somehow managed to accidentally discard that important document. If you were wise enough to make a copy of the paper, you could just get out the backup paper and be none the worse for wear.

Even on your CE device, documents and files can suddenly disappear. (At some point, you'll inevitably delete a document that you need to keep.) The possibility exists that something could go wrong with your CE device, and if the machine were to totally reset itself, you would lose all the files that had been stored on it. The chances of that happening are slim, but if everything on your CE device is backed up, you can always restore the backup and continue working as if nothing happened.

This chapter explains how to use Windows CE Services on your personal computer to back up all the information stored on your CE device. I discuss the different options that you can select to specify the type of backup you want to perform. I also look at how you can quickly restore a backup file and replace the current information with a previous copy.

Performing a Backup

The Windows CE Services program that runs on a personal computer gives you the capability to back up your CE device on a regular basis. When you back up your CE device, the Windows CE Services program copies all the stuff that you have placed on your CE device since you originally set it up. This backup file is stored on your personal computer so that if anything ever goes wrong on your CE device, you can restore the backed-up copy. Of course, your CE device must be connected to your personal computer in order to create or restore a backup.

 You can back up your CE device at any time, as long as the unit is connected to your personal computer, by clicking the Back Up Now button on the toolbar of the Windows CE Services program. (Don't forget that the Windows CE Services program is on your personal computer.) The Back Up Now button looks like a stack of papers with a red arrow on top of them.

 Windows CE Services frequently turns off your toolbar. To turn the toolbar back on, choose View➪Toolbar.

 Before you start your backup, make sure that all programs on your CE device are closed. After you start the backup, take a break while Windows CE Services completes the process. The backup process ensures that you have a complete backup file if you ever need to restore one.

To back up the contents of your CE device, follow these steps:

1. **Click the Back Up Now button on the Windows CE Services toolbar, or choose Tools➪Backup Now.**

   Windows CE Services automatically selects a location for the backup file and displays the default location in the Confirm Backup dialog box, as shown in Figure 13-1. You can accept this default location or specify a different location for the backup file.

   Remember: The backup file needs to be stored on your personal computer so that it can be copied onto your CE device if any type of problem occurs.

   When you click the Back Up Now button, you get either an incremental or a full backup of your CE device. The type of backup that is performed is determined by the settings you choose in the Backup/Restore Properties dialog box. The following section discusses this dialog box in detail.

Figure 13-1:
To perform
a backup
in the
specified
folder, click
the OK
button.

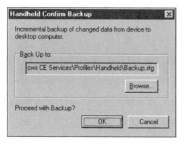

2. **If you want to place the backup in a different folder, click the Browse button to display the Select Backup Set dialog box, shown in Figure 13-2. Specify the location for the backup file and then click the Save button to use the specified location for the backup file.**

Do not use your CE device while the backup file is being created. If you are using files on your CE device, Windows CE Services cannot make a backup copy of those files.

Figure 13-2:
Indicate the
name and
location of
the backup
file on your
personal
computer.

As the backup file is created, the Backup In Progress window shows you the status of the process (see Figure 13-3). The length of time required to back up your device is based on the amount of stuff you have stored. If at any time you want to stop the backup process, simply click the Cancel button. Keep in mind, however, that if you cancel the process, you do not have a complete backup file.

3. **Click the OK button on the Backup Complete alert box.**

The Backup Complete alert box, shown in Figure 13-4, tells you that you can now safely use your CE device.

Before you can back up your CE device, you must install the Windows CE Services program on your personal computer and establish a relationship between your CE device and the personal computer that is running the

Figure 13-3:
The Backup
In Progress
window.

Figure 13-4:
Click the OK
button to
close the
backup
process.

Windows CE Services program. For more information about setting up
Windows CE Services, refer to Chapter 10.

If something happens to the stuff you have stored on your CE device, you
can restore only the items you last backed up. Anything you have done
on your CE device since the last backup is lost. The more often you back up
your CE device, the less likely you are to lose something important.

Setting the Backup Options

You can select specific options for each backup by choosing Tools⇨Backup/
Restore. After you choose the Backup/Restore option, the Backup/Restore
Properties dialog box appears, as shown in Figure 13-5. (By the way, I
discuss the Restore tab in the next section of this chapter.)

The Backup tab enables you to do the following:

- ✔ Indicate the type of backup that is performed each time you request a
  backup.
- ✔ Specify that the CE device is backed up every time you run the Windows CE Services program.
- ✔ Indicate the default location on your personal computer for the
  backup file.

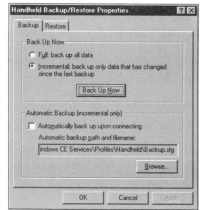

Figure 13-5:
Specify the
type of
backup
performed
by
Windows CE
Services.

To specify the type of backup, click either the Full or Incremental option in the Back Up Now section of the Backup tab. The option you select determines the type of backup that is performed whenever you click the Back Up Now button or choose Tools⇨Back Up Now:

- ✔ **Full:** When you make a full backup of your CE device, all the information on your CE device is copied into the backup file. The backup file is just another type of file that is created on your personal computer. Windows CE Services automatically creates this file when you do a backup of your CE device.

- ✔ **Incremental:** An incremental backup copies only the files that have changed since the last time you performed a full backup on your CE device. This type of backup is much quicker than a full backup because you only have to wait for the new stuff to be backed up. Windows CE Services provides the option of having an incremental backup performed whenever you connect your CE device to the personal computer. This can be a valuable option to use, because it eliminates the need for you to keep track of when you last backed up your CE device.

To ensure that your CE device gets backed up on a regular basis, you can request that Windows CE Services always back up the device when you connect to it. To have an automatic backup, you need to select the Automatically back up upon connecting option.

If you want the backups to be placed in a folder other than the default one on your computer, click the Browse button to display the Select Backup Set window. Specify the folder location for the backup file. You can even change the name of the backup file, although I would recommend keeping a name that reminds you that the file contains a backup of your CE device.

Restoring a Backup

When you restore a backup, all the stuff currently on your CE device is replaced with the files in the backup that you restore. For this reason, make sure that you really want to restore the backup before you perform the following steps on your CE device. The only way to undo the process is to restore another backup, assuming that you have one for your current settings.

Make sure that you close all programs that are currently running on your CE device before restoring the backup file; the restore process does not run properly if a file is open on your CE device.

1. **In Windows CE Services, choose Tools⇔Backup/Restore.**

   The Backup/Restore Properties dialog box appears.

2. **On the Restore tab of the Backup/Restore Properties dialog box, click the Restore Now button (see Figure 13-6).**

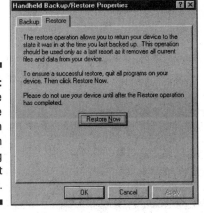

Figure 13-6: Click the Restore Now button to begin restoring the last backup.

3. **In the Confirm Restore dialog box, click the OK button if you want to restore the specified file onto your device.**

   The Confirm Restore dialog box indicates which backup file will be restored onto your CE device, as shown in Figure 13-7. If this file is not the one you want to restore, you can click the Browse button to display the Select Backup Set window, where you can specify the path of the backup file.

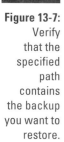

Figure 13-7:
Verify
that the
specified
path
contains
the backup
you want to
restore.

4. In the alert box labeled Proceed with Restore, click the <u>R</u>estore button to start the restore process.

This alert box asks whether you really want to perform this restore, as shown in Figure 13-8. You have essentially reached the point of no return — when you click the Restore button, the process starts. Do not use your CE device while the information is being restored.

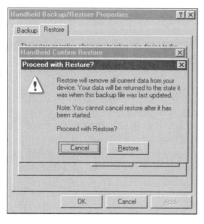

Figure 13-8:
Select the
Restore
button to
restore
all the
backed up
information.

5. If you get a message about programs running on your CE device, close the specified programs on your CE device and click the <u>C</u>ontinue button.

If you have left any programs running on your CE device, the restore program will not be able to restore some files onto your CE device and the Restore: Programs Running alert box appears, as shown in Figure 13-9. To resolve the problem, close all running programs on your CE device and click the Continue button. If you are not sure which programs are running, check for any programs listed in the status bar at the bottom of the screen. If you see any buttons (other than the Start button), the corresponding program is still open. You may also need to close a program sitting in the Status portion of the taskbar (the bottom-right corner of the screen); to close these programs, simply double-tap the corresponding icon.

Figure 13-9:
You must close all program files on your CE device so that the files can be properly restored.

6. **When you see the Restore Complete alert box, click the OK button, disconnect your CE device from your personal computer, and press the Reset button.**

   You must reset your CE device before the restored settings take effect. If you are not sure where the Reset button is located on your CE device, refer to the hardware documentation that came with your CE device.

To properly restore all the files onto your CE device, you must make sure that all programs are closed before running the restore process.

Chapter 14

Adding New Software
to Your CE Device

*O*ne of the most attractive features of CE devices, when compared to other mobile devices on the market, is that with Windows CE you can easily add new programs to your CE device. This capability turns your CE device into a literal pocket-sized computer.

This chapter explains how to locate and install new Windows CE programs on your CE device. It also illustrates how easily you can remove anything that you have added to your CE device to allow storage space for something new.

Locating Windows CE Programs

Because Windows CE is still fairly new to the market, locating software to add to your CE device can be tricky. But believe it or not, several programs have already been created for Windows CE.

Although you can locate some software at computer stores, one of the best sources for locating programs available for your CE device is the Internet. One good place to look for software and other happenings in the Windows CE world is the Mobile Worker Magazine, at www.microsoft.com/windowsce/hpc/mobile/, shown in Figure 14-1. Another good site is Mobilesoft; check out www.mobilesoft.com.

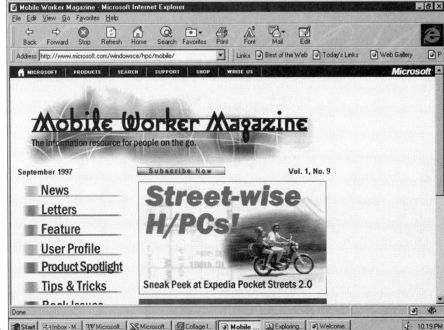

Figure 14-1:
A great deal of information about Windows CE is available on the Internet.

Because most programs have to be installed onto your CE device from your personal computer, use a personal computer to search for software for your CE device. Normally, you download the software to the personal computer, not your CE device (although you may find a site where you can download directly to your CE device, so keep your eyes open). New sites that contain information about Windows CE programs are constantly being added to the Internet, so the best thing to do is to use one of the search engines and look for all references to Windows CE.

Before you download or purchase anything, make sure that the program is specifically designed to run on Windows CE. You can often get away with placing a Windows 95 program on Windows NT, and almost all Windows 3.1 programs run on Windows 95 and Windows NT. But that is not the case with Windows CE — the program must be specifically created for Windows CE, or you will not be able to use that program on your CE device.

The other thing that you must keep in mind is the type of processor that you have in your CE device. The processor (the CPU, in computer lingo) is the heart of your CE device, and it controls everything that occurs on your CE device. The processors that are available for CE devices are almost as varied as the CE device manufacturers. Essentially, the software developer is required to make a different version of the program for each processor, so check to see if the program works with the processor on your CE device before you purchase the program.

Installing a New Program

Common knowledge says that no two things are exactly alike, and this adage definitely holds true when it comes to installing new software programs on your CE device: No two installation programs are the same. Software developers create their own unique installation programs for their specific products. Although the installation programs all differ from one another, you do find some consistency as to how the programs are actually installed on your CE device.

Keep in mind that in order to install new software, you normally need to connect your CE device to a personal computer. The computer needs to have Windows CE Services set up on it. (For more information on setting up Windows CE Services, refer to Chapter 10.) Depending on the software developers' installation instructions, though, you may not need to have Windows CE Services running before you run the installation program.

You normally add programs to your CE device in one of two ways. Both methods require using a personal computer connection:

✔ **Copying required files:** You add some programs by simply copying a file from your personal computer to the appropriate folder on your CE device. To do so, you use Windows Explorer and click the program icon in the folder on your personal computer and then drag the program icon into the desired CE Device folder.

✔ **Running an installation program:** Most software developers create an installation program that you run on your personal computer to install the necessary files on your CE device. This method is probably the easiest way to install new software because typically, the installation program requires very little input from you.

Other methods exist for placing programs on your CE device. If you have a LAN connection, you can transfer the files from your personal computer to the CE device. You can also use the infrared port to copy a program file from another CE device. Finally, you can copy the files from the Internet onto your CE device, if you find a site that provides this capability.

Copying the program file to your CE device

You can copy most Windows CE programs to your CE device in the same manner as you would copy a file to your CE device. You usually use this method if only one file is required to run the program on your CE device, and the program does not require any changes to the system settings for Windows CE. If this is the case, you simply copy the program file onto your CE device.

The following steps illustrate how to copy a program file to your CE device:

1. **Make sure that you have a connection established between your CE device and the personal computer.**

   Usually, all you need to do is connect your CE device to the computer with the serial interface cable and then run the Windows CE Services program on your personal computer. Windows CE Services automatically establishes the connection with your CE device. For additional information about establishing a connection, refer to Chapter 10.

2. **Open Windows Explorer on your personal computer and then open the folder containing the program file that you want to place on your CE device.**

   The easiest way to open the folder is to click the appropriate folder in the folder list on the left side of the window, as shown in Figure 14-2. The right side of the Windows Explorer window shows the contents of the selected folder.

Figure 14-2: To open a folder, click its icon on the left side of the window.

3. **In the tree-view list on the left side of the window, locate the folder on your CE device where you want to place the program.**

   For the sake of consistency, consider putting it in your Program Files folder so all programs will be in the same location.

4. **Click the program file and drag it until it is on top of the CE Device folder.**

   Remember: To drag and drop, you must position the mouse pointer on the item, hold down the left mouse button as you drag the item to the appropriate location and then release the mouse button when the item is in the new location. When you release the mouse button, the Copy & Convert to Mobile Device window appears on your personal computer to display the progress as the program is copied to your CE device.

5. **To run the program, simply double-tap the program icon on your CE device.**

    Remember that you need to use the Windows CE Explorer to locate the program icon in the folder where you copied it. If you need some pointers on using the Windows CE Explorer, refer to Chapter 2.

Running an installation program

Quite often, the software developer creates an installation program that you run to install the new program on your CE device. These installation programs are almost always designed to be run from the computer that is connected to the CE device. An installation program is probably the easiest way to install a program on your CE device, because the program does all the work of copying the required files to your CE device and placing the files in the appropriate directories.

Removing a Program from Your CE Device

You have only a limited amount of storage space on your CE device. To ensure that you don't run out of space for the things you want, you will probably want to eliminate programs that you no longer use.

 The easiest way to remove a program is to select the Remove Programs icon in the Control Panel folder. The Remove Programs icon looks like an Explorer window with an X through a program icon. The Control Panel folder displays after you choose Settings⇨Control Panel from the Start menu.

When you double-tap the Remove Programs icon on your CE device, the Remove Program Properties window appears, as shown in Figure 14-3. To remove a program in the list from your CE device, tap the selected program to highlight it and then tap the Remove button. You see a message verifying that you want to delete the program, as shown in Figure 14-4. To continue the process, tap the Yes button.

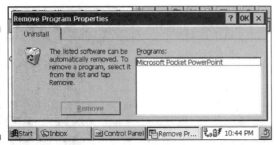

Figure 14-3:
The
Remove
Program
Properties
window.

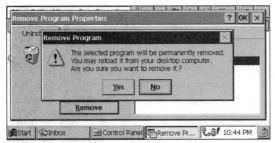

Figure 14-4:
Windows CE
verifies that
you want to
remove a
program.

If you do not see the program you want to remove listed on the Remove Program Properties window, the program was probably installed by copying the appropriate file onto your CE device, as discussed earlier in this chapter. To remove any programs not listed on the Remove Program Properties window, locate the program file by using Windows CE Explorer, highlight the program file icon, and tap the Delete button.

Part IV
Getting Online with Windows CE

The 5th Wave   By Rich Tennant

"OH YEAH, AND TRY NOT TO ENTER THE WRONG PASSWORD."

In this part . . .

In this electronic age, sending e-mail messages and connecting to the Internet are probably the most commonly performed tasks of the mobile professional. With Windows CE and your CE device, you have capabilities for sending and receiving e-mail from any location, all in the palm of your hand. Imagine being able to surf the Net while watching Monday Night Football! You find all the secrets for dealing with modems, e-mail accounts, and the Internet within this part.

Chapter 15

Connecting to a Remote Location

● ●

In This Chapter

▶ Setting up remote connections

▶ Changing the configuration setting

▶ Connecting to a computer at another location

● ●

*O*ne of the most widely mentioned capabilities of Windows CE devices is that they enable you to use a modem and connect to other sites, such as a company network or even to the Internet. To connect to a remote site, you need to create a remote connection on your CE device for that site.

In this chapter, I explain how to connect to another location from your CE device. I outline the basic requirements for creating a remote connection, and I take you step by step through the process of creating a remote connection.

Creating a Remote Connection

Windows CE comes with the built-in capability to connect to a remote location with your CE device. Using your CE device and a modem, you can connect to a computer network or even to an Internet service provider. To connect to a computer network at your work or another location, the network computer must be

✔ **Set up as a remote access server.** A remote access server is basically just a computer that is responsible for handling the connections made to the network using modems.

✔ **Using PPP (point-to-point protocol).** PPP is how your CE device communicates with the remote computer. Because PPP is the only protocol that your CE device supports, you need to make sure that the network to which you are connecting also supports PPP. (*PPP* is just another nerdy computerese term that describes the way the machines communicate across modems.) The system administrator at the location to which you want to connect can verify whether the machine is using PPP.

Before you can connect to a remote location, you need to create a remote connection specifically for that location, by completing the following steps:

1. **Tap the Start button and then choose Programs⇨Communication⇨ Remote Networking, as shown in Figure 15-1.**

   Windows CE opens the Remote Networking folder, shown in Figure 15-2. If this is the first remote connection you've created, the Remote Networking folder contains only the Make New Connection icon. After you create remote connections, they are listed in the folder, like the Internet connection shown in Figure 15-2.

Figure 15-1:
The Communication menu contains options for communicating with other computers.

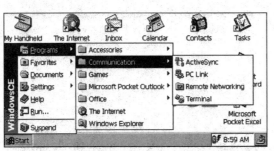

Figure 15-2:
The Remote Networking folder is home to the settings for connecting to other computer networks.

2. Tap the Make New Connection option.

After you select the Make New Connection option, the Make New Connection dialog box appears, as shown in Figure 15-3. You use this dialog box to name your new remote connection and to specify the connection type. You can actually create two different types of connections from this dialog box:

- **Dial-Up Connection:** Select this remote connection type if you plan to use your modem to make the connection.

- **Direct Connection:** Select this type if you plan to connect your CE device to a computer by using the serial interface cable or the infrared port. You normally only select this connection type if you are setting up a connection between your CE device and a personal computer.

3. Type the name of your new remote connection.

Type a name that is different from any other connections that you have on your CE device. Remote connections are just like files — you cannot have two with the same name on your CE device.

REMEMBER

Figure 15-3:
Type a
unique
name for
your new
remote
connection.

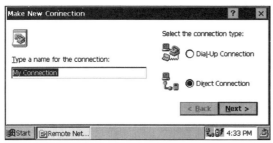

4. Tap the Dial-Up Connection option.

Doing so enables you to create a remote connection for your modem. You will probably select this option most often because the direct connection between your computer and CE device is created when you set up the Windows CE Services software on your computer. So the only time you select the Direct Connection option is if you need to create a connection to a different personal computer.

5. Tap the Next button.

The Make New Dial-Up Connection dialog box appears, as shown in Figure 15-4.

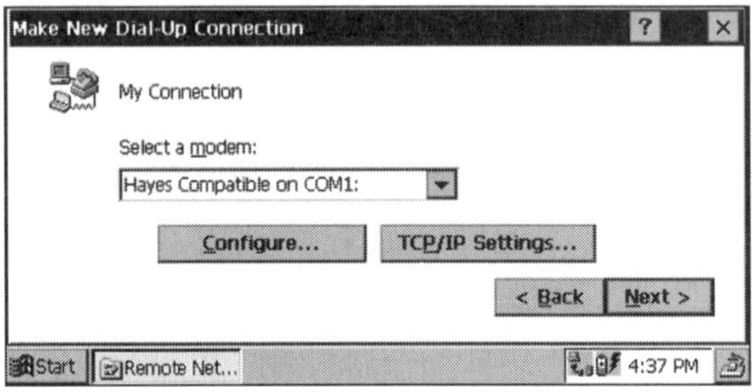

Figure 15-4:
The Make
New
Dial-Up
Connection
dialog box.

6. **Make sure that the Select a modem drop-down list box contains the name of your modem.**

   If your modem is not listed, tap the down-arrow button and highlight the name of your modem. If your modem is not listed in the drop-down list, it may not be properly connected to your device. You need to make sure that the modem is connected to your CE device properly, based on the installation instructions that come with the modem.

   You can enter special settings for your dial-up connection by tapping the Configure button and the TCP/IP Settings button. I provide specific information about each of these buttons in the following sections.

7. **Tap the Next button to display the next screen, shown in Figure 15-5.**

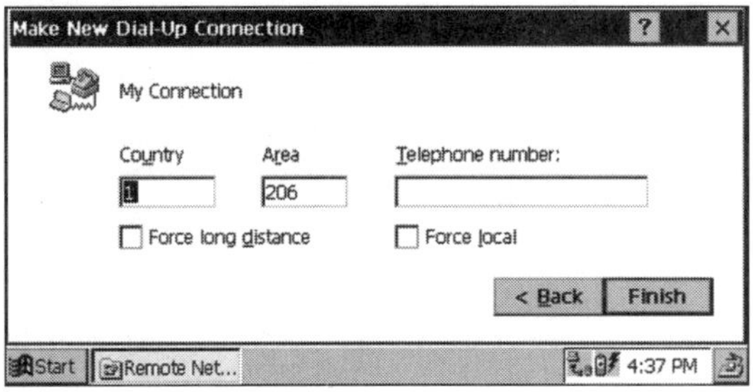

Figure 15-5:
Indicate the
dialing
information
for the
remote
connection.

8. **Type the country code for the remote connection in the Country field.**

   The country code is only necessary if you are dialing from one country to another. If you are calling a location within your country, the Country field contains the long-distance access for your country. For example, in the United States, this code is 1.

9. **Type the area code for the remote connection in the Area field.**

   You can find out the area code for most cities, as well as country codes, in the World Clock program on your CE device. The quickest way to run this program is to double-tap the time display in the bottom-right corner of the desktop. (For more information, see Chapter 19.)

10. **Type the phone number for the remote connection in the Telephone number field.**

11. **Select the Force long distance check box if necessary.**

    If the phone number for your remote connection is a long-distance number, you need to make sure that the check box next to this option contains a check mark. This step is especially important to remember if the connection number shares the same area code as you do, but the phone call is still considered long-distance.

12. **Select the Force local check box if necessary.**

    If the phone number for your remote connection has a different area code from your current location, but it is not a long-distance call, you need to make sure that the check box next to this option contains a check mark.

13. **Tap the Finish button to save the new remote connection.**

Before you save the connection, you can tap the Configure button and configure the connection, or you can tap the TCP/IP Settings button and change the TCP/IP settings for your remote connection. If you are not sure of these settings right now, you can set or modify them at any time after you create the remote connection. In the following sections of this chapter, you can find more information about entering the proper information for these settings.

Configuring a connection

You may need to change the configuration settings for the remote connection. This step is necessary if you need to change the connection settings for the modem, make sure that the terminal window appears during the connection, or even indicate how long Windows CE should let the phone ring before a connection is made. To modify the connection settings, tap the Configure button in the Make New Dial-Up Connection dialog box to display the Device Properties dialog box, shown in Figure 15-6.

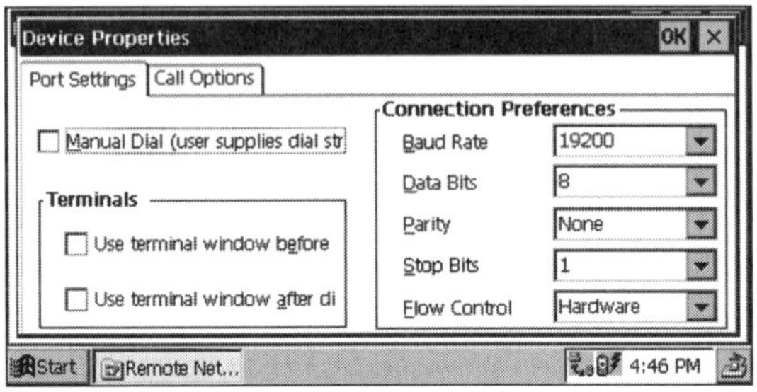

Figure 15-6: Indicate how the modem should connect to the remote connection.

Dialing patterns

You may need to use different dialing methods with your modem when you are connecting from different locations. For example, if you are making a connection from a pay phone, you probably want to use a calling card, so you need to tell the modem to wait for the calling card tone and then dial the calling card number.

You use a standard list of characters under Windows CE to send added instructions to your modem. You normally enter these extra characters in the Extra Settings field on the Call Options tab of the Device Properties dialog box. You may use any combination of the characters listed in the following table.

Character	Purpose
0–9	Indicates a numeric character that is part of the dialing string.
E	Dials the country code that is indicated by the program that is dialing the modem.
F	Dials the area code that is indicated by the program that is dialing the modem.
G	Dials the local number that is indicated by the program that is dialing the modem.
P	Indicates that the digits that follow should be pulse dialed.
T	Indicates that the digits that follow should be tone dialed.
W	Waits for a second dial tone. You normally want to use this code after entering a credit card number to wait for the next dial tone.
$	Waits for the credit card tone.
,	Inserts a pause in the dialing string. The length of the pause is determined by the specific modem, but it is usually about two seconds.
!	Transfers to another extension.
@	Waits for a quiet answer — no noise on the other end of the line. This quiet answer normally indicates that the modem has made a connection.
A,B,C,D,*,#	Used on some tone systems for special control characters. The purpose of these characters varies. You will probably rarely use these characters.

Port settings

You use the options on the Port Settings tab of the Device Properties dialog box to specify how the modem actually connects to the remote location.

Some types of remote connections may require you to manually log into the machine. Manually logging in is normally done by using a *terminal window,* which means that you basically get a blank screen on which you enter the information required to connect to the network. For most Internet connections, manual login is not required, although if you know or have been informed by a system administrator that the connection you are making requires a manual connection, you probably need to select one of the terminal options. Select the first check box to display the terminal window before the call is placed so that you can type in any required strings; the other check box displays a terminal window after dialing the number — this is probably the most common selection.

The Connection Preferences section contains different preferences that you can select to inform the modem how to connect to the remote location. The fields in this section automatically contain a default set of values. If you need to change any of the values in those fields, tap the down-arrow button next to the appropriate field and tap the value you want to input for the field. Again, you should change these fields only if you have been informed that you need to connect with a different set of values (or your modem requires them — refer to the modem documentation). Use only the values you are provided for each of these fields. Each of these fields affects the way your CE device makes the connection.

The best recommendation I can offer for setting the baud rate is to set it to the maximum speed your modem can attain when using compression. For example, your 33.6 Kbps modem may be capable of 57,600 bps with compression. Refer to the hardware documentation for your modem to figure out its full capabilities.

Call options

Figure 15-7 shows the options on the Call Options tab of the Device Properties dialog box. These options enable you to indicate how much time should elapse between certain events during the call.

You can indicate a specific amount of time that the modem should wait for a connection before hanging up. You do so by selecting the check box next to the field Cancel the call if not connected within and then typing the appropriate number of seconds in the seconds field.

To ensure that the modem does not start dialing without a dial tone, select the check box next to the Wait for Dial Tone before Dialing option. Of course, if you are going to make a credit card call, you want to wait for a dial tone, so specify the amount of time that your modem should wait for a dial tone in the field next to the option Wait for credit card tone.

Figure 15-7:
Indicate the
amount of
time that
the modem
should wait
for different
events to
transpire.

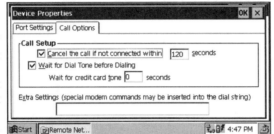

You may want, or even need, to add some special strings of characters to the characters that the modem dials to connect to your remote connection. These characters can be used to indicate that you are placing a credit card call, to insert a pause when attempting to access an outside line, or to wait for a second dial tone. You specify these special characters in the Extra Settings field. Check out the "Dialing patterns" sidebar for more information about the different dialing pattern characters that you can use.

Modifying the TCP/IP settings

When you create a remote connection under Windows CE, another button you can select in the Make New Dial-Up Connection dialog box is the TCP/IP Settings button. When you tap this button, the TCP/IP Settings dialog box appears, as shown in Figure 15-8. The settings in this dialog box are required for most types of remote connections.

TCP/IP deals with the communication between different types of computers. This standard communications protocol was developed so that computers with different operating systems could talk to each other. TCP/IP is used as the standard communications protocol on the Internet. In case you are really curious, TCP/IP stands for Transmission Control Protocol/Internet Protocol. (Test that one out on your friends.)

Quite often, the remote connection that you want to use requires you to specify certain addresses so that your device can connect properly. These address settings are specified by selecting the TCP/IP Settings button on the Make New Dial-Up Connection dialog box.

The TCP/IP Settings dialog box has two tab options: General and Name Servers. The first tab deals with the IP address, and the second tab, Name Servers, deals with setting DNS and WINS addresses. You can refer to the descriptions in Table 15-1 to determine the purpose of each field. Before you type any values in these fields, check with your systems administrator (if connecting to an internal company network) or with your Internet service provider to get the required values for each field.

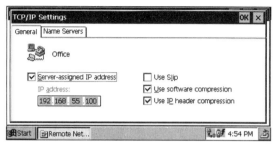

Figure 15-8:
Indicate the
server
addresses
for your
remote
connection.

Table 15-1	TCP/IP Settings
Setting	***Description***
IP address	This address, specified on the General tab, tells the Internet where to send information you request while connected to an Internet service provider. If you have a *static IP address,* you need to remove the check mark from the Server-assigned IP address check box and type the address in the IP address field. A static IP address means that the address for your CE device connection on the Internet is always the same. This type of situation normally only occurs if you have a machine that is constantly connected to the Internet. With most Internet service providers, the IP address is assigned to you each time you connect to the Internet, so you will want to keep a check mark in the Server-assigned IP address check box.
DNS address	This is the address of a machine, running the *domain naming system,* that is responsible for converting the name you request to a physical IP address on the Internet. It is specified on the Name Servers tab. For example, if you type www.microsoft .com, in Pocket Internet Explorer, the DNS server converts it to the physical address of 207.68.156.73. You may need to specify the location of the DNS server that you need to use. If so, remove the check mark from the Server-assigned addresses check box and type the address in the Primary DNS field. Some Internet service providers have more than one DNS address for converting IP addresses; if you receive more than one address, type the second one in the Secondary DNS field.

(continued)

Table 15-1 *(continued)*

Setting	Description
WINS address	This is the address of a Windows NT server, running the Windows Internet Naming Service, that is responsible for resolving the IP addresses for Internet sites that you request. It is specified on the Name Servers tab. The server also normally assigns IP addresses to computers within the internal computer network of a company. You may need to specify the location of the WINS server that you need to use. If so, remove the check mark from the Server assigned addresses check box and type the address in the Primary WINS field. Again, some Internet service providers have more than one DNS address for converting IP addresses; if you receive more than one address, type the second one in the Secondary WINS field.

Changing the settings for a remote connection

 Doesn't it seem that as soon as you get something set up, it needs to be modified for one reason or another? Windows CE has planned for just such an occurrence. You can change most of the information for a remote connection by locating the desired connection in the Remote Networking folder and selecting the Properties icon on the toolbar. The Properties icon resembles a list with a hand at the top of it. (Or you can choose File➪Properties from the Remote Networking folder.)

After you tap the Properties icon, the Dial-Up Connection dialog box appears with the information for the selected remote connection, as shown in Figure 15-9. In this dialog box, you can modify the phone number settings, configure the connection, or change the TCP/IP settings for the connection.

Figure 15-9:
Make modifications to a remote connection in the Dial-Up Connection dialog box.

To modify the way the modem actually connects to the remote location, tap the Configure button. Doing so displays the Device Properties dialog box, which you can use to adjust your settings.

Connecting to a Remote Location

After you create a remote connection on your CE device, you can quickly connect to the remote site at any time. The following steps tell you how to connect to the remote site:

1. Locate the icon for your remote connection.

The remote connection icons are normally located in the Remote Networking folder, as shown in Figure 15-10. You can find this folder by tapping the Start button and then choosing Programs➪Communication➪Remote Connections.

Figure 15-10:
Double-tap the appropriate remote connection icon.

2. Double-tap the selected remote connection icon.

After you double-tap the icon, the Dial-Up Connection dialog box appears, enabling you to type the connection information for your account, as shown in Figure 15-11.

Figure 15-11:
Connect your modem to the phone line before tapping the Connect button.

3. Type your user name in the Underline-U-ser Name field.

Use the user name that was assigned to you by the remote site to which you're attempting to connect. This user name is the one that you received when you set up your remote login account; if you are connecting to a machine at work, quite often this is the same user name that you connect with at work.

4. Type your password in the Underline-P-assword field.

5. If required, type a domain name in the Do_m_ain field.

This field is normally not needed for Internet connections. The Domain field is normally used when connecting to an internal network at a company. If you need to type a value in this field, you should receive that information when you set up your account with either the Internet service provider or the systems administrator.

6. Select the check box next to the Underline-S-ave password field.

By having your CE device remember your password and user name information, you don't have to type the information each time you want to connect to the Internet. However, if you share the CE device with someone else, you may not want to select this check box.

7. Tap the Connect button.

The modem dials the phone number and connects to your remote site.

By using the Save password option, you don't have to worry about forgetting or mistyping your user name, your password, or even the domain name. Your device automatically remembers this information, and if other people look at the screen, they won't be able to figure out your password because Windows CE displays asterisks in place of the characters in your password.

Turning off call waiting

If you are lucky enough to have access to that ever-popular calling feature known as call waiting, you will soon find that it is not much of a blessing when it comes to using a modem. Those little beeps indicating that someone else is on the line can cause your modem to hang up. To eliminate this problem, you can either cancel your call waiting service, which is probably not the answer you want to hear, or you can have your CE device disable call waiting when you are using your modem.

To disable call waiting temporarily, you need to get the code that disables it from your local phone company. Each phone company has its own code that you can enter before placing a phone call to temporarily disable the call waiting service during that call. For example, some phone companies have you enter the code *70 before dialing a phone number to disable the call waiting feature.

After you know the code for disabling call waiting, tap the Dial Properties button in the Dial-Up Connection dialog box to display the Communications Properties dialog box, shown in Figure 15-12. Or you can double-tap the Communications icon in the Control Panel folder.

Figure 15-12:
Select the option Disable call waiting by dialing and then specify the disable code.

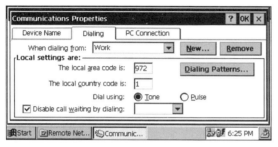

Select the check box next to the option Disable call waiting by dialing. In the drop-down list box next to the option, select the code that your phone company uses to disable call waiting. If you don't see the correct code in the list, type the code in the field next to the down-arrow button.

Don't worry about turning your call waiting back on. With most phone companies, the call waiting option is only disabled during one phone call. As soon as you hang up the phone, call waiting starts working again.

Connecting from a different location

Because your CE device is so mobile, you'll probably use it in all kinds of places. For example, you may be on vacation in Florida and want to check your e-mail messages at work (not that anyone would do that on vacation, but it's a good example). You can set up different locations on your CE device from which to dial, thus enabling you to dial into the office from Florida without altering the settings for your home location.

To set up a new dialing location, you need to use the Dialing tab on the Communications Properties dialog box. This dialog box appears after you tap the Dial Properties button in the Dial-Up Connection dialog box. The field labeled When dialing from, at the top of the dialog box, indicates the name of the current *dialing from* location. To create a new location, tap the New button and type the name of the new location in the window, as shown in Figure 15-13.

Figure 15-13:
Type a
unique name
for the
dialing
location and
tap the OK
button.

Remember to specify the local area code for the new location and the local country code. If you are unsure of the area code, check the World Clock program — it contains area codes and country codes for many locations.

After you create a location, you can select it by simply tapping the down-arrow button next to the When dialing from field and highlighting the appropriate location in the drop-down list.

You can remove dialing locations from the list by selecting a location from the drop-down list and then tapping the Remove button.

Chapter 16

Connecting to the Internet

● ●

In This Chapter

▶ Setting up your Internet connection

▶ Locating information on the Internet

▶ Customizing the way you view information on the Internet

● ●

Connecting to the Internet has gone from being a casual pastime to a way of life for many people. Now with Windows CE, you can connect to the Internet from any location.

This chapter explains the basic requirements for connecting to the Internet. I also explain how to connect to the Internet and locate the information you want — all from the comfort of your CE device.

Setting Up Your Internet Connection

You are almost ready to start exploring the Internet; but before you can start, you need to figure out how you are going to connect to the Internet. Unfortunately, nothing these days is ever really free, and the same goes for connecting to the Internet. If you are lucky enough to have access to an Internet connection through your work, I guess you may be able to connect for free and let your boss pick up the tab. But for the rest of us, getting on the Internet is similar to subscribing to cable television.

If you don't currently have Internet access, you need to locate an Internet Service Provider (commonly referred to by Internet geeks as an ISP). You can find an ISP by looking in the yellow pages or on billboards or even by checking with your local computer store.

Internet Service Providers normally charge a monthly access fee for you to use their Internet connection so that you can send e-mail messages and explore the Net. This monthly charge is usually either for a set number of hours a month or a flat fee for unlimited usage. The ISP market is competitive and so are the rates. Base the type of service that you choose on your own personal needs. If you plan to spend a lot of time on the Internet, for example, you will probably find an ISP that provides you an unlimited number of connection hours more economical.

After you establish an Internet account with a provider, you're ready to connect to the Internet. To do so, you need to create a remote connection for your Internet service provider's site by using the Remote Networking options, which I cover in Chapter 15. To create the remote connection, you need to know the phone number that your modem dials to connect to your ISP.

Keep in mind that most ISPs will tell you that their service doesn't support Windows CE or your CE device. This assertion is more a result of ignorance than fact. Many ISPs just don't have a clear understanding about the capabilities of CE devices. All CE devices can connect to the Internet through an ISP. I suggest that you set up an Internet connection on your personal computer along with your Windows CE connection. That way, if you do have a problem connecting to the Internet on your CE device, you can test things with your personal computer before calling your ISP's support department. Based on my own experience, most ISPs aren't going to be much help when you're having trouble connecting with your CE device, for the simple fact that they can't visualize what you are actually doing. Of course, as Windows CE becomes more widely used, this will become less of a problem.

Manually connecting to the Internet

After you create a remote connection on your CE device to your Internet service provider, you can quickly connect to the Internet at any time. Remember, you must have a modem that is connected both to your CE device and to a phone line; otherwise, your efforts to connect to the Internet will be in vain. The following steps illustrate the process of manually connecting to the Internet:

1. **Double-tap the remote connection icon for your Internet service provider.**

   You can find the icon in the Remote Networking folder — choose Programs➪Communication➪Remote Networking from the Start menu. When you double-tap the icon, the Dial-Up Connection dialog box appears and enables you to type the connection information for your account, as shown in Figure 16-1.

2. **Type your user name in the User Name text box.**

   Type the user name that your ISP assigned you.

3. **Type your password in the Password text box.**

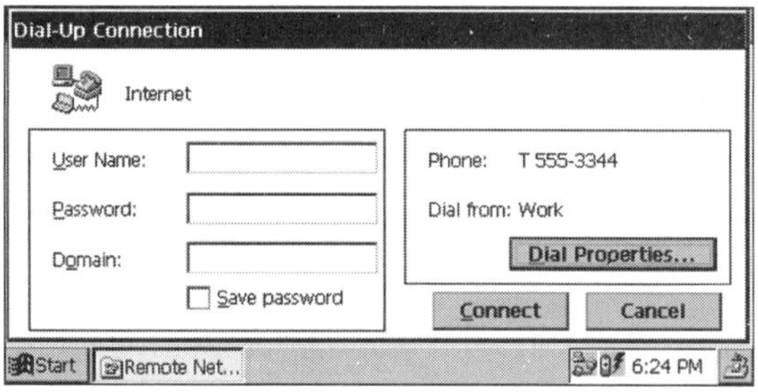

Figure 16-1:
Connect
your
modem to
your CE
device
before
tapping the
Connect
button.

4. **If required, type a domain name in the Domain text box.**

   Most Internet connections don't require this field. Normally, you use the Domain text box only when you are connecting from an internal network at a company. If you need to type a value in this field, you can receive that information when you set up your Internet account.

5. **Select the Save password check box.**

   By using the Save password option, you don't have to worry about forgetting or mistyping your user name or password. Your CE device automatically remembers this information for you. If other people look at this screen, don't worry — they can't figure out your password, because Windows CE displays asterisks in place of the characters in your password. If you share your CE device with someone else, however, you may not want to select this check box.

6. **Tap the Connect button**.

   The modem dials the phone number and connects to your Internet Service Provider.

7. **Double-tap the Pocket Internet Explorer icon.**

   This icon is located on your desktop. If you can't find it, choose Programs➪The Internet from the Start menu. When you double-tap the Pocket Internet Explorer icon, you get your default Web page loaded within the Pocket Internet Explorer. You are now ready to start browsing the Web.

Setting the automatic dialing option

With Windows CE, you can set up Pocket Internet Explorer to automatically dial out to your ISP whenever you want to view a site on the Internet. This is a handy feature to use because it eliminates the need for you to go and locate your Internet connection. Whenever you request to look at a Web site, the Dial-Up Connection dialog box automatically appears and enables you to quickly connect to the Internet.

You can also specify the amount of time that you want your CE device to remain connected to the Internet if you are not using it. This option eliminates the risk of your forgetting to disconnect when you finish surfing. This option is especially valuable if you have to pay an hourly rate for your Internet service.

To set up the automatic dialing options for your Internet connection, follow these steps within the Pocket Internet Explorer program:

1. **Choose <u>V</u>iew⇨<u>O</u>ptions.**

   The Options dialog box appears.

2. **Tap the Auto Dial tab (see Figure 16-2).**

   By using the Auto Dial options, when you close the Pocket Internet Explorer program, Windows CE automatically disconnects from your ISP.

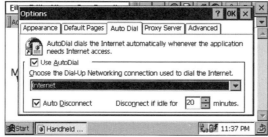

Figure 16-2:
The Auto
Dial option
automatically
connects
you to the
Internet.

3. **Select the Use <u>A</u>utoDial check box.**

   Remember, you simply need to tap the check box with the stylus to select or unselect an option.

4. **Select the remote connection that you want to use to connect to your Internet service provider.**

   To select a connection, tap the down-arrow button and highlight the appropriate connection in the drop-down list box.

5. **Select the Auto <u>D</u>isconnect check box.**

   This selection is optional. By using it, you ensure that your CE device always disconnects after a specified amount of time has passed since you used it.

6. **Specify the amount of time the CE device should sit idle before hanging up.**

7. **Tap the OK button to close the Options dialog box and save the settings.**

Browsing the Internet

Well, if you're reading this section, you have probably jumped through all the proper hoops and are ready to start exploring the Internet. If you have never experienced the Internet, you are in for quite an adventure.

Surfing the Internet essentially means looking at different locations on the Internet that both companies and individuals have developed. These Internet locations are commonly referred to as *Web sites*.

Working with proxy servers

Quite often, companies set up proxy servers for their employees to use when connecting to the Internet. A proxy server essentially provides a means for the company to keep employees from viewing nonbusiness-related web sites. It basically filters out sites that employees should not be browsing. Use of a proxy server also provides a performance gain because commonly accessed Web sites are cached on the proxy server.

If you are attempting to connect to the Internet by using an Internet connection at your company, you may find it necessary to use a proxy server. If you're unsure whether this is required, check with your network administrator. If you need to use a proxy server, get the proxy server address information from your network administrator.

To set up the proxy server information, choose View⇨Options in Pocket Internet Explorer.

When the Options dialog box appears, tap the Proxy Server tab, as shown in the figure.

Select the Use Proxy Server check box. Then type the proxy server address in the Proxy Server field and the port information in the Port text box.

Keep in mind that Pocket Internet Explorer works only with proxy servers that comply with the CERN proxy server standard. I know this sounds like Greek, but essentially, before attempting to set up the proxy server information, double-check to see if the proxy server is compliant with this standard to avoid any additional headaches. If the proxy server is not compliant with this standard, you need to find another method for connecting your CE device to the Internet.

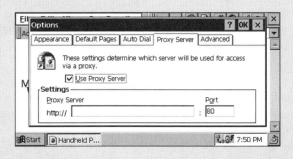

Using the Pocket Internet Explorer toolbar

Pocket Internet Explorer provides several buttons on the toolbar at the top of the screen. The only drawback to using the toolbar buttons is trying to figure out what each button does. Unfortunately, the buttons are not labeled. So to help ease the frustration of tapping the wrong button, you can find a description of each button in Table 16-1.

Table 16-1	Pocket Internet Explorer Toolbar Buttons
Button	**Description**
⬅	Scrolls back to the previous Web page.
➡	Scrolls forward to the next Web page.
⊗	Stops a process. You tap this button if you want to cancel a Web page you requested or to stop a search.
↻	Reloads the Web page that you are viewing, commonly referred to as *refreshing the page*.
⌂	Displays your home page, which is whatever page you specify as your default start page.
⊙	Displays your default search page. This page helps you look for specific information on the Internet.
A	Changes the size of the characters displayed on the Web page. Five different sizes of characters are available (Largest, Large, Medium, Small, and Smallest). Each time you tap this button, the characters change to a different size. Simply continue tapping the button until you find a size that you like. You may find that you need to change the size of the characters as you go to different sites.
?	Provides help information for Pocket Internet Explorer. (Of course, it won't be as helpful as this book, but nothing is perfect.)

Keep in mind that all the toolbar buttons are also listed in the menus. So if you don't want to decipher little pictures, go ahead and use the menus. But after you use the buttons a few times, I'm sure you'll realize that tapping a button is much faster than finding a menu option.

Jumping to a new location

Nowadays, it seems everyone has an Internet address. How often have you heard someone say "Come visit us on the Web at www..." and then proceed to list a long string of characters? Well, those long character strings are commonly referred to as *Internet addresses* or, if you want to sound really technical, *URLs* (uniform resource locators). You use these addresses to locate information on the Internet. Each person, business, organization, school, and so on, on the Internet has a unique address. For example, if you want to visit the Microsoft Web site, you simply type the address **www.microsoft.com**.

To make it simple to jump to an address, Pocket Internet Explorer comes with an Address field in which you can type the desired address, as shown in Figure 16-3. Simply type the desired address in this field and press the Enter key; Pocket Internet Explorer locates the Web site you specified.

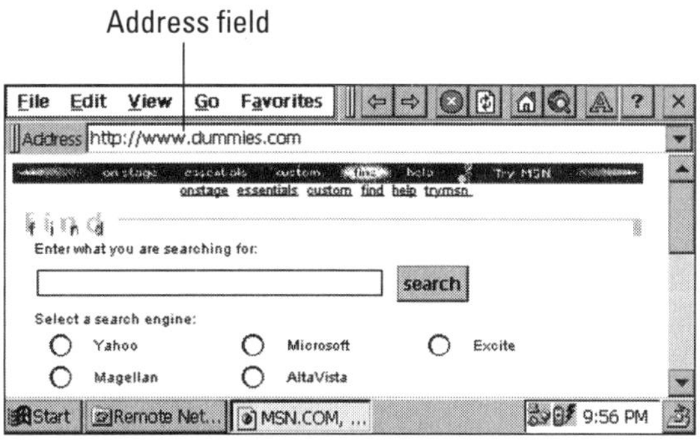

Address field

Figure 16-3:
Type the
exact
address of
the location
you want to
explore.

Typing an Internet address is a lot like dialing a phone number: If you don't type the characters exactly right, you are going to end up getting a wrong number. To view the desired Web site, type the correct address in the Address field. If you have visited this Web site before, it may be listed in the Address drop-down list box. Tap the down-arrow button to see which addresses Windows CE has saved.

If you have already typed the desired address in the field, you can try tapping the down-arrow button and selecting the address from the list of past addresses.

You can also open up a document on your CE device by typing the location of the document in the Address line. This option is useful for people who have created HTML documents on their CE device. By the way, an HTML (hypertext markup language) document is a document created in a format that can be viewed using an Internet browser program, such as Pocket Internet Explorer. Although these documents are normally placed on Web sites, they can also exist on any computer or CE device.

Searching for a specific site on the Internet

You have no way of knowing the address of every Web site that you may want to look at, and luckily you don't have to. Several programs, commonly referred to as *search engines,* keep track of different Web sites. If you are looking for information on a specific topic, you simply type the topic on the search engine page, and you get a list of several Web sites that discuss your topic. For example, Figure 16-4 shows the results of using a search engine to locate Web sites that discuss scuba diving.

Figure 16-4:
You can locate all the sites that discuss a topic by using a search engine.

Your Pocket Internet Explorer program comes set up to use a default search site whenever you request a search. To display the search site, you can either tap the Search button or choose Go➪Search the Web. Because search engines look at Web sites all around the world to find your specified topic, the Search button resembles a world with a magnifying glass over it. After you tap the Search button, your default search page appears, as shown in Figure 16-5. This page has links to several different search engines available on the Internet.

Figure 16-5:
Enter the information you want to find and then tap the Search button.

If you don't find the information you are looking for with the first search, try selecting a different search engine. Your search page comes with the capability to search the Internet by using any one of seven different search engines, and each one is bound to locate different Web sites. To select a search engine, simply tap its radio button. If you cannot see the radio buttons for the search engines, tap the scroll bar to scroll down the page until the radio buttons are visible. By the way, when you first open the default search page, none of the radio buttons are selected, and it just randomly picks a search engine for the search; selecting a radio button ensures you get a search from the desired search engine.

Deja view: Returning to a page you've previously viewed

Viewing Web sites on the Internet is similar to reading a book: At any time during the process, you may decide you want to go back and read the information on a previous page again. To make it easy to return to a previously viewed Web site, Pocket Internet Explorer comes with a couple of different options.

The easiest way to jump back to a previously viewed page is to tap the Back button on the toolbar. This button enables you to scroll back through the different Web sites you have visited during your current Internet session. The only drawback is that you have to wait for each site to reload while you look for the one you want to see.

To move forward through the previously viewed Web sites, tap the Next button on the toolbar. This button enables you to scroll forward until you get to the last new page that you viewed.

Another way to locate a previously viewed Web page is to look at your viewing history. Pocket Internet Explorer keeps a list of the Web sites that you have visited and calls it your history. To view the history list, choose Go⇨History to display the History window, shown in Figure 16-6. On the History window, select the page you want to go back to and then tap the OK button. Pocket Internet Explorer displays the selected page without forcing you to scroll through all of the previously viewed pages.

Saving Your Favorite Sites

You can keep track of Web sites that you may want to visit again by storing their addresses in your list of favorites. Storing a favorite site is as easy as setting a bookmark in a favorite book. To store the address of the Web site that you are currently viewing, choose Favorites⇨Add to Favorites to display the Add To Favorites dialog box, shown in Figure 16-7.

Figure 16-6:
Highlight
the Web
site to
select it
and then
tap the OK
button.

Figure 16-7:
Tap the OK
button to
add the
current
Web page
to your list
of favorites.

The Name field provides the name of the Web site that you are currently viewing. This is the name that is stored when you tap the OK button. If you want to use a different name to refer to this Web page, type that name in the Name field. You can call the page anything you want — after you select the name you assign, Pocket Internet Explorer jumps to the page you want to view.

In the Add To Favorites dialog box, you can also create different folders to store related favorite Web sites. For example, you could create a Windows CE folder where you could place all the Web sites that relate to Windows CE. To create a new folder, simply tap the New Folder button in the Add To Favorites dialog box. Remember, the New Folder button looks the same in all Windows CE programs (it resembles a folder with a starburst behind it). When you tap the New Folder button, a folder is added with the words New Folder highlighted. Simply type the desired name for the folder you are creating.

Jumping to a favorite Web site

If you have created bookmarks for your favorite Web sites, you can display them anytime you want to review the information they contain. To view your list of favorite Web sites, tap the Favorites menu and then select the name of the Web site you want to view, as shown in Figure 16-8.

Favorite sites

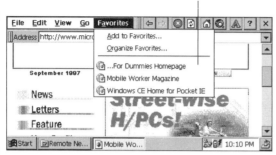

Figure 16-8: On the Favorites menu, tap the name of the site you want to view.

If you are not currently connected to the Internet but you have set up the Auto Dial option, Windows CE attempts to connect to the Internet. If Windows CE connects, it then displays the Web site you selected.

You can also see your list of favorite sites by selecting the Favorites option on the Start menu. When you tap a site, Windows CE attempts to connect to the Internet and show you the site.

In a process called *caching,* Pocket Internet Explorer actually keeps a copy of each Web site you visit in the Temporary Internet Files folder. When you select a favorite site, if a copy of the Web site is in your cache file (the Temporary Internet Files folder) that copy of the Web site is loaded and Pocket Internet Explorer does not connect to the Internet. Unfortunately, this copy may not contain the most recent information for the Web site. To force Pocket Internet Explorer to update the Web site, tap the Refresh button on the toolbar. This causes Pocket Internet Explorer to connect to your ISP (if you have Auto Dial selected) and locate the selected Web site.

Creating shortcuts on the desktop

If you have a Web site that you visit often, you may want to create a shortcut for that Web site on your desktop. For example, you may regularly check a particular Web site to see the latest stock prices. If you have a shortcut for that site on your desktop, you can load Pocket Internet Explorer, and it will connect to the Internet and quickly locate the Web site you selected. Creating the desktop shortcut saves you the trouble of manually opening Pocket Internet Explorer and then locating the desired Web site in your favorites list.

All right, that all sounds nice. But you want to know how to accomplish this astounding feat — right? To create a desktop shortcut for a Web site, you need to make sure that the Web site is displayed on the screen in Pocket Internet Explorer. Then choose File⇨Send To⇨Desktop as Shortcut. An icon is added to your Windows CE desktop with the name of the current Web site, as shown in Figure 16-9.

Web site shortcut

Figure 16-9:
You can easily add icons for your most frequently visited Web sites.

 Don't add too many different Web site shortcuts to your desktop, or it will become cluttered and locating information will be a hassle. If you want to remove a Web site shortcut from your desktop, drag-and-drop it into the Recycle Bin.

Customizing Your Browser

Although Pocket Internet Explorer comes with several standard settings, you can customize the browser to fit your own needs. For example, you can have a specific page loaded whenever you run Pocket Internet Explorer.

You can accomplish most of your Pocket Internet Explorer customization tasks by using the Options dialog box. This dialog box appears when you choose View⇨Options.

Specifying a different home page

 Your home page is the page that is always loaded first when you run Pocket Internet Explorer on your CE device. It is also the page that is loaded when you tap the Home button. The Home button is easy to spot because it looks just like a little house.

When you install Pocket Internet Explorer on your CE device, a default home page is also loaded onto your CE device. The default page that is loaded when you run Pocket Internet Explorer is called default.htm.

You may decide that you want to use a different page for your home page whenever you run Pocket Internet Explorer. For example, you may want to use a company page as a home page or even a favorite Web site.

Keep in mind that if you set your home page as a page that is not loaded on your CE device, you will be prompted to connect to the Internet immediately when you run Pocket Internet Explorer. To eliminate this problem, make sure that the Save Password check box is checked in the Dial-Up Connection dialog box.

To set your home page, choose View⇨Options and tap the Default Pages tab, as shown in Figure 16-10.

Figure 16-10:
You can
quickly
select a new
home page
for Internet
Pocket
Explorer.

To set a Web page you are currently viewing in Pocket Internet Explorer as your new home page, follow these steps:

1. **Make sure the drop-down list box has the value Home Page selected.**

   If you do not see the words Home Page in the field next to the word Your, tap the down-arrow button and select the Home Page option.

2. **Tap the Use Current Page button.**

   The address of the Web site you are currently viewing in Pocket Internet Explorer appears above the Use Current Page button as the address of your home page.

3. **Tap the OK button to close the Options dialog box and save the settings.**

To switch back to the default home page that came with Pocket Internet Explorer, tap the Use Default Page button on the Default Pages tab of the Options dialog box.

Specifying a different search page

 Your search page is similar to the appendix in a book: You tell it a certain word or phrase that relates to the information you are looking for and it provides you a list of the closest matches to that word. You can load the search page when you tap the Search button on the toolbar. The Search button looks just like a world with a magnifying glass sitting on top of it.

When you install Pocket Internet Explorer on your CE device, you already have a default search page. The default search page is a Web site that Microsoft established to give you access to several of the major search engines on the Internet. Search engines are actually just programs that run on the Internet and keep track of different Web sites containing the information that you are looking for.

You may decide that you want to use a different page for your search page within Pocket Internet Explorer. To set your search page, choose View⇨ Options to display the Options dialog box. In the Options dialog box, tap the Default Pages tab, as shown in Figure 16-11.

Figure 16-11:
You can quickly select a new search page for Pocket Internet Explorer.

To set the Web page you are currently viewing in Pocket Internet Explorer as your new search page, follow these steps

1. **Make sure that the drop-down list box has the value Search Page selected.**

   If you do not see the words Search Page in the field next to the word Your, tap the down-arrow button and then select the Search Page option.

2. Tap the Use Current Page button.

The address of the Web site you are currently viewing in Pocket Internet Explorer appears above the Use Current Page button as the address of your search page.

3. Tap the OK button to close the Options dialog box and save the settings.

To switch back to the default search page that came with Pocket Internet Explorer, tap the Use Default Page button on the Default Pages tab of the Options dialog box.

Changing the appearance of Web pages

Unfortunately, with a screen smaller than the one on your personal computer, it's not as easy to view Web pages as it is on your personal computer. You may even find that certain added features, such as pictures and sounds, slow down your CE device's capability to display Web pages adequately.

To change the way Web pages appear on your CE device, choose View⇨Options and tap the Appearance tab, shown in Figure 16-12.

Figure 16-12: You can modify the way a Web page displays on your CE device.

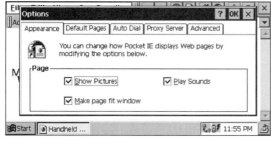

You can use three options to specify how you want different Web pages to appear on your CE device. To select one of these options on the Appearance tab, simply tap the check box next to the desired option to add or remove the check mark. Table 16-2 provides a description of the effect that each one of these options causes on your Web pages.

Table 16-2	Web Page Appearance Options
Option	*Description*
Show Pictures	Displays all the Web page's pictures. If you turn off this option, the site loads without taking the time to download the pictures that normally appear on the Web site. You can still see the locations where the pictures normally appear.
Play Sounds	Plays all the Web site's sounds. If you turn off this option, Web sites with sounds load faster because the sound files don't have to download.
Make page fit window	Adjusts the sizing of the Web page to make sure that the entire page appears within the width of your screen. If you select this option, you may find that some tables and images are too small and difficult to see; to resolve the problem, unselect this option.

Chapter 17

Sending and Receiving E-Mail

*T*hese days, e-mail is a way of life in the workplace. Quite often, whole meetings transpire solely through the use of e-mail. Windows CE affords you the luxury of maintaining constant contact via e-mail from any location, either at your company, on the Internet, or both.

This chapter explains how to send and receive e-mail messages by using Windows CE. I also discuss customizing your e-mail environment by doing such things as creating folders for related mail messages.

Connecting to a Mail Server

To send e-mail messages, you must connect to a mail server. The *mail server* is a machine at the remote connection that is responsible for sending your messages to the appropriate addresses and delivering messages that you receive into your mailbox, or *e-mail account*. You can find out more about creating remote connections in Chapter 15.

Most people compose the messages they want to send and then connect to the mail server to send the messages, which is commonly called *working offline*. You can connect to the server and then create your messages while online, but if you are charged for connect time to your Internet service provider, you probably want to remain connected for the minimum amount of time necessary.

Before you connect to a mail server, you need to set up your e-mail account information by using the Inbox program on your CE device. The following sections describe how to locate the Inbox program, create an e-mail account, and use your CE device's modem to send and receive messages.

Locating the Inbox program

Before you can send e-mail messages from your CE device, you need to locate the Inbox program. The Inbox icon looks like a letter with an envelope sitting on top of it. After you locate the icon, double-tap it to display the Inbox program.

If you cannot find the Inbox program icon sitting on your desktop, don't despair; you should be able to locate it by following these simple steps:

1. **Use your stylus to tap the Start button (in the lower-left corner of the screen).**

2. **On the Start menu, tap the Programs option.**

   Windows CE displays a list of the programs and program folders on your CE device.

3. **Tap the Microsoft Pocket Outlook option.**

   You should be able to locate the Inbox program option on the Microsoft Pocket Outlook menu, as shown in Figure 17-1.

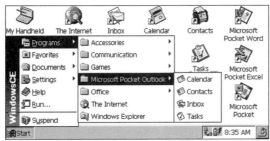

Figure 17-1:
You can find the Inbox program on the Microsoft Pocket Outlook menu.

4. **Tap the Inbox option to display the Inbox program, shown in Figure 17-2.**

   You can send and receive e-mail messages here by using a company e-mail system or the Internet. You can also transfer messages between your CE device and your personal computer.

Figure 17-2:
The Inbox program enables you to check e-mail messages from any location.

Before you can send or receive e-mail messages, you need to set up your e-mail account information in the Inbox program, as I describe in the next section of this chapter.

Specifying your e-mail address

Before you can send or receive e-mail messages, you need to tell the Inbox program some information about the e-mail account to which you want to connect. In essence, the Inbox program needs to know where you want it to look for your e-mail messages as well as the location of the mail server (which is similar to a post office) to which it should transfer the messages you send so that they can be routed to the appropriate location.

The following steps illustrate how to set up the e-mail account information on your CE device:

1. **Tap the Options button on the toolbar. (The Options button resembles a list with a stylus on top of it.)**

   The Options dialog box appears, sporting four tabs full of options.

2. **Tap the Services tab.**

   The Services tab, shown in Figure 17-3, is where you create and modify the e-mail account information for your CE device.

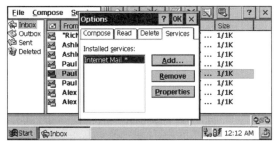

Figure 17-3:
The Services tab of the Options dialog box.

3. Tap the Add button.

The Services dialog box displays the types of e-mail accounts that you can create.

4. Tap the Internet Mail option and then tap the OK button.

The Service Name dialog box appears, as shown in Figure 17-4.

Figure 17-4:
The Service
Name
dialog box.

5. Type a unique name in the Enter a unique name field and then tap the OK button.

You need to assign a unique name, such as My Internet Mail, in the field in the Service Name dialog box. For ease of use, you may even want to use the name of your access provider as the name; this can be useful if you get your mail from different locations. This name is displayed when you select the e-mail account to connect to. When you tap the OK button, the Service Definition wizard appears, as shown in Figure 17-5. Here you actually indicate your e-mail address, the remote connection to use to locate your e-mail, and logon information.

The actual name of the Service Definition wizard changes based on the name you specified in the Service Name dialog box. For example, if you called it Personal Mail, the wizard would be named Personal Mail Service Definition, as shown in Figure 17-5. If you name it Internet Mail, it will be Internet Mail Service Definition.

Figure 17-5:
Specify the
e-mail
account
information
on this
screen.

6. In the Connection field, tap the down-arrow button and then tap the remote connection to use for your e-mail.

All the remote connections you have created on your CE device are listed in the drop-down list. If you don't find the connection you want, you need to create the connection before you can select it on this screen. For more information about creating remote connections, refer to Chapter 15.

7. Type the address of the mail server in the POP3 host field.

This is the part of your address that comes after the @ sign. If your address is john@xyzinc.com, you probably need to type **xyzinc.com** in this field. Verify this with your ISP; ISPs often assign a different name to the mail server.

8. Type your e-mail user ID in the User ID field.

The User ID is the part of the e-mail address before the at symbol (@). Therefore, if your mail address is john@xyzinc.com, you simply type the characters that precede the @, which is **john** in this example, in the User ID field. Most e-mail addresses have all lowercase characters.

9. Type the password for your e-mail account in the Password field.

Depending on how your account was set up, this password may be the same as the password that you use to connect to your Internet service provider. If you want to avoid the drudgery of always typing your password, select the check box next to the Remember Password field to have your CE device remember your password. If you are concerned about someone using your CE device to make a remote connection when you're not around, however, you may want to avoid selecting this field so that the password is requested each time.

10. If your Internet service provider uses a different server to send outgoing messages, type the address in the SMTP Host field.

To reduce the demand on the mail server that is receiving your mail from other locations, some Internet service providers use a different machine to handle mail messages that people send out. Not all providers exercise this option, so leave the field blank if the information is not applicable.

11. Type your return address in the Return address field.

Indicate the address you want used when someone selects the reply option for your message. You probably just want to place your Internet mail address here, although you may have occasion to have mail returned to another address, such as a company Internet account. If so, type that address in the field.

12. Tap the Next button to continue the setup process.

You get the second set of steps for setting up your e-mail service, as shown in Figure 17-6.

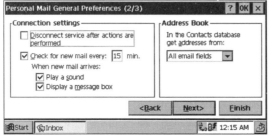

Figure 17-6:
The second set of steps for setting up your e-mail service.

13. Specify the connection settings.

In the Connection settings section, indicate whether you want the modem to hang up after sending and receiving messages, how often to check for messages, and finally how you want to be notified when you receive a message.

If your Internet Service Provider charges you a fee based on the number of minutes that you are connected to the Internet, select the Disconnect service after actions are performed option.

14. In the Address Book section, indicate which e-mail addresses you want to display when you select the Address Book button while creating a message, and then tap the Next button.

You get the final set of steps for setting up your e-mail service, as shown in Figure 17-7.

Figure 17-7:
The final set of steps for setting up your e-mail service.

15. On the third page of the Inbox Preferences wizard, indicate whether you want to see just the message headers or the entire message.

I recommend that you download just the message headers, because you have a limited amount of memory on your CE device. If you decide to read a message, additional lines of the message are downloaded when you double-tap the message.

16. **If you selected the Message headers radio button, select the check box next to the Include field, and indicate the maximum number of lines that you want to download for a message.**

    I recommend setting this field to about 50 lines, which is more than enough lines for most messages.

17. **If you selected the Full copy radio button, select the desired check boxes indicating whether you want to download meeting requests and file attachments.**

    Because file attachments can be quite large, I recommend that you consider not selecting this option. Due to the limited amount of memory on your CE device, it is possible to get one message with an attachment too large to fit on your device.

18. **Tap the Finish button to save the new e-mail service.**

    You are now ready to connect to your Internet Service Provider and get your e-mail messages.

These steps only set up the e-mail portion of your Internet or other remote connection account. You must also establish a remote connection that you can use to access this account. For more information on creating remote connections, refer to Chapter 15.

You may only have the ability to set up an e-mail service for an Internet e-mail account. This option comes standard on all CE devices. As you add other types of software and services to your CE device, you can set up e-mail for other types of services. For example, a popular add-on to CE devices is a paging card, which provides you with the capability to set up an e-mail server for paging messages.

The menacing file attachment

If you have used e-mail at all, you have probably experienced the process of getting file attachments with your messages. A file attachment is essentially a file that is sent along with an e-mail message. This file can be a simple little page of text, or a huge color picture from a friend's latest cruise (I say "huge" because pictures are usually fairly large files).

Pocket Inbox lets you decide whether you want to receive attachments that may be sent with your messages. This is specified when you create the e-mail service by selecting the File Attachment check box in the Inbox Preferences dialog box. To change this option at any time, simply choose Service⇨Properties, and then tap the Next button until you see the Inbox Properties dialog box, where you can select or unselect this option.

Remember: If you tell Pocket Inbox that you want attachments, you are going to get every attachment, no matter how large.

Making the connection

To connect to your e-mail service, tap the Connect button on the toolbar of the Inbox program. The Connect button is the last one on the toolbar; it resembles a hand holding up a computer monitor. (You may have to think deep thoughts to find the correlation there.)

If you have set up multiple e-mail services, Windows CE connects to the last e-mail service that you selected. The current e-mail services for your CE device are listed on the Service menu between the Connect option and the Retrieve Full Copy option, as shown in Figure 17-8. A small dot appears next to the currently selected service. To select another service, simply tap the one you want.

Figure 17-8:
You can
switch
between
different
e-mail
services on
the Service
menu.

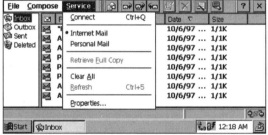

When you tap the Connect button, the Dial-Up Connection screen appears if you are not already connected to the remote location, verifying that you desire to make a connection. When you tap the Connect button, you are connected to the remote location. After you are connected to the location, Windows CE connects to the appropriate mail server and sends and receives your messages.

Handling E-Mail

The Inbox program on your CE device enables you to quickly send and receive e-mail messages from any location. You can send a message to anyone who has an e-mail account. After you receive a message, you have the option of sending a response back to the person who sent the message. You can find more information about sending and receiving e-mail in the following sections in this chapter.

Creating an e-mail message

When most people use an e-mail program for the first time, the first thing they want to do is figure out how to create a message. To send an e-mail message, all you need is the recipient's e-mail address.

Creating an e-mail message is easy. Simply tap the New Message button — it's the first button on the toolbar — and a window in which you can compose your new e-mail message appears, as shown in Figure 17-9.

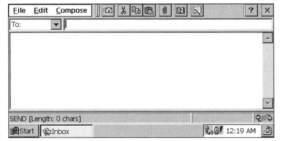

Figure 17-9: Composing a new e-mail message.

In the window where you create your e-mail messages, you have basically three different fields or areas for information:

- ✔ The top two fields on the window are used for specifying the heading information for the message.
- ✔ The bottom section contains the actual message that you are sending.

Typing the message

You type the message that you are trying to send in the bottom portion of the window (the big section). The message section is free-form, like the main window of a word processor, which means that you can type information on any line of the section.

You can use the Cut, Copy, and Paste buttons on the toolbar to copy and move information around in your message. If you're like me, you probably don't always like the way the message looks when you first type it. By using these toolbar options, you can move information around in the message without retyping any of it.

Specifying the message headings

The top two fields are used for specifying the heading information for your message, such as the address where the message should be sent, the address where you would like to send a copy of the message, the subject of the message, and so on. The To field is the only field that must have a value when sending a message. It needs to contain the address where the message should be sent.

To check the values assigned to the different message header fields for your message, tap the down-arrow button to view a drop-down list, as shown in Figure 17-10. If any of the fields contain values, the values are listed next to the fields. For all the heading fields, you can simply type the information in the text box on the right side of the screen.

Figure 17-10:
Checking the
values
assigned to
the message
header
fields.

 To make typing an e-mail address even easier, the Inbox program is linked to the Contacts program, enabling you to add an e-mail address from your contacts database. To find an e-mail address from your contacts database, tap the Address button on the toolbar. This button looks like an open address book.

When you tap the Address button, the Choose Address dialog box displays a list of the e-mail addresses that you have added to the Contacts program and the name that corresponds with each address, as shown in Figure 17-11. You can tap the Address button to select addresses for the To, Cc, and Bcc heading fields. When you select an address, it is added to whichever heading field you selected.

Figure 17-11:
Tap an e-
mail address
and tap the
OK button.

The e-mail addresses that are actually displayed on the Choose Address dialog box are determined by the value you assigned the Address Book section when you set up your e-mail service. For example, if you requested that only Email2 addresses be displayed, you do not see any of the Email1 addresses that you may have added to the Contacts program on the Choose Address dialog box.

Reading a message

After you receive messages, you can open them and read them. To open a message, double-tap the message with the stylus. The selected message opens in a window, as shown in Figure 17-12.

Figure 17-12:
Double-tap
a message
in the Inbox
to view the
message
text.

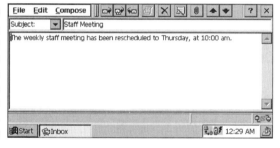

> You can use the up- and down-arrow keys to scroll through the messages in your Inbox. Tapping the up-arrow button displays a previous message and tapping the down-arrow button displays the next message in the Inbox.

Retrieving a copy of a message

Windows CE always tries to help by adding only a minimal amount of stuff to the memory on your CE device. The amount of each message that is copied to your CE device is determined by the settings you specify when you set up the e-mail service. Normally, you get only the headers to the messages copied to your CE device, and then you can copy the messages you select to your CE device. By copying only the messages that you want to read, you do not fill your storage memory with messages you are not interested in.

To copy the text of a message to your CE device, select the message that you want to copy and choose Service⇨Retrieve Full Text Copy.

Replying to a message you received

You can reply to the message while it is listed in the Inbox or reply to a message that you are currently viewing. Windows CE provides options that enable you to respond to a message in three ways, as I describe in Table 17-1. You can also find these options in the Edit menu.

Table 17-1	Replying to a Message
Tap This Button	**To Do This**
	Send a response to the person who sent the message.
	Send a response to everyone who received the original message.
	Forward a copy of the message to someone else.

When you select one of the reply options, a copy of the message may appear on-screen, as shown in Figure 17-13. You can add information to the message and then tap the Send button to send the message.

TIP

The copy of the message appears on-screen only if you've selected the Include body check box on the Compose tab of the Options dialog box; otherwise, you just get a blank screen. To open the Options dialog box, choose Compose⇨Options.

Send button

Figure 17-13: Type the text and tap the Send button.

REMEMBER

If you can't connect to your e-mail service when you create the reply, the outgoing messages sit in your Outbox folder until you connect again. Basically, the Outbox is just like putting mail in the mailbox at home — it sits there until the letter carrier picks it up.

Organizing Your E-Mail

The Inbox program provides options for organizing your messages. For example, you can create new folders and move the messages you want to keep into these folders. You can also delete any unnecessary messages as soon as possible to ensure that you have plenty of storage space for other things on your CE device.

You can read about all the cool tools for organizing e-mail in the following sections. You even find out how to move messages from your CE device onto your personal computer.

Finding new places to store copies of messages

You may find that you want to keep copies of certain messages that you have either received or sent. The best way to store messages is to create a folder in which to place them. By creating a folder, you can separate the old messages that you want to keep from the new messages in your Inbox. Doing so helps to eliminate the possibility of accidentally deleting a message that you want to keep.

The following steps illustrate how to create a new folder called Work on your CE device and then use the drag and drop options to copy a message from your boss into that folder.

1. **On the left side of the screen, tap the Inbox folder to select it.**

2. **Choose File⇨Folder⇨New Folder.**

   The New Folder dialog box appears, as shown in Figure 17-14.

Figure 17-14: The New Folder dialog box.

3. **Type a name for the new folder (for example, Work) in the Folder name field and tap the OK button.**

   The new folder is added to the list of folders on the left side of the Inbox screen, as shown in Figure 17-15. The Inbox program always lists the four main folders first, and then your personal folders in the order that you created them. In other words, the list is not alphabetized in any fashion.

4. **Tap the message you are moving, drag it across the screen, and drop it in the new folder.**

   The message is copied from the Inbox folder to the Work folder.

Figure 17-15:
Your new
Work folder.

Only messages that exist on your CE device can be moved into new folders. If you try to move a message of which only the message heading has been copied to your CE device, it is marked to move, but it does not actually move until you connect to the server where the message is located.

Copying and moving messages

Windows CE gives you the capability to copy messages between folders by using the Move to and Copy to commands on the Edit menu. These two commands work almost the same way. The only difference is that the Move to command moves the message, whereas the Copy to command places a copy of the message in the specified folder. So in deciding which command to use, you need to decide exactly how attached you are to that message. In other words, do you like that message enough to keep two copies?

Each message you save takes up some of your storage space. You may decide you want to keep a copy of a message in a separate folder for backup purposes.

When you select a message and choose either the Move to or Copy to command, a window appears, as shown in Figure 17-16. In this window, you can select the folder where you want the message to go. Keep in mind that dragging and dropping a message between folders produces exactly the same result as the Copy to option.

Figure 17-16:
Highlight the
desired
folder and
tap the OK
button.

Deleting unwanted mail

Everyone needs to do a little bit of housecleaning from time to time. Doing so is especially important when you are dealing with your e-mail. Each message that you keep takes up valuable memory on your CE device.

 To delete an item, select the item you want to delete and then tap the Delete button on the toolbar. (Remember, this button looks like a giant X.) The confusion comes after the message is deleted. Windows CE tries to be helpful by coming up with all sorts of ways to determine when to actually delete the message. Some messages are moved to the Deleted Items folder, and others are immediately deleted.

You can have some say in how Windows CE handles the messages you choose to delete, and I would suggest that you make a few changes. The settings for deleted messages are determined based on the options that you select on the Delete tab in the Options dialog box, shown in Figure 17-17.

Figure 17-17: Set deleted message options on the Options dialog box.

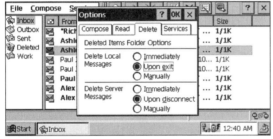

 You can restore a deleted message from the Deleted Items folder by making sure that the *local messages* you delete (the ones that are sitting on your CE device) are not deleted until you exit the Inbox program. This feature helps to ensure that you do not accidentally remove something that you intended to save. Also, make sure that the messages that are sitting on the server are only deleted when you disconnect from the server. These two steps will save some heartache in the future.

Transferring messages between your CE device and a personal computer

Windows CE offers the capability to copy messages between your CE device and a personal computer. This feature can be especially useful if you have messages on your CE device that you want to keep for an extended period of time. You can move them to your personal computer and save them with other related messages.

Transferring messages can be accomplished using either the Inbox program or the Outlook program under Windows 95 or Windows NT 4.0 on your personal computer. Follow these steps to transfer messages from your CE device to your personal computer:

1. **In either Inbox or Outlook, simply choose Tools⇨Windows CE Inbox Transfer.**

   The Windows CE Inbox Transfer dialog box appears on your personal computer. Of course, you must have a connection between your personal computer and your CE device to make this transfer possible. Refer to Chapter 10 for more information about connecting to your personal computer.

2. **Select the check box next to the Copy or move selected messages to your desktop computer option.**

3. **Select the folder on your CE device that contains the messages, and then highlight each message that you want to copy or move.**

4. **Tap either the Copy messages or Move messages radio button to indicate whether you want to copy or actually move the messages from your CE device.**

5. **After you make the transfer selections, tap the Transfer button to move or copy the messages to the specified locations.**

If you want to transfer messages from your personal computer to your CE device, you need to highlight the messages before choosing Tools⇨Windows CE Inbox Transfer. In the Windows CE Inbox Transfer dialog box, select the check box next to the Copy selected messages to your mobile device option and specify the name of the folder that should contain the selected messages on your CE device in the Mobile device folder drop-down list box. To make sure that the messages are not too large, I recommend that you select the option to transfer only the first 50 lines of each message.

When you transfer messages from your CE device to Windows 95, the date on the message is changed to the date you transferred the message, which can be confusing when trying to determine exactly when you received the message.

If, for some reason, you cannot locate the Windows CE Inbox Transfer option when you run the Inbox program or Outlook program on your computer, you probably did not install on your personal computer all the options loaded with the Windows CE Services 2.0 programs. The Inbox program update is one of the options that you can select when installing the Windows CE Services on your computer — the install program just isn't clear about what is actually occurring. You may need to rerun the installation for the Windows CE Services 2.0 in order to get the proper stuff installed on your computer. For more information about the installation, refer to Chapter 10.

Part V
Personalizing Your CE Device

The 5th Wave   By Rich Tennant

In this part . . .

*W*hether you don't like the wallpaper, need to turn down the volume, or want to set a password for your CE device, you can find options to perform all these tasks and more in the Control Panel folder on your CE device. The chapters in this part look at various ways you can personalize your CE device to fit your own unique tastes.

Chapter 18

Protecting Vital Information

. . . .

. . . .

I'm betting that at an early age you were taught the importance of labeling your personal belongings so that others would know that your stuff belonged to *you*. With that same theory in mind, Windows CE enables you to equip your CE device with your own personal information. To make your CE device more secure, you also can set a password on your CE device to keep confidential information totally and completely confidential.

This chapter explains how to go about setting up your personal information and then takes things one step further and tells you how to protect your CE device by using a personal password.

Labeling Your CE Device with Your Personal Information

Nothing is equal to the frustration of finally getting all of your pertinent stuff entered into your Windows CE device and then realizing you don't have a clue as to where you put your CE device. Now, if you label your CE device and someone finds it, that person knows where to return your CE device. Makes sense, doesn't it? (Of course, I can't guarantee that the person who finds it will return it — so don't lose it.)

Anyhow, Windows CE provides the capability to display your name, address, and phone number on the first screen that appears when you turn on your CE device. So all anyone has to do is turn on your CE device, and they will immediately know who owns it. This initial screen is known as the Owner Identification screen, and it provides a way to display personal information, such as your name, address, and phone number.

To set or modify the Owner Identification screen, you need to select the Owner icon in the Control Panel folder. The Owner icon illustrates its purpose by looking like a couple of luggage tags.

The following steps describe how to set up your personal information to display whenever someone turns on your CE device:

1. **Double-tap the Owner icon in the Control Panel folder.**

   The easiest way to get to the Control Panel folder is to select the Settings option in the Start menu. When you double-tap the Owner icon, the Owner Properties dialog box appears, as shown in Figure 18-1. This dialog box is where you type all your personal information.

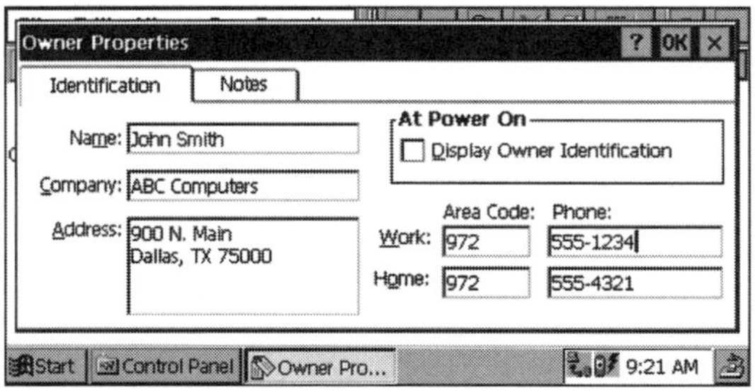

Figure 18-1:
Anyone who turns on your CE device will see the information you specify.

Owner Properties	? OK ×
Identification Notes	
Name: John Smith	At Power On
Company: ABC Computers	☐ Display Owner Identification
Address: 900 N. Main Dallas, TX 75000	Area Code: Phone:
	Work: 972 555-1234
	Home: 972 555-4321
Start Control Panel Owner Pro...	9:21 AM

2. **Type the appropriate information in the Name, Company, Address, and phone number text boxes.**

   Remember, whatever you enter in this dialog box appears when someone turns on your CE device. You do not have to type information in all of these fields. If you are really worried about other people figuring out your home phone number, you may not want to put it in this screen.

3. **Select the Display Owner Identification check box.**

   You must select this check box if you want the information to appear whenever your CE device is turned on.

4. **In the Notes tab, type any additional information that you want to appear.**

   The Notes tab provides a text box where you can type additional information that you may want to appear in the Owner Identification window, as shown in Figure 18-2.

5. **Select the Display Owner Notes at Power On check box.**

   Select this option so that anything you type in this tab appears in the Owner Identification screen.

6. **Tap the OK button to save the changes to the Owner Properties screen.**

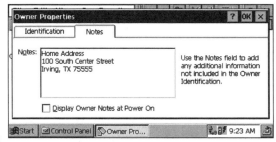

Figure 18-2:
Put extra
information,
such as a
home
address,
in the
Notes tab.

You may find that this information is already set up on your CE device. When you turn on your CE device for the first time, you can set up all this information. The Owner option lets you make modifications to the information at any time.

Password-Protecting the Contents of Your CE Device

If you work for a large company, you probably have heard how important it is to protect your computer by using a password. You may have even seen videos illustrating how easily someone can copy sensitive information from your computer if you don't take precautions to make sure that it is locked with a password whenever you walk away from it.

Well, the information contained on your Windows CE device is every bit as vulnerable as the information on your personal computer. All someone has to do is turn on your CE device, and they instantly have access to all the stuff that you think you have hidden. To help protect your sensitive information, Windows CE enables you to password-protect your CE device. If you password-protect your CE device, the first screen that appears when someone turns on your device requires a valid password before any other information can be viewed. This screen also contains owner information, if you select that option.

Whether you decide to password-protect your CE device is up to your own discretion. If you want to set a password for your device, perform the following steps:

1. In the Control Panel folder, double-tap the Password icon.

Don't forget, the easiest way to find the Control Panel folder is to tap the Settings option in the Start menu. The Password icon looks like a couple of keys. When you double-tap the Password icon, the Password Properties dialog box opens.

2. Type your password in the Password text box.

Don't be concerned if you are unable to see what you type in the
Password field. The field is encrypted, meaning that Windows CE
substitutes an asterisk for each character typed (see Figure 18-3). This
ensures that someone cannot find out your password by looking at the
Password Properties screen.

Figure 18-3:
Windows
CE displays
asterisks
whenever
you type a
password.

3. Type your password again in the Confirm Password text box.

Make sure that you type exactly the same password as you typed in the
Password text box.

4. Select the Enable Password Protection check box.

This ensures that your CE device will request your password whenever
someone turns it on. Anyone who does not know the password will not
be able to get beyond the initial screen.

5. Tap the OK button to save the password settings.

One thing to remember: If you have a password on your CE device and you
plan to interface your CE device with your personal computer, you need to
type in your CE device's password on your computer before you can access
your CE device. This step helps ensure that someone cannot bypass your
password security and access your CE device by using your personal
computer.

Make sure you select a password that is easy for you to remember. If, for
some reason, you forget your password, the only way to reset the password
is to totally reset your CE device. Totally resetting your CE device also
erases everything that you have stored on it, and your CE device appears as
if you have never used it before. If you are really worried about forgetting
your password, make sure that you write your password down in a safe
place so that you can find it if you ever forget it. The despair of forgetting
your password will be nothing compared to the shock of losing everything
on your CE device.

Chapter 19

Personalizing Your Desktop

● ●

In This Chapter

▶ Hanging new wallpaper on your desktop

▶ Adding new sounds

▶ Adjusting the volume

▶ Modifying the time settings

▶ Changing the keyboard settings

● ●

*O*kay, get ready to do some redecorating. Do you have your paint cans ready? Oops, I guess I got the wrong book. But Windows CE does let you personalize the look and feel of the operating system by changing the wallpaper on your desktop, changing sounds, and adjusting the volume. The great thing about these adjustments is that they don't require all the work needed to redecorate your office.

This chapter explains how to use some of the options in the Control Panel folder to change the look of your Windows CE desktop, modify the sounds you hear and the volume at which you hear them, adjust the keyboard settings, and change the time and date settings.

Locating the Control Panel Options

The Windows CE Control Panel folder is full of options that you can use to customize the settings on your CE device. If the sounds coming from your Windows CE device are attracting too much attention in the company meeting, for example, you can adjust the Volume and Sounds setting to make the sounds softer or even turn the sounds off.

The easiest way to open the Control Panel folder is to tap the Start button and then choose Settings⇨Control Panel. In the Control Panel folder, you see several icons for adjusting the settings on your CE device, as shown in Figure 19-1.

Figure 19-1:
Use the
icons in the
Control
Panel
folder to
customize
your CE
device.

You use the options in the Control Panel folder to control everything from how your desktop looks to the way your stylus selects items. Table 19-1 provides a brief description of when to select each icon.

Table 19-1	Control Panel Options
Double-Tap This Icon	**To Do This**
	Set the communication properties for your CE device. This icon controls how the CE device connects to your personal computer as well as how it connects to a remote location, such as the Internet. For more information about setting communication properties for your remote connection, refer to Chapter 15.
	Specify what your desktop looks like by selecting the desired desktop wallpaper.
	Tell Windows CE how fast to type repeating characters by using the keyboard. In other words, if you hold down a key on the keyboard for too long, the character repeats on the screen. This option lets you specify how fasssssssst that happens.
	Create the identification information that appears when you turn on your CE device. Check out Chapter 18 for more information.
	Set a password for your CE device. Chapter 18 has more information on setting passwords.
	Check the battery level for the main and backup batteries on your CE device. You can also indicate how long your CE device may sit idle before shutting off. Refer to Chapter 1 for more information on using this option.

Double-Tap This Icon	To Do This
	Specify how various values display based on the settings used in your specific country. For example, if you are in the United States, currency is represented with the $ symbol, whereas in France you would use the F symbol.
	Get rid of programs that you don't want to keep on your CE device. Keep in mind that you cannot remove the standard Windows CE programs that were originally installed on your CE device, such as Pocket Excel and Pocket Word. Refer to Chapter 14 for more information about removing programs.
	Recalibrate your stylus, and adjust the double-tap setting. If your stylus is not selecting the items you want, use this option.
	Adjust the memory settings for your CE device. This option also gives you a bunch of technical information about your device, such as the processor type, and the version of Windows CE that you are using. Refer to Chapter 1 for more information on using this option.
	Change the sounds that you hear from your CE device. You can also adjust the volume for all sounds with this option.
	Set the date and time for your CE device. You can also select a city that you visit often as your visiting city.

You can also display some of these options by tapping the items in the status bar (the bottom-right corner of the screen). If you double-tap the time, for example, the World Clock dialog box, where you set the date and time, appears.

Changing the Look of Your Desktop

You probably have already noticed that Microsoft has been nice enough to remind you that Windows CE is loaded on your desktop by painting it across your desktop. For those of you who are a little bored with that look, you can change the *wallpaper* (a generic term used to refer to the background of your desktop) on your desktop.

To modify the wallpaper for your desktop, double-tap the Display icon in the Control Panel folder. The Display icon looks like a miniature computer monitor. The Display Properties dialog box appears, as shown in Figure 19-2. In this dialog box, you can change the background settings for your desktop.

Figure 19-2:
Use the Display Properties dialog box to select new wallpaper for your desktop.

To select an image for the background of your desktop, tap the down-arrow button next to the Image drop-down list box and tap the picture you want to display on your desktop. The selected image appears on the sample display in the center of the screen.

If the image you select is quite small, you may want to have that image repeated across the desktop. This process of duplicating the same image all over your desktop is called *tiling*. To tile the selected image, tap the check box next to the Tile image on background option. When you tap the OK button, your desktop wallpaper changes to show the image you just selected.

If you want to use a picture for the desktop background that does not appear in the drop-down list, tap the Browse button to display the Browse dialog box, shown in Figure 19-3. You'll probably need to tap the Previous Folder button (which looks like a folder with an arrow pointing up on the front of it) to navigate through the folders and find the filename for the picture you want. When you find it, select the filename and tap the OK button.

You can use just about any bitmap image as the background on your CE device, as long as the image is in the Windows CE bitmap format of .2BP or .BMP. If you have a bitmap image on your personal computer that you want to use, you can transfer it to your CE device.

Figure 19-3:
You can
select any
picture on
your CE
device
as the
background
for your
desktop.

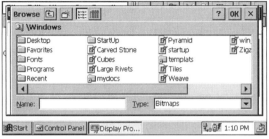

Changing the Sounds

You have probably noticed by now that your CE device makes different
sounds depending on what is happening or even which option you have
selected. On some CE devices, these sounds may seem a little too loud,
especially if you use your CE device in meetings where other people can be
easily distracted.

 Luckily, you can adjust the volume of the sounds that come out of your CE
device and change or eliminate any sounds that you don't care for by
double-tapping the Volume and Sounds icon in the Control Panel folder. This
icon looks like a loudspeaker sitting on top of a volume control.

When you double-tap the Volume and Sounds icon, the Volume and Sounds
Properties dialog box appears (see Figure 19-4). This dialog box has two
tabs: one for setting the volume of your CE device, and the other for indicating the specific sounds that occur for different events on your CE device.

Figure 19-4:
Indicate
how loud
you want
the sounds
to be on
your CE
device.

(figure showing Volume & Sounds Properties dialog box)

Adjusting the volume

The options on the Volume tab in the Volume and Sounds Properties dialog box let you specify how loud sounds are on your CE device and whether sounds occur for specific events or programs or when you press certain keys or tap the screen with the stylus.

You adjust the volume by using the slider on the left side of the screen. You can tap the up-arrow button or the down-arrow button to make sounds louder or softer, or you can drag the slider itself up and down.

The check boxes on the right side of the screen indicate whether sounds occur for different events on your CE device. If you do not want to be interrupted with sounds as you work, simply remove the check marks from all the check boxes.

Sounds are a great way to confirm that the action you just performed (typing or tapping) was recognized by your CE device. I recommend keeping these options selected. You may decide that you want to select the Soft radio button next to each option so that the sound is not quite so loud, however.

Selecting new sounds

You can use the options on the Sound tab of the Volume and Sounds Proper-ties dialog box to specify the exact sound you hear when various things happen under Windows CE. For example, you can select which sound you hear every time Windows CE starts.

As shown in Figure 19-5, the Event Name list box indicates all the Windows CE events that currently have an associated sound. The events with a sound have the little speaker icon next to the event name.

To listen to the sound that plays whenever a specific event occurs, tap the sound in the Event Name list box and then tap the right-arrow button. The Event Sound list contains the name of the selected sound.

If you want to change the sound, tap the down-arrow button next to the Event Sound drop-down list box, and highlight the sound you want to use for that event. If you don't want a sound for that event, make sure that you select the (None) option.

Figure 19-5:
The Event
Name
list box
indicates
which
events
have an
associated
sound.

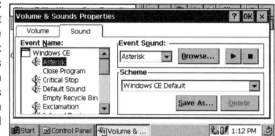

You may want to use different sounds on your CE device depending on your location. At home, for example, you may want to use sounds for every event; and, at the office, you may want to use only a few sounds. The good news is that you do not need to manually switch the sounds each time; you can create what is referred to as a *scheme,* which is basically a group of selected sounds. The scheme information is shown in the Scheme drop-down list box. If you have never created or switched schemes, you probably see the Windows CE Default scheme in the list box. To create a new scheme, select the sounds you want for various events, type a name for the scheme in the list box, and then tap the Save As button. When you change the sounds for a scheme, make sure that the scheme name is displayed in the drop-down list box and then tap the Save As button. To switch to a scheme that you've created, select the desired scheme in the Scheme drop-down list box on the Sound tab and then tap the OK button.

If you have used the options on the Volume tab to turn off the volume or indicate that you do not want certain types of sounds, you may not hear the sounds you select on the Sound tab. If you are having problems with the sounds you've selected, recheck the settings on the Volume tab.

Changing the World Clock Options

You have probably noticed by now that the current time always appears in the lower-right corner of your CE device screen. If you double-tap the time display, you see the World Clock dialog box, which contains a calendar indicating today's date and clocks for the current time in both your home and visiting locations (see Figure 19-6).

Figure 19-6:
Set your
date and
time infor-
mation in
the World
Clock
dialog box.

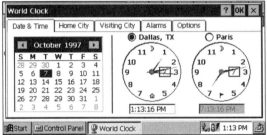

 You can also display the World Clock dialog box by double-tapping the World Clock icon in the Control Panel folder. The icon looks like a globe with a clock in the center of it.

The World Clock dialog box provides five different tabs for setting the date and time, selecting the home and visiting cities, adding special alarms, and creating custom cities. I discuss these tabs in the following sections of this chapter.

 Windows CE can keep track of date and time information for two locations simultaneously. You set one location as your home city and the other as your visiting city. For example, if you live and work in Dallas, but you frequently visit your company's headquarters in Los Angeles, you can set Dallas as your home city and Los Angeles as your visiting city. For the full scoop, see the next sections.

Setting date and time information

When you tap the Date & Time tab at the top of the World Clock dialog box, you are presented with a calendar and clocks for setting the date and time in two locations. The first clock is for the city that you have selected as your home city. It should be labeled with the name of the location where you live (or at least the closest city within your time zone). The other clock indicates the time in the visiting city that you have selected. This clock is normally used to keep track of the time in another city that you visit frequently.

The selected radio button indicates the clock that is currently being used to determine times on your CE device. To change the clock, simply tap the radio button above the desired clock.

 To change either the home city or the visiting city, you need to select the city you want on the Home City or Visiting City tabs, as I describe in subsequent sections in this chapter.

To change the current date, simply tap the correct date on the calendar. If you need to select another month, tap the left and right arrows at the top of the calendar to move through the months of the year.

To change the time on either clock, you can either drag the hands of the clock to the appropriate location or type the correct time in the time field under the clock. Note that when you change the minutes on one clock, the minutes automatically change to match on the other clock as well.

The clock that is currently selected is the time that Windows CE uses for different events on your CE device. For example, the Calendar program uses this time to determine when it should notify you of a meeting or appointment. If you are in your visiting city, be sure to select the radio button for that clock.

Selecting your home city

When you select the Home City tab on the World Clock dialog box, you are presented with options that let you select the specific home city location. This screen provides added information about the selected city, such as the area code, current time, and even the sunrise and sunset times for the current date, as shown in Figure 19-7.

Figure 19-7:
The Home City tab provides information about the city you selected.

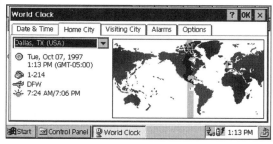

If you want to change the home city, simply tap the down-arrow button next to the City drop-down list box and select the appropriate city in the list. If you really want to have fun, try tapping the desired location on the world map; the information shown on-screen changes to the city you select. You see a little house icon on the world map identifying your home city location. If multiple cities are located close to the spot where you tap, you see those cities listed so you can select the correct one.

If you are unable to locate the city you want, you can create a custom city by using the Options tab. For more information, refer to the section "Setting other clock options," later in this chapter.

Selecting your visiting city

The Visiting City tab on the World Clock dialog box includes options that let you select your visiting city location. This screen provides added information about the selected city, such as the area code, current time, and the sunrise and sunset times for the current date.

If you want to change the visiting city, simply tap the down-arrow button next to the City drop-down list box and select the appropriate city in the list, as shown in Figure 19-8. Alternately, tap the world map and the desired location; the information shown on-screen changes to the city you select. You see a little flag icon on the world map identifying your visiting city location.

Figure 19-8:
Select the desired city from the drop-down list box of available cities.

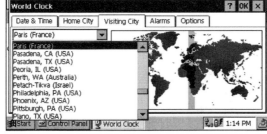

Setting alarms

When you select the Alarms tab on the World Clock dialog box, you are presented with options that enable you to set alarms for every day at a specific time (see Figure 19-9). For example, you may want to set an alarm to ring every morning at 10:00 to remind you to take your medication.

You can create as many as five alarms. The alarms are turned on if a check mark appears in the check box next to the alarm. You can type a description for an alarm in the fields that say `<Alarm Description>`. Make sure that the time field contains the appropriate time; you can either type a time or tap the down-arrow button and highlight the appropriate time for the alarm.

Figure 19-9:
Create an
alarm to
ring daily
at the
specified
time of day.

You can specify the type of alarm that occurs by tapping the Options button next to the alarm. When you tap the Options button, the Notifications Options dialog box appears, as shown in Figure 19-10. Select the alarm type and then tap the OK button.

Figure 19-10:
Select the
type of
alarm you
want for the
specified
time.

Setting other clock options

The Options tab on the World Clock dialog box, shown in Figure 19-11, enables you to set additional options that you can use when setting up your information. For example, if you do not find the city you want for your home or visiting city, you can add that city to the list in the Custom Cities section.

Figure 19-11:
Add new
cities to the
city list
using the
Options tab.

If you cannot find the city you want on the Home City or Visiting City tab, you can create a new city by performing these steps.

1. Tap the <u>A</u>dd button on the Options tab of the World Clock dialog box.

When you select the Add City option, the Choose Nearby City dialog box appears, as shown in Figure 19-12.

2. Tap the appropriate city in the list box and then tap the OK button.

Select a city that is located close to the city you want to add. When you tap the OK button, you see the Add City dialog box.

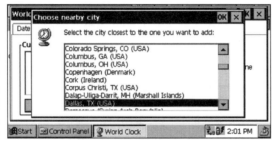

Figure 19-12:
The Choose Nearby City dialog box.

3. In the Add City dialog box, type the name of the city in the City <u>N</u>ame field.

The Add City dialog box copies most of the information it displays from the city that you selected in the Choose Nearby City dialog box. If you know any of the other information, simply type the information in the appropriate fields and then tap the OK button (see Figure 19-13).

Figure 19-13:
Type the information for the new city and tap the OK button.

You cannot modify the information for any of the cities that are already set up within Windows CE. If some of the information changes for these cities, such as a new area code, you have to create another city with the same name and modify the appropriate information.

If you want to see roman numerals displayed on the clocks in Windows CE, select the Roman Numerals check box on the Options tab.

Customizing the Regional Settings

If you have traveled at all to other countries, you have probably noticed that not only do people speak different languages, but they also use different symbols to represent currency, numbers, time, and even dates. For example, if you are from the United States, you are used to seeing a dollar sign ($) as the currency symbol. When you go shopping in Paris, you find items marked with an F, which represents the franc.

Because Windows CE is designed to be used in countries throughout the world, it also is designed to enable users to change various settings to match those for their region.

To change these settings, you need to double-tap the Regional Settings icon in the Control Panel folder. This icon looks like a globe. Selecting this icon displays the Regional Settings Properties dialog box, shown in Figure 19-14.

Figure 19-14: Choosing settings appropriate for your region of the world.

The Regional Settings Properties dialog box has five different tabs that you can use to specify the desired settings. On the Regional Settings tab, you indicate the region of the world where you live (or at least the area that uses the symbols you are most accustomed to working with). If you want to change some of the settings (for example, the symbol used to represent a decimal point), you can use the other tabs to make these changes.

Table 19-2 provides a quick overview of the different things you can do with each of the tabs in the Regional Settings Properties dialog box.

Table 19-2	Tab Options for Regional Settings
Use This Tab	*If You Want To*
Regional Settings	Select the region of the world that most closely matches the international settings that you are accustomed to using.
Number	Customize the way numeric values are shown in Windows CE. For example, you can specify the symbol used for decimal values.
Currency	Customize the way that currency values appear in Windows CE.
Time	Customize how time values display in Windows CE.
Date	Customize the way dates display in Windows CE.

Adjusting the Keyboard Settings

You cannot change the location or size of the keyboard on your CE device, but you can adjust the key repeat settings. The key repeat settings specify the amount of time you need to hold down a key before the keyboard assumes that you want to repeat the character. These settings also indicate how quickly the keyboard repeats the character on-screen, after it actually starts to repeat that character.

You can totally eliminate the capability to have a key repeat when you hold it down, but you may find this capability useful — you don't have to press a key repeatedly. Most people find that the repeat rate set on the CE device is adequate, but if you get lots of duplicate characters when you type on your CE device, you probably want to adjust these settings.

 To set the repeat properties for the keyboard on your CE device, you use the Keyboard Properties dialog box, shown in Figure 19-15. To open this dialog box, choose S̲ettings⊏⊅C̲ontrol Panel from the Start menu and then double-tap the Keyboard Properties icon in the Control Panel folder. The Keyboard Properties icon resembles a miniature keyboard. You also can open this dialog box by pressing the Windows key+K.

A check mark in the box next to Enable Character Repeat indicates that a key will repeat when you hold it down on the keyboard. Remove the check mark from the box only if you do not want keys to repeat.

Figure 19-15:
Use the
Keyboard
Properties
dialog box to
modify the
keyboard
repeat
settings.

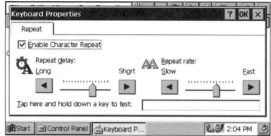

The Repeat delay slider indicates the amount of time that should elapse before the key that is held down on the keyboard is repeated. To adjust the setting, tap either the Long or the Short arrow until the pointer is in the location you want. After you adjust this setting, test it to make sure that you like the new adjustment.

The Repeat rate slider indicates how quickly the key repeats after the specified delay has elapsed. To adjust the setting, simply tap either the Slow or the Fast arrow until the pointer is in the location you want.

You can test the repeat rate by using the field at the bottom of the dialog box labeled Tap here and hold down a key to test. If you want to use this feature, tap in this field, and then hold down a key to check the repeat rate. The selected key is repeated in the field. Although this field provides you with an immediate test, you will probably need to use the keyboard more to determine whether the setting is exactly what you want.

If you decide to change these settings, you probably will have to make a few adjustments before you find the setting that works best for you.

Setting the Stylus Properties

When you originally set up your CE device, you also set up the way the stylus responds to your taps on the screen. You may find that these settings no longer seem right or that your CE device does not seem to respond when you double-tap an option. To adjust the stylus settings, double-tap the Stylus icon in the Control Panel folder to open the Stylus Properties dialog box, shown in Figure 19-16.

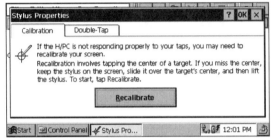

Figure 19-16:
Adjust your
stylus
settings in
the Stylus
Properties
dialog box.

To recalibrate the stylus, tap the Calibration tab (if it is not already selected), then tap the Recalibrate button. Doing so displays a screen where
you can again tap the cross symbol to adjust the settings. The cross symbol
looks like a large plus sign in the center of the screen. When you tap it, it
moves to another location so you can tap again. Continue tapping until you
get a message indicating the calibration is complete. When you see that
message, simply press the Enter key to save you new settings, and tap the
OK button to close the Stylus Properties dialog box.

On the Double-Tap tab in the Stylus Properties dialog box, shown in Figure
19-17, you can adjust the way Windows CE responds when you double-tap an
item. To adjust the double-tap setting, simply double-tap the checkerboard
pattern, then test the settings on the bottom image.

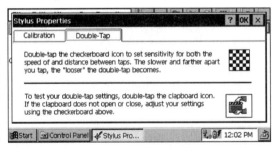

Figure 19-17:
Adjusting
the double-
tap settings.

Part VI
The Part of Tens

The 5th Wave   **By Rich Tennant**

"Hey Dad.- guess how many Milk Duds fit inside your disk drive."

In this part . . .

You have stumbled across the much-acclaimed Part of Tens found in all *...For Dummies* books. If you are a person who likes to make lists, this part is for you. You can find lists containing approximately ten related items, all dealing with Windows CE.

In this part, you can figure out what else you can get for your CE device and find answers to some of the most common problems you may encounter with Windows CE.

Chapter 20

Ten Ways to Spend Money on Your Windows CE Device

. . . .

In This Chapter

▶ Spend some more bucks to become connected

▶ Purchase more memory

▶ Save money on battery purchases — by spending some money

▶ Pick up a stylus to match your attire

. . . .

Surely when you bought that Windows CE device you didn't think that you were finished spending money. After all, what good is buying a CE device with so much expansion capability if you never expand? Every day, more and more items are available that you can add to your CE device; I'm just including some of the major ones in this chapter.

Modem

Okay, the box said that your CE device can connect to the Internet; what it may not have mentioned is that in order to do so, you must have a modem connected to your device. Some of the CE devices do come with a built-in modem; if this is the case with your device, you probably don't need to worry as long as you don't want to add a faster modem or even a wireless one.

If your CE device does not have a modem, you definitely need to acquire one before you can connect to another remote location. If you run down to your local computer store to purchase a modem, you'll quickly find that modems come in all shapes and sizes, and the salesperson is immediately going to start asking you how fast you want the modem to be, whether you want internal or external — and have you considered a wireless modem? Enough to make your head spin yet?

You should consider three types of modems for your CE device:

- ✔ A **PC Card modem** (also known as a PCMCIA card) is a modem that is about the size of a credit card. The modem is inserted into your CE device in a PC Card slot. Most of the CE devices come with a PC Card slot. This slot is designed to accept any of the standard PC Cards. If you purchase a PC Card modem for your CE device, be sure to look for one with a low power rating.

- ✔ You can also use an **external modem** with your CE device. An external modem is a good option if you already own a modem and don't want to purchase a PC Card modem. The only drawback is the fact that an external modem is more bulky to haul around. The only requirement for using an external modem is that you need to purchase a null-modem cable and a 9-pin to 25-pin adapter. (Your local computer store can help you with these items — don't worry about knowing what they are; just ask for them by name.) To use the external modem, connect one end of the null-modem cable to the end of your serial interface cable that normally connects to your computer, attach the 9-pin to 25-pin adapter to the other end of the null-modem cable, and then plug the adapter into the external modem.

- ✔ A **wireless modem** is one of the newest breed of modems available. This type of modem is similar to a cellular phone in that you do not need to plug the modem into a telephone line like other modems. A wireless modem transmits a signal through the air by using a small antenna. Probably one of the only drawbacks with the wireless modem is that it requires some type of monthly contract to pay for your wireless service. But if you are looking for freedom to use the modem when you are away from home, this solution is definitely one to consider.

If you do not want the expense of purchasing a wireless modem, but you own a cellular phone, then you do have another option to consider. Some modem cards come with the option of plugging into a cellular phone. If you're interested in this capability, be sure to read the modem box carefully to see if it comes with this option before purchasing the modem card. This option probably requires the purchase of a special cable to connect the modem card to your specific cellular phone.

When using a modem with your CE device, use an electrical adapter if at all possible. A modem causes an extreme power drain on your CE device. In fact, some modems won't even work without the electrical adapter.

Memory Card

No matter how much memory you have available on your CE device, sooner or later you'll inevitably run out. At that point, you can remove all the old files from your CE device. But if you're like me, you prefer to hold on to everything. Before you run out and plop down more money for the latest CE device with double the amount of storage space, you do have another option.

You can purchase a *PCMCIA storage card*. This card fits in the PC Card slot on your CE device. By adding one of these cards, you can move all the files onto the card and use your CE device's memory (RAM) for storing programs.

These storage cards come in an array of sizes. Keep in mind that you can only use them for file storage — most programs will not run off a storage card.

Before you run out and purchase a PCMCIA storage card, you need to make sure that your CE device has a slot for this type of card. If you own a Velo 1, for example, you may want to consider purchasing the miniature memory cards — called *Compact Flash* — used by that device. You can use PCMCIA cards if you own a V-Module, however.

Docking Station

Docking stations are one of those things that may or may not have some importance to your CE device. If you decide to purchase one, you must purchase one designed specifically for your unit. For example, a NEC docking station will not work with a Cassiopeia.

Some CE devices come with docking stations, and they're available as add-on options for other devices. On most devices, the docking station serves as a method for plugging the unit into the power adapter and connecting to your personal computer.

Refer to the hardware documentation that comes with your device to determine whether a docking station would be useful for you.

Storage Case

If you are going to be carrying around your CE device (which is probably a dumb statement, because I'm sure that's why you bought it), you may want to consider purchasing a storage case for it. Several types of storage cases are available for CE devices. Some just carry your CE device, and others give you the ability to carry everything but your desk. A storage case ultimately helps protect your CE device, and after spending all that money, I suspect that you'd like to protect your investment.

Rechargeable Battery

If your CE device didn't come with a power adapter, you have probably purchased enough batteries to own stock in a certain battery company. To eliminate the need to constantly buy new batteries, most CE devices have a rechargeable battery available that can be used to replace the main batteries in your device.

Make sure that you follow the instructions for recharging the battery. Some types of rechargeable batteries do not hold a full charge if they are not drained before recharging. Always make sure that you recharge the batteries immediately when you get a low battery message; otherwise, you drain the backup battery.

AC Adapter

As convenient as it is to own a device that can be carried everywhere, you will find occasions when you want to plug it into an outlet. For example, when you use a modem with your CE device, you should plug in the CE device, if at all possible, to reduce the battery drain caused by the modem.

Unfortunately, not all CE device manufacturers package AC adapters with CE devices. If your handheld did not come with one, you should definitely look into purchasing one.

Stylus

Okay, so that little plastic stylus just isn't your style. Don't despair: Many types of styluses are available on the market, designed to fit anyone's taste.

Whatever type of stylus you purchase probably will not fit in the stylus holder on your CE device, so you may want to go ahead and keep the stylus that came with your CE device stored in the stylus holder. That way, if you forget your new, fancy one, you still have a stylus to use with your CE device.

Additional RAM

When you first got your CE device, that 2MB or 4MB of RAM probably seemed more than adequate. After all, you only wanted to put so many programs on that little CE device. But by now, you may be sorry you didn't pick up a CE device that had more memory.

Luckily, most Windows CE device manufacturers kept that in mind when designing the CE devices. Most of these devices can be expanded to have more memory. Although the memory expansion may not be cheap, it is definitely cheaper than purchasing a new CE device.

For more information about increasing the RAM on your device, contact the technical support group for the company that developed your specific CE device. Most of the upgrades require taking your CE device into a service center.

Paging Equipment

If you're the type of mobile professional who is lucky enough to be able to carry a pager, you definitely will be interested in the paging equipment available for your CE device. You can buy paging equipment that lets you receive a message on your Windows CE device.

To take things one step further, you can even get two-way paging units that let you send and receive pages by using your Windows CE device. Imagine being able to type in a response to a page. These paging units even enable you to send e-mail messages to Internet accounts, and all of this is done through your pager, not a modem.

GPS

The *GPS* (global positioning system) is a gadget that you may want to consider adding to your Windows CE device, especially if you're a gadget nut or if you tend to get lost easily. A GPS's sole purpose is to determine your exact location on earth by using satellite signals.

These types of devices are being added to automobiles, and now you can carry one with you wherever you go.

Chapter 21

Ten Common Problems You May Encounter with Your CE Device

In This Chapter

▶ Figuring out why your battery bill has gone up

▶ Fixing a blank screen

▶ The horrors of forgetting your password

▶ Determining why personal computer files won't work on a CE device

▶ Why doesn't my CE device connect to the outside world?

Sometimes it seems as if no matter what you do, something goes wrong. Nearly everything that goes wrong with your CE device can be dealt with, although you may not always get the resolution that you want. This chapter provides a look at some of the common problems you may encounter when using your CE device, as well as a few suggestions about how to resolve the problems.

The Batteries Run Down Too Quickly

The box your CE device came in said that you would get 20 hours of battery life, yet you're getting a low-battery message after using the device for a considerably shorter period of time. This problem is actually a common one. Unfortunately, when the manufacturers determine battery life, they base it on optimal conditions, such as using the CE device without PC Cards, a backlight, or an internal modem. When you use any of these additional features, your batteries are used up at a much faster rate.

To help conserve your batteries, always use an AC adapter when you use a modem. Modems tend to use a great deal of extra power. Even the modems that claim to use low power cause your CE device to use more battery power than when you are not using the modem. Also, the backlight causes a considerable drain on the batteries, so try to reduce the use of this feature; if at all possible, move to a location where you don't need the backlight.

The CE Device Won't Turn On

You have tried in vain to turn on your CE device, and now you're probably sure that you made a mistake spending all that money on it. Take a deep breath before you go throwing it against the wall. You can perform a very easy step that will probably solve the problem.

Try tapping the Reset button with your stylus. The Reset button is located in a different spot on each CE device, so if you don't know where it is, you may need to check your hardware documentation. On most CE devices, the button is either on top, near the display, or on the bottom of the device.

When you shut down your device, it remembers exactly where you were and what you were doing so that the next time you turn it on, you can continue at that location. Occasionally, all this information just seems to jumble up its brains and the device does not want to turn on. By pressing the Reset button, you tell the device to forget about what you had open and start as if all the programs were closed.

If you had a file open that you had not saved before shutting down your CE device, you may lose the contents of that file when you reset. Always save before shutting down the CE device to eliminate the possibility of losing important information.

I Can't Remember My Password

Windows CE does a fantastic job of protecting your CE device when you have password-protected it. If someone doesn't know your password, that person cannot view any information you may have stored on the CE device, no matter what steps he or she takes.

The only way to get around a password is to totally reset the CE device. This type of resetting differs from pressing the Reset button, which just restarts your CE device. When you totally reset your CE device, everything you have stored on the device is erased. In fact, when you turn on your CE device, it appears as if you have never used it before. If at all possible, try to figure out your password first — after you reset your CE device, you can't undo the results.

If you have a backup of your CE device before you forgot your password, you can restore that backup after you reset your CE device. For more information on restoring from a backup, refer to Chapter 13.

For information about how to totally reset your specific CE device, refer to the hardware documentation that came with the device. For some CE devices, totally resetting the device is simply a matter of removing the main and backup batteries for a certain amount of time.

In the future, keep your password written down in a safe place. That way, if you ever forget it again, you know where to look for it. Just make sure that you can remember where that safe place is.

I Can't Install Windows 95 Programs

Although Windows CE very closely resembles Windows 95, only Windows CE programs can be installed on your CE device. If you have a favorite program that you run on your personal computer, chances are that a version may be available for your CE device. Check with the software developer to see if it has developed a Windows CE version.

The Device Can't Locate My Personal Computer

If you're having problems getting your CE device and your personal computer to communicate, you can try a couple of things. Before doing anything else, you need to make sure that the serial interface cable is properly connected between your CE device and the personal computer. Without the cable, the two units can't communicate.

If the two units are turned on with the cable connected, your personal computer immediately tries to make a connection to the CE device, but for some unknown reason, it does not always make the connection. To remedy the situation, try running the PC Link option on your CE device at the same time your personal computer is attempting to connect, or at least after it has failed the connection. Sometimes when the personal computer is still booting up and attempting to connect to the CE device simultaneously, it cannot successfully connect to the CE device.

If you are still having problems, and the cable is definitely connected correctly, you may have a *hardware conflict* on your personal computer. In other words, another item inside your computer is trying to use the same serial port where you plugged in the cable. If you have another serial port, try it; otherwise, you may have to break down and ask one of the nerdy computer people to look at your personal computer and determine why you cannot use that serial port.

To find the serial port on your personal computer, look for a small port with either 9 or 25 small pins poking out of it. Serial ports are normally used to connect hardware devices, such as a modem or a mouse.

My Microsoft Word File Won't Open in Windows CE

When you copy either a Microsoft Word or Microsoft Excel file to your CE device that you want to be able to open on your CE device, you must convert the file to the appropriate Windows CE format. For Microsoft Word documents, the .DOC and .RTF file formats are converted to .PWD file formats — the file format recognized by Pocket Word.

To make sure that the Windows CE Services program is properly converting the file as it is copied to your device, perform the following steps:

1. Choose Tools➪File Conversion.

The Windows CE Services program runs on your personal computer. When you select the File Conversion option, the File Conversion Properties dialog box appears. Make sure that the check box next to the Enable file conversion option is selected.

2. Click the Desktop -> Device tab in the File Conversion Properties dialog box and highlight the Microsoft Word Document option in the list box.

You should see that all .DOC files are converted to .PWD files in the File conversion details section at the bottom of the screen.

3. If the appropriate file conversion type is not selected, click the Edit button and make the appropriate selection in the Edit Conversion Settings dialog box.

4. Click the OK button to close the Edit Conversion Settings dialog box and save your selections.

5. Click the OK button to close the File Conversion Properties dialog box and save all your changes.

I Want to Send E-Mail to Several People at Once

You have an e-mail message that you want to send to several different people simultaneously from the Inbox. If you have used other e-mail programs in the past, you may have accomplished this feat before. The easiest way to send a message to more than one address is to hold down the Ctrl key while you tap the addresses you want to select in the Choose Address dialog box; this places a semicolon between each address in the To field, indicating that the message should be sent to each address.

If you often send e-mail to a standard group of people, such as the people in your department, here is another trick you can try. Create a contact in the Contacts program for the desired group (you may call the group Coworkers, for example). In the e-mail field, type the e-mail addresses for the members of the group and place a semicolon between each address. To send to that group, simply select the Address book option in the Inbox program and highlight the Coworkers option.

I Need Storage Space for a New Program

You may get an error message if you try to add a new program and your CE device is set up so that most of the memory is available for program memory rather than storage memory, or vice versa. To change the memory settings, double-tap the System icon in the Control Panel folder. On the Memory tab, slide the little slider so that it indicates that more memory is available for storage. You want to make sure that plenty of memory is still available for running programs.

If you still don't have enough memory available for the program you want to add, you can try adding some more storage, such as PC Card storage. Remember that you will probably have to move your files to the card and keep all the programs in the regular memory on your CE device.

The Device Turns Off by Itself

If your CE device is running on battery power, Windows CE is designed to shut it down automatically if the machine sits idle for a specified amount of time. This option is designed to help conserve your batteries when the CE device is not in use. The default time that the CE device sits idle before shutting down is about 3 minutes, but you can modify this time if you want.

To change the amount of time that your device waits before shutting down, select the Power icon in the Control Panel folder and change the number of minutes on the Power Off tab.

If your CE device is connected to the personal computer, whether or not it is running on batteries, the device remains on and does not shut down. Don't leave the CE device connected too long, or you may end up running down your batteries.

I Can't Connect to the Web

If you are trying to connect to the World Wide Web through your Internet service provider and are able to connect to the provider but not to the Web, you may be able to use a fairly simple solution. It may just be that you have accidentally selected the proxy server setting when it is not required. To correct this problem, perform the following steps:

1. **Make sure that your Internet Explorer program is open.**

    To open it, simply double-tap the Internet icon on your desktop.

2. **Choose Options⇨View to display the Options dialog box.**

3. **Tap the Proxy Server tab.**

4. **Make sure that the Use Proxy Server check box is not selected.**

If this change does not correct the problem, your Internet service provider may have a temporary connection problem. Try connecting at a later time.

For more information about proxy servers, refer to Chapter 16.

Index

YOUR ONLINE RESOURCE

WWW.DUMMIES.COM

Discover Dummies Online!

The Dummies Web Site is your fun and friendly online resource for the latest information about ...*For Dummies*® books and your favorite topics. The Web site is the place to communicate with us, exchange ideas with other ...*For Dummies* readers, chat with authors, and have fun!

Ten Fun and Useful Things You Can Do at www.dummies.com

1. Win free ...*For Dummies* books and more!
2. Register your book and be entered in a prize drawing.
3. Meet your favorite authors through the IDG Books Author Chat Series.
4. Exchange helpful information with other ...*For Dummies* readers.
5. Discover other great ...*For Dummies* books you must have!
6. Purchase Dummieswear™ exclusively from our Web site.
7. Buy ...*For Dummies* books online.
8. Talk to us. Make comments, ask questions, get answers!
9. Download free software.
10. Find additional useful resources from authors.

Link directly to these ten fun and useful things at
http://www.dummies.com/10useful

SURF THE NET

WWW.DUMMIES.COM

For other technology titles from IDG Books Worldwide, go to
www.idgbooks.com

Not on the Web yet? It's easy to get started with *Dummies 101*®: *The Internet For Windows*® *95* or *The Internet For Dummies*, 4th Edition, at local retailers everywhere.

IDG BOOKS WORLDWIDE

Find other ...*For Dummies* books on these topics:
Business • Career • Databases • Food & Beverage • Games • Gardening • Graphics • Hardware
Health & Fitness • Internet and the World Wide Web • Networking • Office Suites
Operating Systems • Personal Finance • Pets • Programming • Recreation • Sports
Spreadsheets • Teacher Resources • Test Prep • Word Processing

The IDG Books Worldwide logo and Dummieswear are trademarks, and Dummies Man and ...For Dummies are registered trademarks under exclusive license to IDG Books Worldwide, Inc., from International Data Group, Inc.

IDG BOOKS WORLDWIDE
BOOK REGISTRATION

Register This Book and Win!

We want to hear from you!

Visit **http://my2cents.dummies.com** to register this book and tell us how you liked it!

- ✔ Get entered in our monthly prize giveaway.

- ✔ Give us feedback about this book — tell us what you like best, what you like least, or maybe what you'd like to ask the author and us to change!

- ✔ Let us know any other ...*For Dummies*® topics that interest you.

Your feedback helps us determine what books to publish, tells us what coverage to add as we revise our books, and lets us know whether we're meeting your needs as a ...*For Dummies* reader. You're our most valuable resource, and what you have to say is important to us!

Not on the Web yet? It's easy to get started with *Dummies 101*®: *The Internet For Windows*® *95* or *The Internet For Dummies*®, 4th Edition, at local retailers everywhere.

Or let us know what you think by sending us a letter at the following address:

...*For Dummies* Book Registration
Dummies Press
7260 Shadeland Station, Suite 100
Indianapolis, IN 46256-3945
Fax 317-596-5498

BUSINESS AND GENERAL REFERENCE BOOK SERIES FROM IDG

COMPUTER BOOK SERIES FROM IDG